HEY BABY!
What's Your Name?

A CANADIAN GUIDE TO
NAMING YOUR BABY

SHANDLEY McMURRAY

WILEY

John Wiley & Sons Canada, Ltd.

Library and Archives Canada Cataloguing in Publication Data

McMurray, Shandley, 1976-
        Hey baby! What's your name? : a Canadian guide to naming your baby / Shandley McMurray.

Includes index.
ISBN-13 978-0-470-83687-3
ISBN-10 0-470-83687-3

1. Names, Personal—Canada—Dictionaries. I. Title.

CS2377.M235 2005   929.4'4'0971   C2005-903748-2

Production Credits:

Cover design: Karen Satok
Cover image: Justin Pumfrey/Getty Images
Interior text design: Pat Loi
Illustrations: Kathryn Adams
Printer: Friesens

John Wiley & Sons Canada, Ltd.
6045 Freemont Blvd.
Mississauga, Ontario
L5R 4J3

Printed in Canada

10 9 8 7 6 5 4 3 2 1

To my wonderful husband,
Austin—my best friend and true love.

To my huge, supportive family—for
making me laugh and loving me always.

And finally, to my sweet little Marley Vail—
the new and forever love of my life.

Table of Contents

Acknowledgements		**ix**
Introduction		**1**
Chapter 1:	**Getting Started**	**6**
	Don't Do It	8
	Definitely Do It	10
	Choose It Anyway	13
	Should You Tell?	14
	Who to Tell	16
	When to Tell	16
	James Junior	17
	What's Your Baby-naming Personality? quiz	18
Chapter 2:	**Just For Dad**	**25**
	Sports Heroes	26
	Car Names	34
Chapter 3:	**Truly Canadian**	**38**
	Acadian Names	40
	First Nations Names	46
	French Canadian Names	49
	Inuit Names	53
	Métis Names	54

Chapter 4: **Literary Names**   **64**
Author Names   66
Character Names   76

Chapter 5: **Ethnic Names**   **86**
African Names   87
Chinese Names   92
English Names   94
German Names   97
Greek Names   102
Irish Names   105
Italian Names   108
Japanese Names   112
Polish Names   114
Russian Names   117
Spanish Names   120

Chapter 6: **Through the Ages: Classical Names**   **126**
Top Names in 1920   127
Top Names in 1950   128
Top Names in 1960   129
Top Names in 1970   131
Top Names in 1980   134
Top Names in 1990   135
Top Names in 2000   135

Chapter 7: **Celebrity Names**   **138**
Avoid the Dramatic   139
Be Realistic   139
Choose Carefully   139
Beware of the Mob   139
Celebrities' Names   140
Celebrities' Kids' Names   152

Chapter 8: Around the World   **161**

Australia   162
Austria   163
Canada   164
Denmark   164
England   165
Finland   166
France   167
Germany   167
Iceland   168
Ireland   168
Italy   169
Japan   169
Norway   170
Poland   170
Scotland   172
Spain   173
Sweden   173
Switzerland   173
United States   174

Chapter 9: What's In a Name?   **176**

Still Want to Choose an Unusual Name?   178
Living Up to Expectations   179
Names to Avoid at all Costs   182

Chapter 10: Popular Names   **183**

Popular Names   186
Popularity Charts   212

Chapter 11: Traditional Names   **216**

Religious Names   216
Old-Fashioned Names   231
Last Names as First Names   246

Chapter 12: Trendy Names 250
Trendy Boys' Names 251
Trendy Girls' Names 252

Chapter 13: Unisex Names 255
Who's Choosing These Names? 257
The Pros 257
The Cons 259

Chapter 14: Place Names 262
Canadian Place Names 263
International Place Names 275

Chapter 15: Surnames 277
Choosing the Mother's Maiden Name: Why Do It? 280
Choosing the Father's Surname: Why Do It? 281
Choosing a Hyphenated Surname: Why Do It? 284
Giving Siblings Different Surnames: Why Do It? 285

Chapter 16: The Great Canadian Name Quiz 292

Index 301

Acknowledgements

Heartfelt thanks to everyone who helped with this book:

Joan Whitman, my supportive and enthusiastic editor, without whom this book wouldn't have taken shape.

Rick Broadhead, the resourceful agent who helped it all happen.

The extremely helpful people at Vital Statistics offices throughout the country, especially Lenore in Nova Scotia, Claude in Québec, Jason in Ontario, Frances in Manitoba, Pat in Saskatchewan, Gail in Alberta, Linda in B.C., Sylvia in the Yukon, Cathy in the North West Territories and Margaret in Nunavut.

And most importantly, my fantastic friends, family and husband, each of whom has a wonderful name that I love. Thank you for never tiring of reading, editing and answering endless questions about everything to do with baby names.

Introduction

Congratulations! You are now an official people grower (or partner to a people grower). The next few months are sure to be an exciting time for you and your baby, full of important changes inside and out. Between planning for your little one's arrival, deciding whether to paint the nursery pink or blue and worrying over every little thing, life is certainly busy. The last thing you need to stress about is searching for the perfect baby name.

So I've done a lot of the work for you. From traditional to trendy, you're sure to find at least a few names in this book that are worthy of your top 10 list. And a bevy of tips to help you ease through the naming process. All you have to do is keep track of your favourites and make a decision. So sit back, put up your feet and get ready to enjoy *Hey Baby! What's Your Name? A Canadian Guide to Naming Your Baby.*

How This Book Came About

Ever noticed how your interests change at different stages of your life? Boring furniture commercials become interesting when you've bought a house; flyers for flowers become something to look forward to after you've learned to garden. Two years ago, I would have called you crazy if you'd told me that I'd get excited over clipping coupons from Babies 'R' Us catalogues. Today, I find myself glued to baby gear Web sites and how-to parenting books. Another first:

my obsession with baby names. No matter where I go—the grocery store, park or movie theatre—my ears are at constant attention, waiting to hear a parent call her child's name. This is how I judge for myself if a name is too popular.

When I was pregnant, my husband and I loved the name Spencer so much that we were convinced we were having a boy. We'd already given baby Spencer a personality and could see his tiny smile shining back at us when we called his name. Then we started to hear it everywhere—on television, at Wal-Mart, in the schoolyard near our house. And a pregnant friend of ours decided to give this name to her son-to-be. As we sadly crossed Spencer from our list (we're both fans of unpopular choices) we began to get nervous. Would we ever again find a name that we both liked? And what if our baby wasn't a boy after all?

We always thought that picking a name would be a cinch. I mean, everyone can rhyme off names they hate, right? All we had to do was pick one or two that we both liked. Easy! But after lying in bed one morning for two hours with three baby name books, we had only chosen six names, and none of them felt like "the one."

One of the major problems we were having had to do with our choice of baby name books. They didn't seem to speak to us. They were all geared towards Americans and included U.S. statistics and lists of presidential names, things that didn't really interest us as Canadians. Plus, they were set up in dictionary form, which became really tiring after a while. We craved diversity, knowledge about names that were popular in our own country and information about uniquely Canadian names that we could choose from.

At one point, we felt so desperate about the whole baby-naming process and the lack of pertinent Canadian information that we tried to make up our own monikers. Unfortunately, my husband was so drained by then that he could only come up with a description of things he saw in our room—curtain, chaise, dresser—names that would work for Michael Jackson's kids (he has a son named Blanket) but just wouldn't do for our own precious bundle. I wasn't any better. That's when I decided that I'd never name a baby "couch" and that this country needed a baby name book of its own—to help Canucks like us choose the perfect names for our children.

What You'll Find in This Book

Whether you're a fan of fashionable names or desperately want to avoid them, the Popular Names chapter offers a bevy of choices loved by Canadians from coast to coast. Either highlight your favourites or make a mental note of those to steer clear of, depending on your preferences.

Then learn about our nation's naming history and find out what Acadians, French Canadians, Inuit, Métis and First Nations peoples name their children in the Truly Canadian Names chapter. Or widen your scope by reading Around the World to discover which names are the most popular across the globe.

Curious about the popularity of names over the years? Check out Through the Ages to track your faves. Or pay tribute to one of the many cultures that make up our eclectic society by finding a name in the Ethnic Names chapter. I guarantee you'll find at least two winners in this diverse section.

Culture junkie? Don't miss the Literary and Celebrity Names sections. They're full of information about the rich and famous. A dad? You're so special that I've devoted a chapter just to you, complete with names of sports heroes and cars.

More of a conventional type? The Traditional Names chapter is loaded with religious-based monikers. And it also contains an inclusive list of old-fashioned names, some of which are on their way back.

For those looking for a more personal approach to baby-naming, search for the numerous anecdotes peppered throughout the book. When people found out I was writing *Hey Baby!* they often shared stories about the origin of their names. From age three to 73, kindergarten students to retired bankers, Canadians young and old loved telling me tales about their naming likes and dislikes. And I found them so interesting that I've included a few in each chapter.

When you get tired, sick of, or frustrated by looking at names, take a brain break with one of the two fun quizzes. Either test your knowledge of Canadian names (I'm sure at least a few of the questions will stump you), or answer some entertaining queries to discover your own naming personality.

How to Use this Book

Instead of trudging through a tome filled with endless names that become meaningless in their multitude, *Hey Baby!* allows you to choose the types of names that interest *you*. So if you're not a fan of unique or trendy names, you don't have to waste your time reading through them.

Organized by theme, each chapter is unique and packed with lists of names that will appeal to just about everyone: dads, celeb-watchers, literary buffs, eccentrics, traditionalists, history lovers and geography majors. The best place to start is Getting Started, a chapter jammed with useful information about the dos and don'ts of naming a child. Then take the baby-naming personality quiz for a hint about chapters that will work best for you. Otherwise, look through the Table of Contents to find sections that look interesting.

Every chapter contains at least one sidebar that's filled with helpful information and tips on everything from choosing a middle name to making up a moniker of your own (without resorting to names for inanimate objects). So I suggest flipping through each section, even if the topic doesn't interest you, to find the useful advice.

As for the name entries themselves, although not every name is accompanied by its origin or meaning, the majority of them are. Here's how they'll look:

Name (Origin) Meaning. *Variations.*

Overall, this book was created to help you find the perfect name for your baby, a choice that you and your child will be happy with forever. We all know this decision is not one to be made lightly, and that it may take months of deliberation before you find one that fits. So don't try to get through the whole book at once. Take it one chapter at a time, marking the names that could work for your baby and enjoying the quiet time you have now to devote to this important task.

Once you've completed your list of potentials, sit down with your partner and try to find a few that you agree on. If that doesn't

Chapter 1

- ☆ -

Getting Started

Having a baby was your first big decision. Now comes another challenge: choosing the perfect name for your little one. A name is, after all, your child's calling card for life. It's what his friends will base his nickname on and the name he'll write on university exams. It's the signature she'll use on her marriage license and her own child's birth certificate. That's why it's so important to get it right.

Right now, you're probably experiencing many of the joys and fears that accompany a pregnancy. From the elation you feel at having created a new life to the worries you may have about your ability to parent, there's a lot going on in your mind. My husband and I tried for months to get pregnant, so when we first found out about our wee one, we were shocked, relieved, scared and excited all at the same time. These feelings soon turned to concern over the health of our baby, anxiety over our parenting skills and uncertainty about what I should or shouldn't be eating.

As the pregnancy progressed, we found a whole new set of worries: what stroller to get, what size outfits to buy, what colours are the most educational and most importantly, who would be there to teach us how to take care of a newborn? Neither of us knew how to feed a baby or bathe it and my husband had never changed a diaper. In fact, when he was babysitting as a young teenager, he called his dad over for help when the child's diaper was dirty. Definitely not a story that invoked confidence in his parenting ability.

work, you might want to take a break for a week or two and revisit the list, or hit the book again to see if you missed anything. You never know what little treasures could be lurking on these pages.

Good luck and enjoy the search. And best wishes to you and your baby.

But the one constant worry we had throughout the pregnancy was: what on earth are we going to name our baby? Where do we start? Are there rules about what we can and can't do when naming a child? We had so many questions and so few answers. Although we never found an official baby-naming rule book, I was able to find a bunch of tips about things to do and avoid when naming your child. And I've compiled them all in this chapter to help answer some of your own questions about this important, and sometimes stressful, task.

 REAL NAMES

"I like that it isn't common, yet it's recognizable," 27-year-old Cameron says about his name. "I also like that it can be easily abbreviated." The one thing he could do without: being mistaken for a woman over e-mail. Since Cameron is also a popular name for females, this seems to happen quite a bit.

Shianne says people always have a hard time remembering her name. "I usually have to repeat it a few times," complains the 30-year-old. "[And] I've been called Shania, Dianne, Shawna, even Shane. It's a little frustrating." Even Shianne's own twin sister teased her about her name, saying that her parents named her Shianne because she was shy. When they hit university, however, Shianne learned the true motivation behind the teasing. "She confessed that the only reason she did that was because she was jealous that I had the better name," she says.

"When I call somewhere and say it's Cinda, everyone knows it's me. It's fabulous," 38-year-old Cinda says of her name. But, she explains, a distinct name is hard to hide from, which can make it a bit of a problem. "If I screw up on something everybody pretty much knows," she says. "If I was Carol or Sam, people probably wouldn't be so sure which one it was."

Since she was a child, Judith has been known to most as Judy. Problem is, she's always hated the nickname and wishes that her true name was never shortened. "I love the name Judith," explains the 63-year-old. "It's a strong name, a Biblical name and it has pulchritude." She likes her name so much, in fact, that she says she regrets not giving it to one of her daughters.

Don't Do It

From choosing an über popular name to picking one that you think is really funny, here are a few things to avoid when naming your child.

Too Long

Don't pick a name that's too cumbersome. Esmerelda Stephanie Von Morgenstern, for example, is hard enough for a kid to say, let alone spell. Typically, it's best to use a longer first name with a shorter last name. Delaney Reid and Tucker Smith, for instance, sound much more eloquent than Ann Reid and Ted Smith.

Humorous

While naming your child Charlie Brown or Rain Forest may seem cute at first, you should probably think about the gazillion wise cracks he'll get about this later on—not to mention the pent-up resentment he'll harbour against you. And even if you didn't mean to make your child's name into a bad pun (like Holly Wood, Tu Morrow or Bud Wiser) you're still ultimately responsible for the choice. So think twice before you choose.

Too Unique

Although different may seem more interesting, especially in a class full of Emmas and Ethans, giving your child a name that's completely out of the ordinary could set him up for problems later on. Other kids may use little Tambiquono's name as an opportunity to tease him, for instance, simply because they don't understand his moniker. And you might find that your child Kalatenkra will get sick of always having to spell her name for others.

Tainted

Your partner loves the name Sarah, but it reminds you of that cruel girl in high school who stole your friend's glasses and kicked in her locker. Even if you think that you'll be able to get over a tainted name, believing that it will grow on you with time, you could very well be wrong. And it would be horrible to cringe every time you called your own child.

Hard to Spell

So you want to make a common name more original by changing the spelling, huh? You might want to think about the consequences first. Are you prepared to subject your daughter Erycka to a lifetime of correcting people who misspell her name? And don't you think it might be difficult for your son Jheremiah to learn to spell his own name?

Over-Popular

If you don't mind your son being referred to as Matthew C. then by all means give him a popular name. But if you're like me and wince at the thought of your child having to make a name for himself in a class with five other Joshuas, it might be smarter to choose a less popular moniker. Plus, trendy names—like Madison and Ethan—tend to go out of fashion quickly, so it may be best to be safe and choose one that's just under the radar.

Awful Alliteration

Think Alice Adams sounds cute? How about Brian Brampton? You may be right. But then again, the alliteration may be a bit too cutesy, especially for an adult. And think about especially poor selections like Trina Turner or Alice Palace. Such choices can set a kid up for a childhood of teasing and an adulthood of embarrassment. It's probably best to avoid them.

Overly Stereotyped

No matter how hard you may wish it weren't so, some names will never be able to break free of their famous stereotypes. Take Adolph, Osama and Saddam, for instance. Even though these names may have sounded nice at one point, their famous namesakes have given them permanent negative connotations. It would be hard for any child with one of these names to disassociate himself from their politically charged meanings.

Repeating Vowels

Starting a first and last name with a vowel is generally considered a faux pas on the naming circuit. The main reason? Many of these vowel-loving names, like Ava Everhard and Ivor Antanka can turn into tongue twisters, presenting your kids with pronunciation problems.

Easily Teased

Humorous names like the ones mentioned previously definitely fall into this category. But so do any other names such as Nessie (the Loch Ness Monster) and Dick (enough said) that could promote negative nicknames. From wearing the wrong shoes to liking the wrong music, kids have enough to worry about when it comes to teasing. Why add to this with a name that invites mocking?

Too Ethnic

While ethnic names offer a wonderful way to add more history, culture and diversity to our children's lives, choosing the right one can be a bit tricky. You don't want to pick one that's too difficult for others to pronounce, spell or understand. And you definitely don't want to afflict your child with a cultural name that's completely different from her last name. Just imagine how well Yasahiro Jones will go over.

Definitely Do It

Want to ensure that you choose the right name? Here are a few things to keep in mind when making your choice.

Sound it Out

Read each potential name out loud. This helps you to visualize the name and its connotations. Do this with the middle and last name as well to make sure they fit well together and don't make any strange tongue-twisters, rhymes or puns.

Check for Associations

For centuries, we've used people's names to refer to a whole bunch of things—from animals to private parts, which means that a name is no longer just reserved for people. We all know that a Joey is a baby kangaroo, for instance, but did you know that Jenny is the name for a young female donkey? And what do you think Johnson and Willy most often refer to? Because of these associations, it's best to check your favourite names online or with friends to make sure they don't hold any hidden meanings you're not prepared for.

Keep a List

Rate your favourite names on a piece of paper and keep it handy for when new ones come along. That way, you'll never miss out on a last-minute addition or forget one that you heard and liked. This will also help the decision-making process later on and might be an interesting piece of history to add to your child's baby book.

Research the Meaning

While many people don't choose names based on their meaning, it's a good idea to check it out before bestowing a lifelong moniker on your child. You never know what you'll find out. Would knowing that Malloren means a laurel of bad luck or that Mallorie means a bad omen make you think twice about giving these names to your kids?

Look to the Past

Believe it or not, old-time names are becoming new again. Whether we're recycling classics to make up for a lack of new creations or using them to give our children a more distinguished appearance, old-fashioned choices like Spencer and Sophia are making a comeback. And that might not be a bad thing. So check out the "Old-fashioned Names" section in the Traditional Names chapter for a few that you think might work with your little one. Just make sure it's not too old-sounding. Mildred and Gertrude, for instance, may never make it back to popularity.

Consider Siblings

There's nothing worse than feeling like the odd man out. Being named Shandley in a family of children named Debra, Steven, Cynthia and Lindsay would have made me feel like an outsider. But luckily my mother added Taryn, Dawn and Cinda into the mix, making us feel as if we meshed better. In a family of eight kids, though, it's much easier to play around with names like this. If you only have a couple of children, it would sound awkward to introduce Jacinto and

Helen to your friends. So try to pick names that are similar in sound, ethnicity or syllables. It sounds better to have a Samuel, David and Rachel than Felice, Edward and Katrina.

Think About Nicknames

Can't stand the thought of your child being stuck with a horrible nickname? Then think about the potentials before you choose. If you hate the name Harry, for instance, you may want to rethink your choice of Harold as a first name. Or set a rule from day one that no one is allowed to shorten your son's name. But good luck enforcing this when he's off to school.

Check the Initials

So you finally found the perfect name for your little angel. Did you think about what the initials spell? Brandon Andrew Davidson may not like being called bad, for instance. And Rayleen Annie Gordon will probably hate being referred to as a rag.

Honour Your Family

Whether you decide to stick with your mother's first name or choose a variation of your favourite uncle's moniker, keeping your child's name in the family is a great way to honour your ancestral roots. Just make sure the name doesn't sound too old for a new babe. Great Aunt Erma may have told the best stories, but that doesn't mean her name will suit a young girl of today.

Keep your options open

You've finally found a name that's perfect for your baby and you can't wait to give it to him. Hold on a sec. Although you may think that this name is the best fit for your child now, you might change your mind once you actually meet your baby. The reason? Sometimes a child just doesn't look like the name you chose for it. So it's smart to have a backup name or two on hand, just in case.

KIDS' KORNER

Sarah's parents picked her name because they thought it was nice. And she's pretty happy with their decision. "I like that it is not a really long name," says the 13-year-old, "and that it means princess in Hebrew."

Even though five-year-old Tristan likes his first name because it starts with a "t," his favourite name of all is Hotwheels. The reason is simple, he says: "It's because I love Hotwheels."

Joshua thinks his parents named him after someone in the Bible, but he's not sure. And overall, he's pretty happy with their choice. "I like it because it's unique and it has a 'j' and a 'u' in it," says the 14-year-old.

Charissa says her name is very unique and "totally me." When asked where her name originated, the 12-year-old says, "My parents liked the 'rissa' part and they just added the 'cha'." If she absolutely had to choose another name, Charissa says she'd pick Cheniqua (because it sounds like Shaniquwa) or Charisse (because it sounds like Sharèsse).

Tell a Tale

I've always loved hearing stories about how people got their names. From my husband, Austin, who was named after his dad's favourite car to our friend Walter, whose Chinese parents named him after the first newscaster they saw on Canadian television, a story helps bring a name to life. So why not give your child the name of someone with history, like a famous basketball star, inspiring political leader or your favourite friend in grade school? That way you'll always have a tale to tell your child. And we all know how much kids love to hear stories that feature them (or in this case their name) as the star.

Choose It Anyway

Sometimes rules should be broken. And finding a name that you love is definite grounds for busting tradition. The most important thing about the name you choose is that you like it, regardless of the dos and don'ts I've listed in this chapter. So stick with your gut feeling and choose a name that feels right.

Should You Tell?

One of the first questions people asked when they learned I was pregnant was: Have you chosen a name? Most of the time, I simply said "no," hoping that they'd drop the subject. But sometimes, when they really pressed me, I'd cave in and share our favourites-of-the-month. Wondering if you should divulge your own names? Here are a few words of wisdom from one who's been there.

No Way

My best advice about sharing names is: don't do it! No matter how much you may love the person you're telling, that doesn't mean he or she is going to agree with your choice. And ultimately, that's what it is—your choice.

I made the mistake of sharing a favourite girl's name with my sister and good friend once and was shocked by their responses. They both made horrible faces at the name and my sister proceeded to make fun of the choice. I was hoping for a nod of agreement (even if it was a fake one made only to appease me) but they couldn't bite their tongues. My husband and I both like the name and had it on our top three list for months. I was crushed. There was no way I could choose it without always thinking of their reactions to it.

Since I didn't learn from that mistake, I shared another favourite, this time for a boy, with other family members. Our teenaged niece and nephew recoiled at the thought of us naming our child Dexter. The reason was twofold: first, it's the name of their friend's dog and secondly, it's the name of a geeky computer on a show they used to watch as kids. Then my mother said it was the name of a badly behaved kid on a 1940s radio show. So much for that idea.

No matter what the name or who you tell, there's bound to be someone with a negative association to it. So from now on, my husband and I have decided to keep mutually agreed upon names to ourselves. By the time we give it to our child, everyone will be so excited to see the little bundle that they won't be able to say anything bad about our choice.

Should you find out the sex?

So you've found out that you're having a girl. Congratulations! Now you can paint the nursery pink, buy cute little dresses and cut your list down to girls' names only, right? Not so fast. No matter what the ultrasound technician told you, determining the sex of a fetus is not a precise science. Even though all the signs may be pointing to a Caroline and you've had three ultrasounds to confirm it, you could end up with a Charles in the delivery room. So don't get your hopes up too quickly and try not to get too attached to a name because you never know for certain what you're going to get.

If the technician was right, however, finding out the sex beforehand can help you visualize and bond with your unborn baby. And naming your child before it's born can give your baby a personality even before you get to meet it. My good friends Phil and Patricia, for instance, named Adèle months before she was born. Whenever we talked about the baby, we referred to her by her name. So by the time they called to tell us the good news about her arrival, we felt as if we already knew her, which was great.

 FUN FACTS

According to research by a University of Chicago economist, the most popular girls' names in 2015 will include Aviva, Flannery and Linden, while boys will be named Aldo, Bennett, Finnegan and Sumner.

Once a Bedouin woman has a son, she becomes known by his name (e.g., Abu Nassar, which means Nassar's mother) instead of her own.

In Korea, each family member of the same generation shares a certain word, e.g., Jin, in their name. The following generation will incorporate a different name into their own.

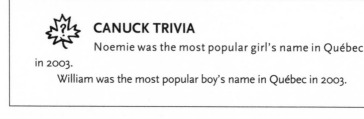

CANUCK TRIVIA
Noemie was the most popular girl's name in Québec in 2003.
William was the most popular boy's name in Québec in 2003.

If You Must

Despite the above listed drawbacks to sharing a name, there are a few bonuses to telling others about your top choices. First, if people like it, you can gloat in your ability to choose a name that appeases pretty much everyone. You and your partner have beaten the odds, finding a name that no one has an aversion to. Second, it's a great way to let mom know the easy way that her name is too old-fashioned for your prodigy and hasn't made it onto your list. This way, there are no surprises for her in the end.

Who to Tell

If you do decide to tell people your names, beware of sharing the information with close friends and family members. Just as you were hoping they'd love your partner as much as you do, you'll probably be rooting for their unwavering enthusiasm over your name choices as well. If you get anything less than a hearty smile and proclamation of love for the name, you may feel hurt and disappointed. Even a split second pause before they respond could cause your heart to sink. So it might be best to test names out on not-so-close friends, acquaintances or colleagues first. That way you can accept their input without becoming emotional and it's much easier to brush off candid comments from people you don't care that much about.

When to Tell

So you've decided to share your favourite picks but aren't sure when to do it. Here's my advice: wait until you've got a semi-final list, narrowed down to a few names for each sex. That way, you and your partner have already argued the pros and cons and settled on a few names you can both live with. In other words, half the battle has been won. By the time you reveal your choices to others, you'll only be discussing names that you both care about instead of wasting time asking for input on one that your partner may cross out immediately anyway.

If you're not planning on keeping your name a secret and aren't looking for other people's input, I'd suggest waiting to share your pick until close to your due date or, even better, after the baby is born. That way, others will be more likely to hold back any negative comments since they know you're really serious about it.

James Junior

Thinking of naming your child after you or your partner? Before you do, it's important to think about the potential downsides of this choice. While some juniors love sharing a moniker with their loved one, others find their names to be unoriginal and confusing. Just think about it. You're totally ticked off because young John didn't feed the dog again and scream for him to "get down here right now." Suddenly, two Johns appear at the door—the big one and the little one—both trying to figure out what they've done wrong. Although this could come in handy at times—you only have to call one name to get both of them to come to dinner or help with the yard work—more often than not, you'll probably find yourself frustrated at having to differentiate between the two.

Another potential pitfall of the junior phenomenon involves a child's psyche. Kids who share a name with someone often live in the older person's shadow. Jenny Jr. may well be seen as a mere extension of her mother rather than as her own person. And, as she grows, young Jenny may believe she has to live up to her mother's achievements, feeling disappointed if she can't measure up to what her mom once did.

One more thing: any child sharing a name with his or her parent is pretty much guaranteed to be called junior at some point in his life. So if you're opposed to this term, you might want to give your child another nickname, like Mikey, if his name is Michael, before Junior can catch on.

Despite the obvious drawbacks, there are some positives to naming your child after a parent. Firstly, it's a way of honouring one of the people responsible for bringing him into the world. And second, it's a wonderful tribute to the memory of a deceased parent. Finally, this may be an important tradition in your family, a way to maintain significant ancestral roots by carrying a name from one generation to the next. But remember, in order for your child to be a true Pierce Manley III, he'll have to have the exact same name (first, middle and last) as his father and grandfather.

What's Your Baby-naming Personality? quiz

Naming a child is rarely an easy task. And even though you've already made the first step—opening this book—it's often hard to know where to start. This fun, light-hearted quiz is designed to make your search a bit easier. Simply answer the questions below to find your baby-naming personality. Then head to the chapters that best suit your naming style.

While you may find quite a few winners in the chapters I suggest, make sure not to limit your search to those sections only. They're merely suggestions to help get you started. You never know what hidden gems you'll find in other areas of the book. And hey, you may find that you actually like a name or two from chapters that you never thought would be of interest. As mom always said, it's best to keep your options open. So get circling!

1. In high school you were:
    a) nerdy
    b) über cool
    c) a loner

2. Your favourite take-out is:
    a) pizza
    b) sushi
    c) Thai

3. Your own name is:
   a) perfect
   b) trendy
   - c) funky and unique

4. Your favourite singer/group is:
   a) Norah Jones
   - b) Coldplay
   c) Radiohead

5. Your favourite novel is:
   a) any English classic
   b) none. I don't have time to read
   - c) *The Life of Pi* by Yann Martel

6. You've always wanted to name a son:
   a) after your father, husband or grandfather
   b) Matthew, Joshua or Ethan
   - c) something creative and original

7. Your favourite children's book is:
   - a) *Goodnight Moon* by Margaret Wise Brown
   b) *Love you Forever* by Robert Munsch
   c) *10 Fat Turkeys* by Tony Johnston

8. Your nursery décor will consist of:
   a) pastel blues and pinks, depending on the sex of our baby
   b) the latest designer crib with Pottery Barn accents
   c) crisp, clean and Zen-like

9. When renting movies, you tend to go for:
   - a) classics
   b) top 10 blockbusters
   c) indie or foreign flicks

10. Your favourite flavour of ice cream is:
    a) vanilla
    b) chocolate
    - c) anything with nuts in it

11. As a kid, you wished your name was:
 a) the same as your mom's or dad's
 b) the same as your best friend's
 c) something wild and outrageous

12. If you had to spend $100 on clothing, you'd buy:
 a) another pair of jeans
 b) the season's trendiest item
 c) a vintage jacket

13. Your favourite class in high school was:
 a) history
 b) English
 ⇒ c) math

14. Your dream vacation spot is:
 ⌐ a) a log cabin on a quiet lake
 b) Hawaii
 c) the Australian Outback

15. Your favourite place to exercise is:
 a) at home with a DVD
 b) at the gym
 ⌐ c) outside

How you Scored

Now it's time to tally your score. The letter you circled most often represents your baby-naming personality. Read on to find out what this means and which chapters are best suited to your naming tastes.

If you answered mostly As, you're a traditionalist. You'd rather spend a weekend in your garden than tour a big city and don't like to draw too much attention to yourself. Organized and intelligent, you're a fan of classic forms of art and culture. And family ties, values and history are extremely important to you.

When it comes to naming your child, you'll probably want to avoid trendy monikers that tend to go out of style shortly after they've made it big. Instead, you may want to choose a name that's stood the test of time, proving over the decades that it's strong and worthy. Other good options for people with your naming personality include monikers that are rooted in religion and history.

The best places to conduct your baby name search include:

Traditional Names—An extensive collection of old-fashioned and religious-based names, this chapter is filled with choices that will appeal to the more traditional parent. It also includes a list of last names (e.g., Mason and Beckett) that can be used as a first.

Literary Names—What better way to celebrate your love of literature than by naming your child after a favourite author or character? This chapter comes complete with character descriptions to help make choosing even easier.

Through the Ages—Browse the trends to find out which names have remained popular throughout the years.

Truly Canadian—Not only for the patriotic, this chapter contains beautiful names valued by the founding peoples of our country— First Nations groups, French Canadians and Acadians included.

Place Names—Although some of these names border on the unique, quite a few have a familiar ring to them. Plus, they're all rooted in our country's history, so how could you go wrong?

If you answered mostly Bs, you're truly fashionable. A pop culture aficionado and lover of all things new, you make it a goal to follow the latest trends. Between work, parties and dinner with friends, you're always on the go. But no matter how rushed you are, you won't leave the house without a well-coordinated outfit and at least a bit of mascara. If you could, you'd name a daughter Manolo Blahnik just because the shoes are so pretty. And a boy could be Ethan because it sounds trendy and is the name of one of your favourite actors.

Names that best suit your hip and with-it personality can be found in the following chapters:

Celebrity Names—From Ashton to Uma, this chapter is packed with names and descriptions of some of your favourite celebs. This is also the place where you'll find the ultra creative (and sometimes downright embarrassing) names of their kids.

Unisex Names—Wondering about the benefits of choosing a unisex moniker for your baby? First, it cuts your work in half. No matter what name you pick, it'll work for either a boy or a girl. Second, they just plain sound cool—especially when used for a girl.

Popular Names—As one who likes to be part of the It crowd, you'll probably love a few of these popular names. While I'd avoid choosing any that have made it into the top 10 (unless you don't mind your son being known as Matt B.), there are plenty of great, hip names to choose from in these extensive lists.

Trendy Names—Totally cool and definitely in, consider these lists *The OC* of names. But beware. Just like the marriage of Julie Cooper and Caleb Nichol, these monikers often have a short shelf life.

If you answered mostly Cs, you're definitely unique. You're passionate about embracing different cultures and like to invent everything from fun new recipes to interesting weekend games. The idea of sitting still on a beach for hours fills you with dread and you'd rather paraglide off Vancouver's Grouse Mountain than take the gondola down. The perfect name for your child would be different, creative and truly individual. There's no way your kid's going to share a name with her classmate.

The best sections for you to start your name search include:

Ethnic Names—Celebrate our nation's diversity by choosing an ethnic name for your child. From African monikers to names favoured in Spain, this chapter gives you a glimpse into a variety of cultures and includes hundreds of gorgeous and unique names to choose from.

Literary Names—Although some of these names border on the classic and traditional, a few, especially in the Characters' Names section, are both interesting and inspiring.

Truly Canadian—Show your Canuck colours by picking a name that represents our heritage. Whether you're motivated by the nature-inspired First Nations names or feel drawn to favoured

Acadian picks, there are sure to be at least a couple of monikers here that'll make it on to your maybe list.

Just for Dad—Okay, so this chapter includes the names of sports heroes and cars. But before you roll your eyes, you might want to check it out. You may be surprised at how different some of these selections are.

Around the World—Find out which names are popular around the globe and discover new international favourites to add to your list.

Place Names—Sometimes, place names are the most interesting choices. In fact, I love place names so much that I consulted an atlas during a search for my own baby's name.

What's in a Name—Exercise your creative muscle by making up a name of your own. Not sure how? This chapter offers tips to help you create the perfect name for your little one.

Grandma or Queenie?

These days, choosing a name for your child's grandparents can be almost as difficult as picking a name for your baby. In a time in which people are terrified of aging, old-sounding names like Grandma and Grandpa are being ditched for jazzier versions like Nan and Pops. Even celebrities have caught on. Goldie Hawn's known as Glamma by her grandson Ryder.

Here are a few alternatives to the traditional Grandma and Grandpa. Mull them over and ask your parents what they think. Or feel free to invent your own.

Alternatives for Grandpa

Abuelo	Daddo	Dziadzia
Ataataga	Dadu	Famor
Avô	Dedushka	Gramp
Boompa	Dyido	Gramps
Bubbe	Dzia	Grampy

Granddad	Papa	Poppy
Granddaddy	Papaw	Saba
Halaboji	Pap-ou	Seneli
Lolo	Pappous	Taid
Morfa	Papps	Tito
Nonno	Pappy	Ye Ye
Oompa	Pepe	Zayde
Opa	Pop Pop	Zeidy

Alternatives for Grandma

Aanaga	Glamma	Mormor
Abuela	Gram	Nagyanya
Ammamma	Grammy	Nain
Babushka	Grams	Nana
Bomma	Gran	Nai Nai
Babcia	Granmanny	Nimmie
Buba	Granny	Nini
Bube	Lola	Nokomis
Busia	Grootmoeder	Nonna
Dida	Halmoni	Oba-chan
Elisi	Mammo	Ouma
Fafa	Meemaw	Oma
Gamma	Meme	Queenie
Gigi	Mop Mop	

Chapter 2

-☆-

Just for Dad

Congrats on making the first step—taking time to read this section of the book. Now that you're here you may be wondering why you deserve your own chapter. Well, times they are a changin' and you deserve credit. Men are doing laundry, cooking dinner and Swiffering floors. They're rubbing their pregnant partner's feet, sitting through prenatal classes and delivering ice cream at two in the morning. Although you may not endure morning sickness or give birth to your child, you still play an active role in his or her well being. And you're just as responsible for naming your baby as your partner is.

So I've devised a chapter just for you—one that eliminates "girly" and "cutesy" names and appeals to the strong, sports and car-loving male psyche. This chapter includes names that will appeal to you, like those of popular sports heroes and luxury cars—all of which can be used acceptably for naming children. Simply put down the remote, read through the lists and pick out the names you like best. Then, try to nudge them to the top of her list. Adding a bit of chocolate at the same time can't hurt!

REAL NAMES

Austin has always liked his first name. "It was unique when I was young, people remember it and it has a story to it," says the 29-year-old. "I was named after my dad's favourite car—the Austin Healey." The downside to his now popular name? Bad jokes. From Austin Powers to Austin, Texas, he gets every cheesy nickname around.

If 35-year-old Miranda was naming a child, she'd steer clear of common names like David, Richard, Ann and Jennifer. The reason: she's always liked having a unique name because it gives her a separate identity.

"Short, easy to spell and simple to pronounce" is the way 32-year-old Scott describes his name. Although he does wish his name sounded more majestic and says he could have passed on the teasing he received about toilet paper and tissue (Scotties) as a kid, Scott says, "I wouldn't change my name."

Nicole likes having a common name because it's easy for others to spell and pronounce. "Also," says the 26-year-old, "since my parents chose the name it has added meaning because that is the name that they gave me." If she absolutely had to choose another name for herself, she'd pick Sarah, another popular chart topper, because she likes the way it sounds.

Sports Heroes

Nothing says strength, determination and skill like the name of a high-powered athlete. Here are few of my favourite sporty names to get you revved up.

Athletic Boys' Names

Anfernee (American) Version of Anthony, meaning praiseworthy. An NBA player, Anfernee Hardaway helped the 1996 U.S. Olympic basketball team win gold at the Atlanta games.

Babe (Unique). Who other than baseball's most famous player could pull off a name like this? Babe Ruth hit 60 homers in 1927 and has brought his own meaning to this name: great athlete.

Ben (Hebrew) Short form of Benjamin, meaning son of the right hand. Once known as the world's fastest man, Canadian Ben Johnson's track and field success came to a quick halt when he tested positive for steroid use at the 1988 Seoul Olympics.

Conrad (German) A daring advisor. Canadian professional beach volleyball player Conrad Leinemann won gold at the 1999 Pan American Games with partner Jody Holden.

Daniel (Hebrew) The Lord is my judge. Canadian wrestler Daniel Igali won gold at the 2000 Summer Olympics in Sydney. He's definitely made this name represent pure strength!

Donovan (Irish) Dark warrior. Canadian sprinter Donovan Bailey took home the gold at the 1996 Olympics in Atlanta. He still holds the world record for fastest 50-metres and the Olympic, Commonwealth and Canadian records for 100-metres. Another athlete of this name: Philidelphia Eagles quarterback Donovan McNabb.

Gordie (English) Short form of Gordon, which means cornered or triangular hill. Known as "Mr. Hockey," Gordie Howe played 32 seasons for the NHL and WHA and at 52 was the oldest player to play in an NHL game. Now that's a name with longevity.

Jacques (French) A derivative of Jacob, meaning substitute. At 24, Canada's own Jacques Villeneuve was the youngest driver to win the Indy 500, an Indy Car Championship. This name definitely denotes power and speed.

Jesse (Hebrew) God exists; wealthy. Revived by motorcycle guru and West Coast Chopper bad boy Jesse James, this name represents speed and machismo.

Jody (Hebrew) A believer in God; from Joseph. Rising professional beach volleyball star Jody Holden of Nova Scotia competed at the 2000 Olympics in Sydney and won gold at the 1999 Pan Am games in Winnipeg.

Joe (Hebrew) Short for Joseph, meaning God adds. U.S. quarterback Joe Montana was named MVP for three of the four Super Bowls he helped win. He was also voted MVP of the NFL twice. In 2000, he was inducted into the Pro Football Hall of Fame.

John (Hebrew) God is merciful. Volleyball player John Child and partner Mark Heese brought home a bronze medal from the 1996 Olympic games in Atlanta and placed fifth in Athens.

Kareem (Arabic) Noble and generous. Before retiring in 1989, NBA star Kareem Abdul-Jabbar (born Ferdinand Lewis) was a member of six NBA championship teams, won the NBA MVP award six times and was named an All-Star 19 times.

Kurt (German) A form of Curtis, meaning courteous. Canadian figure skater Kurt Browning has won three Olympic medals and a place in the Guinness Book of World Records for landing the first quadruple jump in a competition.

Kyle (Gaelic, Scottish) Handsome; near a chapel; a narrow channel. Many Canadians were filled with pride when gymnast Kyle Shewfelt won gold at the 2004 Olympic games in Athens.

Lance (French) A variant of the word Lancelot, as in Knight of the Roundtable. Now commonly associated with seven-time Tour de France winner Lance Armstrong, this name represents strength, perseverance and success.

Marc (French) A version of Mark, meaning warlike. Canadian speed skater Marc Gagnon not only won medals (two gold and two bronze) at three Olympics, but also set records in short track. He is the most decorated Olympic athlete in Canadian history.

Mario (Italian) Derived from Marius, this is an old Roman family name. Canadian hockey great Mario Lemieux has won two Stanley cups, six scoring titles and three MVP awards. He's ranked in the all-time top 10 for goals, assists and points.

Mark (Latin) Warlike. Touted as one of hockey's most intriguing personalities, hockey great Mark Messier is the only player to ever captain two Stanley Cup winners, the Oilers in 1990 and Rangers in 1994. Another famous Canadian athlete of this name: beach volleyball player Mark Heese.

Michael (Hebrew) Who is like God. Famous Michael athletes include Canadian golfer Mike Weir, NBA superstar Michael Jordan, track and field pro Michael Johnson, Olympic swimmer Michael Phelps, race car drivers Michael Schumacher and Michael Andretti and tennis player Michael Chang.

Ned (English) Short for Edward, meaning prosperous guardian. Award-winning rower Ned Hanlon was Canada's first international sports hero in the late 1800s.

Patrick (Latin) Noble. NHL goalie Patrick Roy helped win four Stanley Cups while playing for the Montreal Canadiens and Colorado Avalanche. During his 18-year career, Roy also won the Vezina Trophy for best goaltender three times.

Roger (German) A famous spearman. The most famous athlete of this name is baseball pitcher Roger Clemens. Touted as one of the best athletes of all time, Clemens has dominated the game since the mid-1980s.

Ronaldinho (Portuguese) Little Ronaldo. Named FIFA world player of the year in 2004, soccer great Ronaldo de Assis Moreira was given the nickname of Ronaldinho by Brazilian fans.

Sammy (Hebrew) Short for Samuel, meaning God listens. Baseball player Sammy Sosa rose to fame quickly after hitting 66 home runs in 1998. That same year, he won the National League's MVP award.

Shaquille (African-American) Handsome. Labelled as one of the 50 greatest players in NBA history, Shaquille O'Neal has made this name represent lightning speed and impeccable accuracy.

Tie (Unique) Canadian NHL player Tie Domi is known more for his rough play and love of fighting than he is for scoring. Perhaps this name really means scrapper.

Tiger (American) Tiger; ambitious. Best known by his nickname Tiger, Eldrick Woods has won 58 tournaments, 43 of which were part of the PGA Tour. Proof that if the nickname fits, you should definitely keep it.

Tom (English) Short for Thomas, meaning twin. Who could forget star quarterback Tom Brady of the New England Patriots? In just three seasons in the NFL, he led his team to two Super Bowl victories.

Vince (Latin) Conqueror; short for Vincent. Although born and raised in the States, Canadians claimed basketball wonder Vince Carter as their own during his seven-season stint with the Toronto Raptors.

Wayne (English) Wagon maker. Canada's most famous athlete, Wayne Gretzky, made hockey history as the best player of all time. In addition to setting numerous game records, Gretzky also led the 1980s Edmonton Oilers to four Stanley Cup wins. There are more than 99 reasons to name your son after him.

Athletic Girls' Names

Alanna (Slavic) A form of Alana, meaning beautiful. Canadian Olympian Alanna Kraus has won so many speed skating medals there's no space to include them all. She was ranked third overall for the 2003-2004 Canadian skating season.

Beckie (English) Short for Rebecca, meaning tied and bound. Canadian skier Beckie Scott won Olympic medals in both 1998 at Nagano and 2002 at Salt Lake City. It wasn't until 2004, however, that she finally received a well-deserved gold at Salt Lake City—two of her Russian competitors were stripped of their medals for failing drug tests.

Billie (German, English) Defender of justice; of a strong will. American tennis great Billie Jean King was the first woman to win more than $100,000 in one season. In 1972, she was also the first female athlete to be named *Sports Illustrated's* "Sportsperson of the Year."

Catriona (Gaelic, Greek, Irish, Scottish) Pure; a form of Katrina and Catherine. The fastest woman on ice, Canadian speed skater Catriona LeMay Doan sped her way to two Olympic gold medals and one bronze. She currently holds the Olympic record in the 500 metre event and has broken the world record a staggering eight times. There's no arguing that she's made this name mean quick, talented and strong.

Chantelle (French) A form of Chantal, meaning a song; singer. Champion Australian diver, Chantelle Michell won silver and bronze medals for her outstanding dives at the 2004 Olympic Games in Athens.

Charmaine (French) Another version of Carmen, meaning a song; garden. Known as the world's most lethal striker, Canadian soccer player Charmaine Hooper is a scoring superstar.

Chris (Greek) Christian; short for Christina, meaning anointed. American Chris Evert was to tennis as Michael Johnson was to the NBA. Winner of 18 Grand Slam titles and 157 career singles titles, Evert definitely helped bring women's tennis into the spotlight.

Donna (Italian) A lady. Donna Mancuso fought her way to victory for numerous boxing awards including 2000 Boxing Ontario Female Athlete of the Year and the 2000 USA National Golden Gloves champion.

Elizabeth (Hebrew) Consecrated to God. Figure Skater Elizabeth Manley won a silver medal for Canada in the 1988 Calgary Olympics.

Gabrielle (Hebrew) Strength of God. Few pro athletes are as gorgeous as American volleyball wonder Gabrielle Reece. Perhaps that's because she's also a professional model. In 1997, Reece was voted one of the 20 most influential women in sports.

Hayley (English) Field of hay. Canadian Hayley Wickenheiser was the first female hockey player to score a point in a men's game.

Isabelle (Spanish) Sacred to God; a form of Isabel. Another talented Canadian speed skater, Isabelle Charest won three Olympic medals in the short track event.

Jackie (French) Form of Jacqueline, meaning supplanter. U.S. track Olympian Jackie Joyner-Kersee brought home three gold, one silver and two bronze medals from four Olympic Games.

KIDS' KORNER

When asked to describe her name, 12-year-old Mariam used the word precious. "I'm named after my dad's sister who died," she explains, which makes it extra special.

Gillian's parents thought her name "had a nice ring to it and it was a 'jolly hockey sticks' kind of name," says this six-year-old. But she likes it best because "it starts with a 'g,' like the word girl."

Other than being called Daniella at times, 13-year-old Daniel hasn't really been teased about his name. "I like my name because it suits me and it sounds nice. I can't say there is anything wrong with my name," he says. And he likes the numerous nicknames he gets, including Danny, Dan, Dan the Man, and Dodoo.

Jamie (Hebrew) Supplanter; female form of James. Canadian figure skating's it couple, Jamie Salé and partner David Pelletier went professional after winning gold (amidst much controversy) at the 2002 Salt Lake City Olympic games.

Jessica (Hebrew) Rich. Synchronized swimmer Jessica Chase of Montreal is a two-time national champion. She and her team also brought home a gold at the 1999 Pan Am Games and a bronze from the 2000 Olympics in Sydney.

Josée (French) Feminine form of Joseph, meaning God adds. Award-winning figure skater Josée Chouinard won the hearts of Canadians with both her talent and her loveable personality.

Karen (Greek) Pure. One of Canada's most talented ballerinas, Karen Kain danced in performances of *The Nutcracker, Swan Lake, Giselle* and *Romeo and Juliet* among others.

Kristi (Hebrew) Christian. A form of Christine. One of figure skating's most beloved performers, American Kristi Yamaguchi won gold at the 1992 Olympics and was inducted into both the U.S. and World Figure Skating Hall of Fame in 1998.

Marianne (French) Little Mary. Canadian swimmer Marianne Limpert won silver at the 1996 Olympics and two golds at the 1999 Pan Am games. She placed fourth at the 2000 games in Sydney.

Marilyn (Hebrew) Descendents of Mary. Marilyn Bell was the first person to swim across Lake Ontario.

Martina (Latin) Warlike. Tennis superstar Martina Navratilova won over $21 million in prize money throughout her reign. She also took home 18 Grand slam titles, 167 WTA singles titles and 174 WTA tour doubles titles. That's one athlete who really lived up to the meaning of her name.

Mia (Italian) Mine. U.S. soccer player Mia Hamm is the only woman to have won the coveted FIFA World Player of the Year award. She accepted it in 2002 in Madrid.

Mickey (Hebrew) Short for Michael, meaning who is like God. In the 60s, Mary Kathryn Wright, nicknamed Mickey, was the best female golfer in the States. She won 13 majors throughout her career and an amazing 82 victories overall.

Nadia (Slavic) Hope. In 1976, Russian Nadia Comaneci became the first gymnast to receive a perfect score in the Olympics. She was only 14 at the time.

Nathalie (French, Latin) Variant of Natalie; born on Christmas. The most famous Canadian athlete of this name: Nathalie Lambert, three-time Olympic champion in short-distance speed skating.

Sami (Hebrew) Honoured. Canadian women's hockey star Sami Jo Small helped Team Canada to win gold twice at the 1999 and 2000 World Championships. She also won a silver medal at the 1998 Olympics and gold at the 2002 games.

Serena (Latin) Peaceful; serene. A bit more low-key than her exuberant sister, Serena Williams is just as powerful on the tennis court.

Silken (Unique) Canadian rowing champion Silken Laumann is the only Silken we've heard of. Her triumphs over injury define her as courageous, determined and inspirational.

Venus (Latin) Roman goddess of love. Famous athlete of the same name is tennis superstar Venus Williams—stylish, strong, trend-setter.

Veronica (Latin) True image. Canada's dancing queen, Veronica Tennant was born in England but raised in Toronto. She captivated audiences with her skilled ballet performances for more than a quarter of a century. Another Canadian athlete of this name is award-winning aerial skier Veronica Brenner.

Wilma (German) Protector. Track star Wilma Rudolph won gold in three events at the 1960 Olympics in Rome, making her the fastest woman in the world at the time. And she was number 17 of 21 children, thus proving that undivided parental attention is not necessary for Olympic success!

Car Names

Naming kids after cars is hardly a new phenomenon, but it hasn't seemed to fall far out of fashion either. While naming a child Volkswagen is just plain cruel, the following names might be easier to get your other half to agree to. And remember: cars were first named after people (e.g., Ford, Chrysler and Mercedes), so this is just a natural progression, right?

Car Names for Boys

Alto	Elan	Lupo
Asten	Ferrari	Martin
Audi	Fiat	Maserati
Austin	Forester	Mentor
Baleno	Ford	Morgan
Bentley	Healey	Nissan
Cherokee	Jaguar	Passat
Clarus	Jensen	Peugeot
Cobalt	Justy	Polo
Cooper	Korando	Pride
Corrado	Lancer	Proton
Daimler	Leon	Punto

Quattro
Ralliart
Renault
Rexton
Rio

Rover
Scion
Subaru
Suzuki
Targa

Toledo
Touran
Triumph
Wrangler

Car Names for Girls

Alhambra
Altima
Arosa
Audi
Bora
Carens
Carerra
Carina
Camry
Cayenne
Celica
Citroën
Cordoba
Corolla
Corsa
Corvette
Dacia
Elise
Esprit

Fabia
Felicia
Kia
Kelisa
Kenari
Honda
Impreza
Isuzu
Laguna
Legacy
Lexus
Liana
Lotus
Mazda
Megane
Mercedes
Morgan
Niva
Octavia

Odyssey
Prelude
Previa
Porsche
Riva
Samara
Satria
Scenic
Sharan
Shelby
Sienna
Solara
Sorento
Starlet
Tigra
Vitara
Wira

 FUN FACTS

Two American boys have the name ESPN. Their parents bring a whole new meaning to the name sports nuts!

Although his stage name definitely suits him, Sting was born Gordon Matthew Sumner.

In high school, actor Keanu Reeves' hockey teammates nicknamed him "the wall" to reflect his goalie position.

CANUCK TRIVIA

John and Mary were the most popular names in Nova Scotia in 1950.

Group of Seven painter A.Y. Jackson's full name was Alexander Young.

Agree to disagree

As you've probably noticed, you and your partner won't agree on everything—like how to spend that extra $1,000. And no matter how hard you try, it's going to be tough to convince her to do something she doesn't want to—like name your baby Volvo. Here are a few tips to help you on the road to amends.

Use charm

Sometimes all it takes are a few compliments and a nice back rub to change your partner's mind. Remember to mention how beautiful she looks pregnant and credit all the hard work she's doing to carry your baby. Offering to make dinner and clean up might help, too.

Spend cash

Roses, diamonds, a new car. If you're that set on having her agree to the name you choose, spare no expense on buying her over.

Compromise

She likes Camilla, you like Carmella. Either combine the two names to create a new one or agree that she can name this baby and you name the next. Another option: use your favourite as a middle name instead.

Talk therapy

Schedule time to sit down and rationally discuss your individual choices. Ask her to explain why she doesn't think Labatt is an appropriate name for your future son and you can tell her why you're less fond of Pookey for a girl.

Keep trying

Still can't agree? Keep suggesting names until you finally find one you both approve of. This could be a slow process, taking several months, so start early.

Flip a coin

One of the most famous methods of solving arguments is the coin toss. Used in playgrounds, on sports fields and even at the office, this can often be one of the easiest ways to make a decision. Heads is her name. Tails is yours. Just make sure she doesn't find out that it was a double-sided coin.

Take a poll

Make a list of your top three names and ask her to do the same. Then survey friends and family members to find out their thoughts. Poll as many men as women to make the results more equal. And if you lose, do so graciously. There's always the next kid!

Chapter 3

☆

Truly Canadian

Want to prove your patriotism? Why not give your child a homegrown, truly Canadian name? Now I'm not talking about naming your kid Canada, beaver or moose. And I'm not saying you should have his name tattooed in a maple leaf on his left butt cheek. What I mean is: why not choose a name that represents Canadians—the original ones who helped found our country?

What is a Canadian? To some, we're a beer-drinking, hockey-playing, igloo-building bunch. To others, we're compassionate pacificists who may run the risk of being enveloped by the U.S. A more true description of a Canuck, however, must include our tolerance, love of nature and readiness to embrace other cultures.

Sound hokey? Perhaps, but I don't think you can truly define a Canadian without paying homage to the magnificent land we live off and the people who were here first, creating our history and laying the foundation for where we are today. Although we have a short history in comparison to other countries, it is rich in stories about those who settled here before us, fighting for their own freedoms and consequently our own.

While the majority of Canada's early immigrants came from England, France and Eastern Europe (see "Canada's immigrants" on page 62), we mustn't forget those who were here when they

REAL NAMES

Laurie Jean is proud of her Scottish heritage and loves that her name represents it. "[My name] means that I am part of a family," says the 33-year-old. "I have a cousin Laurie. My mother's middle name is Jean and my grandmother's name was Jean."

When Theresa was born 35 years ago, her parents named her after her grandmother, adding an 'h' to make it seem more Canadian. "My name keeps me attached to my heritage," she says. "[But] I have often wished I had a different name because I feel the expectations of being named after someone."

Sixty-year-old John describes his name as "common, unpretentious and unassuming." He was named, traditionally, after the Biblical saint. Sometimes, though, he says he wishes his name linked him to his mother's aboriginal heritage. "Her maiden name was Cadotte, a surname that is well known in Métis history."

Chantel's real name is Marguerite, but her parents decided to call her by her middle name instead. "They were following a tradition they both had of using their own middle names," explains the 29-year-old. Chantel's favourite part about her name is the fact that it's French and reflects her father's heritage. Since she grew up in an English-speaking environment, however, her name's pronounced as "shan-tell," not "shawn-tell" as it would be in French.

Nadine's mother wanted to make sure her child wouldn't develop an English nickname. So she chose Josette (which can be shortened to Josie) as a middle name and Nadine as a first name for her now 28-year-old. Since Nadine spends most of her time around Anglophones and pronounces her name in French, however, she says she often has to spell it in order for people to understand it.

Fergus's name means more to him than it does to most people. "[It] means I'm Irish," says the 31-year-old. "It connects me to the place my ancestors live...my name grounds me there, gives me a home." After Fergus's father moved to Canada, he pined for his homeland of Ireland. So he chose a traditional name to bestow on his son. "He wanted very badly to implant in me the magic of that place," Fergus says. "I believe he has succeeded."

arrived—the First Nations peoples who were the original settlers. And what about the various groups created by the arrival of the immigrants? From Acadians in the Maritimes to French Canadians in Québec and the Métis in Central and Western Canada, a combining of cultures helped create what are now known as truly Canadian identities.

With these groups came a mixing of languages, cultures and, of course, naming traditions. It was these people who created the meaning of true Canadian names. And, as you'll notice from the following lists, some of their traditions are so intertwined that they even share some common names between them.

Acadian Names

"Acadia" was the term once used to describe French colonies in southeastern Québec, New Brunswick, Nova Scotia and Prince Edward Island. "Acadian" was the name given to the French immigrants who settled in these areas. Although inhabitants were said to begin arriving in the early 1600s, it wasn't until 1605, when the French erected Port Royal in Nova Scotia, that true colonization of Acadia began.

In the one hundred or so years that followed, Acadia was passed back and forth between British and French rule. In 1713, the French finally ceded mainland Nova Scotia to the British. In 1755, the Brits deported most of the Acadians to American colonies, while some were sent back to France or imprisoned in England. A few sneaked back into their homeland while others managed to escape the deportation by hiding in Québec. After the Treaty of Paris in 1763, many of the deported Acadians were finally able to return home.

Today, Acadia includes communities in New Brunswick, P.E.I., parts of Newfoundland, Cape Breton and mainland Nova Scotia. While popular surnames of early Acadia included Babin, Gaudet, Morin, Blanchard and Terriot, finding common first names proved a more difficult task. By searching through New Brunswick's genealogy records, I managed to come up with some common names used by the Acadians during the late nineteenth and early twentieth centuries. As you will see, most of them have a strong French influence.

Acadian Boys' Names

Abel (Hebrew, Assyrian) Breath; child.

Aimé (French) Masculine form of Amy, meaning beloved.

Alphe (French) Form of Alfie, a form of Alfred, meaning wise counselor.

Alphie (French) Form of Alfie, a form of Alfred, meaning wise counselor.

Anthony (Latin, Greek) Praiseworthy; priceless; flourishing.

Antoine (French) Form of Anthony, meaning praiseworthy and priceless.

Armand (French) In the army.

Auguste (German, Latin) Form of Augustus, meaning magnificent.

Beulah (Arabic) Married.

Calixte (Greek) Beautiful.

Cecil (English, Latin) Blind.

Charles (English) Strong and manly.

Clarence (Latin) Clear.

Denis (Greek) Form of Dennis, meaning follower of Greek god of wine Dionysus.

Domitilde (French) From Domitius, meaning a home.

Édouard (French) Form of Edward, meaning prosperous guardian.

Elie (Hebrew) Form of Eli, meaning uplifted.

Elzear (French) Patron saint of farming.

Emelien (French) From Amelius, meaning to rival; compete.

Eutrope (French) From Eutropia, meaning good; honour.

Felix (Latin) Privileged; happy.

François (French) Form of Francis, meaning free and from France.

George (Greek) Farmer of the earth.

Germain (French) From Germany.

Harris (English) Short for Harrison, meaning son of Harry.

Harry (English) Form of Harold, meaning ruler of the army.

Hedley (English) Meadow filled with heather.

Hilaire (French) Form of Hilary, meaning happy; cheerful.

Hilarion (Latin) Happy.

Hillas (Latin) Form of Hilary, meaning happy.

Hypolite (French) Unknown.

Jacques (French) Form of Jacob, meaning supplanter.

Joseph (Hebrew) God adds.

Jules (French) Young; youthful.

Leonide (Latin) A lion.

Léonie (French) Form of Leonius, meaning lion.

Levite (Hebrew) Form of Levi, meaning harmonious.

Llewellyn (Old English, Welsh) Ruling; lion-like.

Lucien (French) Form of Lucius, meaning bright light.

Nelson (English) The son of Neil.

Onesime (French) Profitable.

Onezime (French) Profitable.

Orell (English, Slavic) An ore hill; eagle.

Pacifique (French) Peaceful; peace-loving.

Perley (English) Prized gem of the sea.

Pierre (French) Form of Peter, meaning rock.

Prudent (Latin) Form of Prudence, meaning cautious.

René (French) Form of Renatus, meaning reborn.

Theddy (Greek) Form of Theodore, meaning God's gift.

Tiburce (Hungarian) From the name Tibor, meaning holy place.

Acadian Girls' Names

Adele (French, German) Noble; a Québec place name.

Albertine (French, German) A feminine form of Albert, meaning bright and noble.

Alice (Greek, German) Honest; noble.

Alima (Arabic) Wise.

Alma (Latin) Soul.

Barrie (Irish) Feminine form of Barry, meaning spear-maker.

Brigit (Irish, Scandinavian) Form of Bridget, meaning strong.

Caroline (Latin, French, German) Small and feminine.

Catherine (Greek) Pure.

Celia (Latin) Form of Cecilia, meaning blind.

Claudia (Latin) Lame.

Corine (French) Form of Corinne, meaning maiden.

Delia (Greek) Seen from Delos.

Domitilde (French) From Domitius, meaning a home.

Dora (Greek) A gift.

Edna (Hebrew) Delight.

Egline (French) From Église, meaning church.

Elisabeth (Hebrew) Form of Elizabeth, meaning God's oath.

Eliza (Hebrew) Short for Elizabeth, meaning God's oath.

Elodie (Greek) White blossom.

Emelia (German) Form of Emily, meaning industrious.

Emerise (French) From Aimerie, meaning rich ruler or king.

Emille (German) Form of Emily, meaning industrious.

Euphemie (Greek) Form of Euphemia, meaning spoken well of and highly regarded.

Exilie (French) From the word exiler, meaning exile.

Fannie (American) Form of Frances, meaning free.

Fidele (Latin) Form of Fidelity, meaning faithful.

Genevieve (French) A white wave.

Helene (French) Form of Helen, meaning light.

Ida (English, German) Prosperous.

Jeanne (French, Scottish) Feminine form of John, meaning God is merciful.

Leandre (Greek, Latin) A lioness.

Léonie (French) Form of Leona, meaning brave as a lion.

Leontine (Latin) Like a lioness.

Litian (Greek) A form of Lidia, meaning woman from Lydia.

Louisa (English, Greek) Form of Louise, meaning a renowned warrior; honourable fighter.

Margaret (Greek, Latin, Persian) Pearl; child of the light.

Marguerite (French) Form of Marguerite, a form of Margaret, meaning pearl.

Marie Agnès (French) Combination of Marie, a form of Mary, meaning bitter, and Agnes, meaning pure.

Marie Anne (French) Combination of Marie, a form of Mary, meaning bitter, and Anne, meaning gracious.

Marie Denise (French) Combination of Marie, a form of Mary, meaning bitter, and Denise, meaning a follower of Greek god of wine, Dionysus.

Marie Yvonne (French) Combination of Marie, a form of Mary, meaning bitter, and Yvonne, meaning a young archer.

Mary (Hebrew) Bitter.

Melanea (Greek) Form of Melanie, meaning dark.

Nellie (English, Greek) Form of Cornelia, meaning the colour of a horn; form of Eleanor, meaning light; intelligent one.

Olivia (Latin) An olive tree.

Pacifique (French) Pacific; an ocean.

Philomene (Greek) Form of Philomena, meaning a love song; loved one.

Rosabell (French) Form of Rosabel, meaning beautiful rose.

Rosana (English) Form of Roseanne, meaning a gracious rose.

Rosella (Italian) Form of Rosa, which is a form of Rose.

Thadee (Greek) Form of Thaddea, meaning courageous.

Vivine (French) Form of Vivian, meaning lively; energetic.

Zelina (Greek) Zealous; passionate.

 KIDS' KORNER

Brandon's parents gave him his name because "it was the second best name that they thought of," he says. So what does he think of their choice? "I like it because most kids don't have that name," says the 12-year-old, "[but] it is so boring."

Samantha says she has a pretty name. But often the four-year-old wishes it were a bit shorter. If she had to choose another name for herself, she'd pick Sleeping Beauty or Lexia, after a dog she likes from school.

Ryan's name is short and easy to say—two definite pluses in his mind. The downsides? "It sounds like similar names (Bryan, Simon) and it's [too] popular," says the 13-year-old.

Although eight-year-old Sarah doesn't know why her parents gave her this name, she sometimes wishes she had been consulted in the process. "I would like to be called Alex," she says. Not only because it's not as popular as her own name, but "because I just like the name."

"I like everything about my name," boasts five-year-old Kaylyn. "My name is the same as someone famous (Kalan Porter) [and] there isn't anything that I do not like." If she had to choose another name for herself, Kaylyn says she'd pick Katie after her best friend.

Nichole describes her name as plain and simple. But she's definitely proud of the one thing that sets herself apart from other Nicoles in her school. "It's spelled with an 'h'," says the 13-year-old. "No one else I know spells it like that, which makes the spelling unique."

First Nations Names

The true first inhabitants of Canada, members of the First Nations groups, are thought to have originated in Siberia, making their way through Alaska to settle in Northern Canada. Made up of numerous tribes including the Cree, Inuit, Ojibway and Métis, the majority of these peoples live in the Yukon, North West Territories, Nunavut and Ontario, while a large number also reside in British Columbia. They boast about 60 Aboriginal languages between them.

Unfortunately, according to Cheryl McLean, Director of First Nation Relations and Aboriginal Languages for the Government of Yukon, you probably won't be able to find any of these languages in a book. The reason? Many of the Aboriginal peoples responsible for carrying on these languages believe that writing them down poses a barrier to keeping them alive. So the likelihood of you finding a Tagish or Tlingit dictionary are pretty slim.

Another well-guarded secret of the First Nations peoples are their names. First names hold extreme significance to members of these groups, says Winona Wheeler, a professor at the First Nations University of Canada in Saskatoon, Saskatchewan. Each name is spirit-given and one person can have as many as three or four. In order to learn the naming history behind these spiritual ties, however, you have to engage in indigenous research methods, namely finding an elder of a First Nations tribe and offering him or her tobacco before discussing naming traditions in person.

Since I am not able to publish any of the spirit names, I've chosen to include a few First Nations words that are used commonly in dialect but not as names. These could be a wonderful way to embrace the culture while giving your child a name that stands out.

First Nations' Words

Aagim (Ojibway) Snowshoe.

Aamoo (Ojibway) Bee.

Aandeg (Ojibway) Crow.

Acahkos (Cree) Star.

Adik (Ojibway) Caribou.

Älaya (Southern Tutchone) My friend.

Amik (Ojibway) Beaver.

Atim (Blackfoot, Cree) Dog.

Bapakine (Ojibway) Grasshopper.

Behanem (Abenaki, Ojibway) Woman.

Bikwak (Ojibway) Arrow.

Digo (Ojibway) Wave.

Dinjii (Gwich'in) Man.

Ehsa (Mohawk) Black ash.

Entie (Mohawk) South.

Esiban (Ojibway) Raccoon.

Gizos (Abenaki, Ojibway) Moon.

Ikwe (Algonquin, Ojibway) Woman.

Inini (Ojibway) Man.

Ishkode (Ojibway) Fire.

Iskwew (Blackfoot, Cree) Woman.

Karihton (Mohawk) Black oak.

Kinosew (Cree) Fish.

Linto (Ojibway) To sing.

Makwa (Ojibway) Bear.

Manicos (Cree) Bug.

Mekwi (Abenaki, Ojibway) Red.

Minis (Ojibway) Island.

Misanwi (Ojibway) Snow falls from the trees.

Miskomin (Ojibway) Raspberry.

Miskwaa (Algonquin) Red.

Mistik (Cree) Tree or stick.

Mitíg (Ojibway) Tree.

Mukwa (Ojibway) Bear.

Nagamon (Ojibway) Song.

Namito (Abenaki, Ojibway) To see.

Nebi (Abenaki, Ojibway) Water.

Nibii (Algonquin) Water.

Nikamew (Blackfoot, Cree) To sing.

Níkánít (Cree) Leader.

Nodam (Ojibway) To hear.

Ogin (Ojibway) Rosehip.

Okinís (Cree) Little rosehip.

Okonhsa (Mohawk) Pansy.

Onehta (Mohawk) Pine tree.

Onerahte (Mohawk) Leaf.

Opichí (Ojibway) Robin.

Owera (Mohawk) Wind.

Pehtam (Blackfoot, Cree) To hear.

Pinesis (Cree) Bird.

Shijàa (Gwich'in) My friend.

Shùh (Gwich'in) Spot.

Sisip (Cree) Duck.

Sonhatsi (Mohawk) Black duck.

Sosê (Mohawk) English translation is Joseph.

Thèna (Southern Tutchone) Little star.

Tsorahsa (Mohawk) Iron wood.

Wadiswan (Ojibway) Bird's nest.

Wahta (Mohawk) Red maple.

Wasko (Cree) Cloud.

Zanôba (Abenaki, Ojibway) Man.

Zhoh (Gwich'in) Snow.

French Canadian Names

French Europeans were among the first explorers to discover our country. In fact, famed explorer Jacques Cartier reached our land in 1535, landing in Newfoundland during his search for a passage to the Pacific. Other French travelers followed Cartier's lead, making the voyage to what is now Canada. And they liked what they saw, especially in Québec and the Atlantic provinces. So they stayed. Now called French Canadians, the new generation of these peoples make up the second largest ethnic group in Canada. And French-speakers compose close to 25 percent of our population.

They've fought for decades to preserve their language and traditions in this country. And their most recent effort to safeguard the culture was the almost successful attempt to declare Québec as a sovereign state, entirely separate from the rest of Canada. For now, however, they remain a part of the country they helped to establish and their names can be heard from coast to coast.

According to Micheline Perreault, Directrice Générale of the Société Généalogique Canadienne-Française, the majority of popular French Canadian names originated from the Catholic religion. For instance, Michel came from the angel Michael, Joseph from the father of Jesus and Pierre from the apostle Peter. The following is a list of those that have been popular in Québec over the past 30 years.

French Canadian Boys' Names

Albert (German) Bright and noble.

Alexandre (French) Form of Alexander, meaning man's defender.

Alexis (Greek) Form of Alexander, meaning man's defender.

Anthony (Latin, Greek) Praiseworthy; priceless; flourishing.

Arthur (Celtic) Bear; noble; follower of Thor.

Charles (English) Strong and manly.

David (Hebrew) Beloved.

Felix (Latin) Privileged; happy.

Francis (Latin) Free and from France.

Gabriel (Hebrew) Devoted to God; strength of God.

Guillaume (French) Form of William, meaning fearless protector.

Henri (French) Form of Henry, meaning household ruler.

Jacques (French) Form of Jacob, meaning supplanter.

Jeremy (English) Form of Jeremiah, meaning uplifted by God.

Jonathan (Hebrew) Form of Johnathan, meaning God's gift.

Joseph (Hebrew) God adds.

Kevin (Celtic) Handsome; gentle.

Louis (German) Renowned warrior.

Mathieu (French) Form of Matthew, meaning a gift from God.

Mathis (French) Form of Matthew, meaning a gift from God.

Maxime (French) The greatest.

Michel (French) Form of Michael, meaning who is like God.

Nicolas (French) Form of Nicholas, meaning the victorious people.

Olivier (French) Form of Oliver, meaning olive tree.

Philippe (French) Form of Philip, meaning horse lover.

Pierre (French) Form of Peter, meaning rock.

Samuel (Hebrew) God listens.

Sébastien (French) Form of Sebastian, meaning respected; admired.

Simon (Hebrew) A good listener.

Thomas (Greek) Twin.

Vincent (Latin) Conqueror.

William (English) Fearless protector.

Xavier (Arabic, Basque) Bright; a new house.

Zacharie (Hebrew) Form of Zachary, meaning remembered by God.

Zachary (Hebrew) Remembered by God; a form of Zachariah.

French Canadian Girls' Names

Alexandra (Greek) Protector of mankind.

Ariane (French) Holy.

Audrey (English) Noble and strong.

Blanche (French) White.

Caliste (French) Form of Calista, meaning the most attractive.

Camille (French) A religious helper.

Caroline (Latin, French, German) Small and feminine.

Catherine (Greek) Pure.

Émilie (French) Form of Emily, meaning industrious.

Gabrielle (Hebrew, French) Devoted or faithful to God.

Jade (Spanish) A green gem.

Jeanne (French, Scottish) Feminine form of John, meaning God is merciful.

Jessica (Hebrew) Wealthy; grace of God.

Julie (English) Form of Julia, meaning young.

Karine (Russian) Form of Karen, meaning pure.

Laurence (French) Feminine form of Laurence, meaning crowned with laurels.

Laurie (English) Form of Laura, meaning crowned with laurels.

Lea (Hebrew) Form of Leah, meaning weary; tired.

Lise (Danish, German) Form of Elizabeth, meaning God's oath.

Louise (German) Famous maiden warrior; female form of Louis, meaning renowned warrior.

Marie (French) Form of Mary, meaning bitter.

Marie-Ève (French) Combination of Marie, a form of Mary, meaning bitter, and Eve, meaning life.

Marie-Pier (French) Combination of Marie, a form of Mary, meaning bitter, and Pierre, meaning rock.

Marion (French) An alternate form of Mary, meaning bitter.

Maude (Hebrew, German) From Madeline, meaning woman of Magdala; a high tower; strong in combat.

Megan (Greek, Irish) Strong; a pearl.

Mélissa (French) Form of Melissa, meaning honey; a bee.

Nicole (Greek, French) People of victory.

Noemie (French) Form of Naomi, meaning pleasant one; beauty.

Roxanne (Persian) Brilliant; sunrise.

Sabrina (Latin) One from a border land.

Sarah (Hebrew) Princess.

Stéphanie (French) Form of Stephanie, meaning a crown.

Valérie (French) Form of Valerie, meaning strong.

Vanessa (Greek) A butterfly.

 **FUN FACTS**

Many Jewish people consider it disrespectful to alter a Hebrew name.

Actress Kate Hudson, whose middle name is Garry, gave son Ryder the middle name Russell after her mother's long-time partner, actor Kurt Russell.

Pope John Paul II was born Karol Jozef Wojtyla in Wadomis, Poland.

Inuit Names

Once known as Eskimos ("eaters of raw meat"), the more aptly named Inuit ("the people") live mostly in Northern Canada, particularly Baffin Island and Nunavut. And they were the last of all First Nations groups to put an end to their nomadic lifestyle. Yet many still live in igloos in the winter, skin tents in the summer and hunt seal, deer and moose to maintain their survival.

Over the years, the Inuit have struggled to maintain power politically. They finally won a major battle in 1999 with the creation of Nunavut ("our land"), a province run and inhabited by a mainly Inuit population.

Like other First Nation groups, the Inuit, too, guard their names as a valuable secret. As a result, I could not uncover any of the spiritual names used by the inhabitants of our far north. Instead, I discovered a variety of non-spiritual, non-sacred words in the Inuktitut language that could work well for naming a child. Since the language varies a bit by region, I've included a few of the areas specific to different words.

Inuktitut Words

Aasaq (West Greenland) Summer.

Aivik (Labrador) Walrus.

Aiviq (North Baffin) Walrus.

Amaguk (Labrador) Wolf.

Amiq Tree bark.

Aputik Snow.

Arvik (North Baffin) Whale.

Aujak (Labrador) Summer.

Elisapie English translation is Elizabeth.

Nanu (West Greenland) Polar bear.

Natsiq Seal.

Pannaq Dry tree.

Piaraq Young animal.

Qau Day; daylight.

Siginik (Labrador) Sun.

Siqniq Sun.

Tatqik Moon.

Timmiak (Labrador) Bird.

Timmiaq (West and East Greenland) Bird.

Tinujuq Half moon.

Tuktu Caribou.

Tuttu (West Greenland) Caribou.

Tuttug (East Greenland) Caribou.

Tuttuk (Labrador) Caribou.

Ukiak (Labrador) Fall.

Ukiuk (Labrador) Winter.

Ukiuq (North Baffin) Winter.

Ulluq (West Greenland) Day.

Uumajuq Animal.

Métis Names

The word Métis, meaning mixed, perfectly describes this Canadian group. Their culture originated in the eighteenth century from relationships between French-speaking European fur traders and women of Cree, Ojibway, Assiniboine and Sulteaux descent in the northwestern part of the country. Their subsequent mixing of a variety of languages and traditions helped set the Métis apart from other First Nations groups. Instead of being merely Aboriginal or European, the Métis are considered a combination of the two. And they make up 20 percent of the First Nations population.

Today, 68 percent of the Métis live in urban areas, mainly Winnipeg, Edmonton, Vancouver, Calgary and Saskatoon. The remaining 32 percent live mostly in rural areas in the western regions of the country, with just over two percent of them residing on reserves. In addition to speaking English and French, the Métis created their own language, Michif, which combines the two dialects.

Darren Préfontaine, a curriculum development officer at the Gabriel Dumont Institute of Native Studies and Applied research in Regina, Saskatchewan, says traditional Métis names often had a strong French Canadian influence. But like they did with the French language, the Métis often changed spellings and pronunciation to make words their own, sometimes adding their Aboriginal roots for even more originality.

Although there are no easily found records of these names, Préfontaine claims that old-fashioned monikers like Albertine, Marguerite, Louis and Pierre were commonly seen in the nineteenth century. Some Métis peoples were also given a First Nations name (e.g., Big Bear) based on a particular familial or personality trait, which they may have chosen to use instead of a birth name. Another popular naming tradition among the Métis was, and continues to be, the use of nicknames. The word chi, for instance, is short for the French petite, meaning small. It's often added to garcon or fille as a term of endearment.

Unfortunately, traditional Métis names have been phased out since just after World War II. The reason? People were influenced by mass culture and began to use names that were the most popular at the time. Regrettably for history and tradition's sake, this trend has continued today.

Since there are few records of popular Métis names, I searched though genealogical archival records at Calgary's Glenbow Museum to find a list of names used by members of this group over the years. Here are a few from those that I found.

Métis Boys' Names

Alexander (Greek) Man's defender.

Alexis (Greek) Short form of Alexander, meaning man's defender.

Amable (Latin, French) Lovable.

André (French) Form of Andrew, meaning manly and courageous.

Andrew (Greek) Manly; courageous.

Angus (Scottish) Excellent.

Antoine (French) Form of Anthony, meaning praiseworthy and priceless.

Archibald (German) Bold.

Augustin (French) Form of Augustine, meaning honoured and exalted.

Augustine (Latin, French) Honoured; exalted.

Baptiste (French) Baptist.

Basil (Greek, Latin) Royal, brave.

Bruno (German) Brown-skinned.

David (Hebrew) Beloved.

Donald (Scottish, Old English) A world leader.

Édouard (French) Form of Edward, meaning a guardian of property.

Étienne (French) Form of Stephen, meaning crown.

Felix (Latin) Privileged; happy.

Finlay (Scottish) A fair hero.

Flett (English) Short for Fletcher, meaning arrow maker.

François (French) Form of Francis, meaning free and from France.

Gengoque (Unique) Form of George, meaning farmer of the earth.

George (Greek) Farmer of the earth.

Hiacynthe (French) Form of Hyacinthe, meaning Hyacinth.

Hugh (English) Intelligent; bright in spirit.

Hyacinthe (French) Hyacinth.

Ignace (Latin) Form of Ignatius, meaning fiery.

James (Hebrew) Someone who replaces.

Jean Baptiste (French) After St. John the Baptist.

John (Hebrew) God is merciful.

Joseph (Hebrew) God adds.

Josepha (Hebrew) Form of Joseph, meaning God adds.

Louis (German) Renowned warrior.

Lucius (Latin) A light.

Magnus (Latin) Large; great.

Nicol (Greek, French) Short for Nicholas, meaning triumphant people.

Oman (Arabic) Place name.

Peter (Latin, Greek) Rock.

Pierre (French) Form of Peter, meaning rock.

Samuel (Hebrew) God listens.

Soloman (Hebrew) Man of peace; peaceful.

Thomas (Greek) Twin.

Toussaint (French) All saints; a last name.

Ulrie (German) Form of Ulrich, meaning ruler of the wolves.

Wesley (English) A western meadow.

Willard (German, Teutonic) Bold; determined; brave.

William (English) Fearless protector.

Métis Girls' Names

Adelaide (Hebrew, German, Latin) Noble; kind; a place name.

Adelgarde (German) A form of Adelaide, meaning noble.

Agathe (Greek) Good.

Angelique (French) Angelic; form of Angela, meaning messenger.

Ann (Hebrew) Gracious.

Annie (Hebrew) Form of Ann, meaning gracious.

Antoine (French) Short for Antoinette, a form of Antonia, meaning praiseworthy.

CANUCK TRIVIA

Hockey legend Maurice "Rocket" Richard's full name is Joseph Henri Maurice Richard.

Former Prime Minister John Diefenbaker's middle name was George.

Barbary (Latin) Form of Barbara, meaning foreigner.

Betsy (English) Form of Elizabeth, meaning God's oath.

Catherine (Greek) Pure.

Christianna (Greek) Form of Christina, meaning Christian.

Elise (French) Form of Elizabeth, meaning God's oath and devoted to God.

Eliza (Hebrew) Form of Elizabeth, meaning God's oath and devoted to God.

Elizabeth (Hebrew) God's oath; devoted to God.

Emile (Latin) Easy to please.

Flora (Latin) A flower.

Francoise (French) Form of Frances, meaning free and from France.

Genevieve (French) A white wave.

Harriet (French) Ruler of the house.

Henrietta (English, German) Ruler of the house.

Hester (Dutch, Persian) Form of Ester, meaning star.

Isabella (Hebrew, Italian) Form of Elizabeth, meaning God's oath.

Jemmima (Hebrew) Form of Jemima, meaning dove.

Jessie (Hebrew, English) Short for Jessica, meaning God sees; God's gift.

Josephte (French) Feminine form of Joseph, meaning God adds.

Josette (French) Form of Josephine, meaning God will increase.

Julie (Latin) Form of Julia, meaning young.

Justine (Latin) Feminine form of Justin, meaning righteous.

Lisette (French) Consecrated to God; form of Elizabeth, meaning God's oath and devoted to God.

Lizette (French) Form of Lisette, meaning consecrated to God.

Madeline (Hebrew) A woman from Magdala; a high tower.

Magdeline (Greek) A form of Madeline, meaning woman from Magdala; a high tower.

Marguerit (French) Form of Marguerite, a form of Margaret, meaning pearl.

Marguerite (French) Form of Margaret, meaning pearl.

Marianne (French) Form of Marie, French for Mary, meaning bitter.

Marie (French) Form of Mary, meaning bitter.

Marie Louis (French) Combination of Marie, meaning bitter, and Louis, meaning renowned warrior.

Mary (Hebrew) Bitter.

Maryan (Hebrew) Form of Mary, meaning bitter.

Monique (French) Form of Monica, meaning solitary; advisor.

Pelagie (Greek) Form of Pelagia, meaning of the sea.

Philomene (Greek) Form of Philomena, meaning lover of song.

Rosalie (English, Spanish) Form of Rosalind, meaning a pretty rose.

Sarah (Hebrew) Princess.

Sophie (Greek) Form of Sophia, meaning intelligence; wise.

Therese (Greek) Form of Theresa, meaning reaper.

Therise (Greek) Form of Theresa, meaning reaper.

Multiple names

So you're having more than one child. That makes choosing a name two, three or even four times as tough! And unfortunately, there's no guidebook to help you navigate the dos and don'ts of naming multiples. But look at the bright side: while parents of singles have to struggle with limiting their "yes" lists to just one name, you have the bonus of being able to choose two or more of your favourites. Just think of the possibilities!

But along with these possibilities can come confusion. Is it too cheesy to give my kids rhyming names? How do I choose names that complement each other? If I choose a common name for one, do I have to do the same for the other? Don't worry. Below are answers to these questions and more, plus a few helpful suggestions to help you decide.

Don't do the rhyme

Steer clear of rhyming names like Nala and Tala. While they may sound cute at first, they'll definitely set your kids up for schoolyard teasing. And just imagine how embarrassing it will sound when they're 30, introducing themselves to a room full of the social elite.

Reverse it

Some names, like Aidan, Eva and Olav, can create another name in reverse (i.e., Nadia, Ave and Valo). This is an easy way to connect your children's monikers without having to make them rhyme.

Use an anagram

Similar to using a name in reverse, choose an anagram when naming your children. Look through the book, find names that you like, and play with the spelling to create something new. Here are a few examples to get you started:

Mary—Myra

Edgar—Gerad

Karen—Renka

Stick with synonyms

With so many names to choose from, you're bound to find at least a few with the same meaning. For example, Margaret and Penina both mean pearl while Alexis and Zander mean defender of mankind. Or you could choose names that have similar connotations; Heather and Dahlia are both types of flowers. This way, your children's names can have the same implication even though the actual words may not look or sound alike.

Opt for opposites

Sometimes twins' personalities are as alike as yin and yang. Why not represent this difference by giving them names with opposite meanings—like Melanie (dark) and Phoebe (bright) or Bavol (air) and Dylan (sea)?

Choose a letter

Another way to create a bond between multiple names is by picking monikers that start with the same letter, like Charles and Chester or Caitlin and Casey. As long as you avoid rhyming names, and make sure that each name goes well with your last, you're in the clear.

Count the syllables

Instead of naming one twin Michelangelo and the other Fred, try choosing names that have the same number of syllables. It'll sound better when people say them aloud and gives the kids something more in common. Some good examples: Milton and Nestor, Rexton and Stanley, Caroline and Katherine and Joan and Leigh.

Keep them similar

Thinking of naming one child Sarah and the other Taniqua? Stop. While giving one child a unique name could help set her apart from her twin, it could also isolate the more commonly named child. Not only could it cause tension between the two—did they give her the "cool" name because they love her more?—but just think about how weird it will sound when you introduce them to people. It's best to avoid tension and misunderstandings by sticking with similar names— either unique or common, but not both—for each child.

Don't think about it

There's no rule that says there has to be a connection between the names of multiple children. Besides, having different names could help your kids to assert their individuality. So choose whatever names you like best. They're sure to thank you for it one day.

Canada's Immigrants

Without immigration, Canada wouldn't be the country it is today. There would be no Métis, French Canadians or Acadians, for one thing. And we'd have no distinct naming traditions of our own. So here's a brief history of Canada's first immigrants to help you understand how important they were—not only to our existence but to our names as well.

The British and Eastern Europeans were the first immigrants to settle in Western Canada during the late 1860s and early 1870s, bringing in names like Heinrich, Hans, Ingvar, Peder and Alfild. Included among them were Russian Mennonites as well as people from Iceland and the Ukraine. While the reasons for their emigration varied—Icelandic peoples were fleeing volcanic eruptions while Ukrainians sought refuge from poverty—their goals were similar: to find work, mainly in the farming industry. It wasn't until the 1880s that Jewish immigrants came, seeking work in the fur trade, gold mining, merchandising and farming sectors. Their landing spot of choice: Winnipeg, which made it a booming metropolis prior to 1900. In fact, this area was so attractive that a large number of Ontario-born Canadians moved there as well. Some of their traditional names included Abraham, Daniel, Esther and Rivka.

The majority of the immigrants up to this point were male, and they often left after saving enough money to make a difference to their lives back home. But some sent pre-paid passes for their families to join them on their new Canadian land, encouraging a large influx of even more foreigners to the country.

As of 1891, only 13 percent of the population was made up of foreign immigrants. They settled mainly in Ontario and the prairie provinces, especially Manitoba and Saskatchewan. Between 1901 and 1913, however, things changed. Canadians noticed an increase of over 34 percent in their country's total population—from 5.4 million to 7.2 million in a mere 10 years, with over 400,800 immigrants entering Canada in 1913. While the reason for this increase in migration is debatable, many believe the closing of the American frontier forced many immigrants to move up north to find work.

By 1921, people of other ethnicities began entering our gates—from Italy to Japan, more and more nationalities settled in our provinces. With them came new foods, knowledge, traditions and, of course, baby names.

Chapter 4

- ☆ -

Literary Names

A good book can have a lasting impact on a person's life.
Whether it's an unforgettable character or an insightful
piece of knowledge, you'll be hard-pressed to find someone who
can't name at least one novel that's had a profound effect on them.
Perhaps that's why naming children after famous authors and literary
characters has been a trend for so many decades—we just can't get
books out of our heads.

Don't believe me? I still remember every detail about John
Irving's *A Prayer for Owen Meany*, which I read over 15 years ago. And
my husband, who almost never reads a novel, suggested the name
Atticus from Harper Lee's *To Kill a Mockingbird* for our baby. Still not
convinced? One of today's most popular baby names is shared by the
protagonist in Jane Austen's *Emma*, which was published in the early
nineteenth century.

I've met numerous people who are named after classic works, like
Catherine (Jane Austen's *Northanger Abbey*), Jane (Charlotte Bronte's
Jane Eyre), Chaucer (Geoffrey Chaucer, author of *The Canterbury
Tales*) and Oliver (Charles Dickens' *Oliver Twist*). Plus, I've heard of
many a Holden (J.D. Salinger's *Catcher in the Rye*), Ahab (Herman
Melville's *Moby Dick*) and Scarlett (Margaret Mitchell's *Gone With
the Wind*).

REAL NAMES

Leigh, never a fan of "girly" names, is thankful that her parents had the foresight to give up on her real first name a few years after she was born. "My full name was Carrie Leigh," says the 30-year-old. "But after a while it was clear to my parents that Leigh suited me better, so by grade two I was Leigh."

Brigitte loves the French. Why? Because they're the only people who pronounce her name correctly, she says. "English people keep pronouncing my name as 'Brigitt'...but it sounds really bad, is quite annoying and is also aggravating," complains the 31-year-old.

Distinct. Different. Uncommon. That's how 37-year-old Lindsay describes his name. "I've never met another male Lindsay," he says proudly. But that uniqueness caused a few problems during childhood. "Growing up, the only other Lindsays were female, like Lindsay Wagner the Bionic Woman," he says. "I got teased a lot." If he had to pick another name, Lindsay says he'd choose Woodman because his father always wanted a Woodman in the family but didn't get one.

Twenty-nine-year-old Joy becomes very philosophical when discussing the meaning of her name. "It's like the chicken or the egg thing," she says. "Am I the way I am because I have the name I have, or does my name just fit with who I am? Either way, my name makes me who I am." Hmmm.

Debra says that her name is versatile. "It's short, two syllables and can be conjugated many ways," she explains. "I was Debbie when I was growing up and Debra when I was at university." Still known as Debra, the 45-year-old says it's now easy to figure out how people know her. "I can tell who's talking to me by what era of name they refer to," she says.

Lucky for Canadians, literature is one of our nation's most highly praised forms of art. From classics like *The Wars* by Timothy Findley to multiple award-winners like Michael Ondaatje's *The English Patient*, Canadian authors have proven time and again that we hold a mighty pen. Whether it's due to the long winters we spend inside or the beautiful landscapes we have outside our front doors, Canadian writers churn out an endless supply of original and captivating works. And for those of us searching for baby names, this means plenty of home-grown options to choose from.

Author Names

From Margaret Atwood to Yann Martel, award-winning Canadian authors have shown the international literary world why Canada should be valued for more than just igloos and Mounties. Here are a few of our greatest contributors.

Male Authors' Names

Al (Purdy) Wooler, Ontario. A poet and spoken-word performer, Purdy has won a Governor General's Award, the Order of Ontario, the Order of Canada and Peoples' Poet Award. He is the author of *The Cariboo Horses, Rooms for Rent in the Outer Planets, Selected Poems, Starting from Ameliasburgh, To Paris Never Again* and *Reaching for the Beaufort Sea*.

Alistair (MacLeod) North Battleford, Saskatchewan. Raised in Cape Breton, Nova Scotia, MacLeod is best known for his highly praised best-seller *No Great Mischief*. He has also written *The Lost Salt Gift of Blood, As Birds Bring Forth the Sun and Other Stories* and *Island: The Collected Stories of Alistair MacLeod*.

Austin (Clarke) Born in Barbados, lives in Toronto. Winner of a 2002 Giller Prize for fiction for *The Polished Hoe* and author of numerous books and poems, including *The Origin of Waves* and *The Question*.

bill (bissett) Halifax, Nova Scotia. bissett is the poetic author of *Loving without Being Vulnrabul, Th Influenza uv Logik, Th Last Photo uv th Human Soul, Inkorrect Thots* and *Hard 2 Beleev*.

Brian (Moore) Born in Northern Ireland, Moore is a Canadian citizen who worked for a while at *The Montreal Gazette*. He is the author of *The Doctor's Wife, The Great Victorian Collection, The Temptation of Eileen Hughes, The Luck of Ginger Coffey, The Mangan Inheritance, The Colour of Blood* and *The Magician's Wife*.

Charles (De Lint) Born in the Netherlands, De Lint moved to Canada as a child and lived in numerous towns. He is the author of many novels, including *The Onion Girl, Memory & Dream, Trader, Someplace to Be Flying, Forests of the Heart, Dreams Underfoot, The Ivory and the Horn* and *Moonlight and Vines.*

Colin (Angus) Victoria, British Columbia. Adventure writer extraordinaire, Angus is the author of *Amazon Extreme* and *Lost in Mongolia.*

Dan (Yashinsky) Born in Detroit, Yashinsky moved to Toronto at 21. He is the author of *Tales for An Unknown City, The Storyteller at Fault* and *Suddenly They Heard Footsteps.*

David (Adams Richards) Newcastle, New Brunswick. Winner of the Giller Prize and a Governor General's Award, Adams Richards is famous for compelling novels such as *Hope in the Desperate Hour, The Coming of Winter, Blood Ties, Small Gifts, The Bay of Love and Sorrows* and *Mercy Among the Children.* Another Canadian novelist of this name is **David Carpenter** of Saskatoon, Saskatchewan. This poet, writer and avid fisherman is the author of works like *Jokes for the Apocalypse, Jewels, God's Bedfellows, Fishing in Western Canada, Banjo Lessons* and *Courting Saskatchewan.*

Douglas (Coupland) Born on a West German airbase, Coupland was raised and lives in Vancouver. Creator of the phrase "Generation X," he wrote *Generation X: Tales for an Accelerated Culture, Shampoo Planet, Life after God* and *Terry.*

Earle (Birney) Calgary, Alberta. During his years as a writer, Birney published eight books of poetry and one memoir, including *The Straight of Anian, Turvey: A Military Picaresque, Down the Long Table* and *Spreading Time: Remarks on Canadian Writing and Writers.*

Edward Dickinson (Blodgett) Edmonton, Alberta. More commonly known as E.D., Blodgett authored poetry collections, such as *Take Away the Names, Sounding, Beast Gate, Musical Offering, Silence, the Word and the Sacred* and *Apostrophes II: Through You I.*

Émile (Nelligan) Montreal, Québec. One of French Canadians' most beloved poets, Nelligan wrote many pieces which were published in *Poèmes choisis, 31 Poèmes Autographes: 2 Carnets D'hôpital, The Complete Poems of Émile Nelligan, Le Recital des Anges: 50 Poèmes d'Émile Nelligan* and *Poèmes Autographes*.

Farley (Mowat) Belleville, Ontario. Mowat's books have been translated into 22 languages. Some of his works include *Lost in the Barrens, The Black Joke, The Curse of the Viking Grave, Canada North, Tundra, The Dog Who Wouldn't Be, Never Cry Wolf, The Polar Passion, The Desperate People* and *The Snow Walker*.

George Elliott (Clarke) Windsor, Nova Scotia. A poet, playwright and literary critic, Clarke's works include *Saltwater Spirituals and Deeper Blues, Lush Dreams, Blue Exile, Whylah Falls, Beatrice Chancy* and *One Heart Broken Into Song*.

Guy (Vanderhaeghe) Esterhazy, Saskatchewan. A celebrated best-selling Canadian author, Vanderhaeghe has written such well known titles as *Man Descending, Homesick, Things as They Are, The Englishman's Boy* and *The Last Crossing*.

John (Irving) Born in the U.S., Irving has made a home in both Toronto and Vermont. Many of his best-selling novels have been turned into movies, including *The World According to Garp, The Hotel New Hampshire, The Cider House Rules, A Prayer for Owen Meany* and *A Widow for One Year*. Irving's latest novel, which is largely set in Toronto, is titled *Until I Find You*. Another author of this name is **John Kenneth Galbraith**. Born in Iona Station, Ontario, Galbraith has published *The Affluent Society, The New Industrial State* and *Economics and the Public Purpose*.

Malcolm (Lowry) Born in England, Lowry spent close to 20 years in Dollarton, British Columbia. He is the author of *Ultramarine, Under the Volcano* and *Lunar Caustic*.

Marshall (McLuhan) Edmonton, Alberta. Besides writing numerous novels, McLuhan coined the famous phrases "the medium is the message" and "the global village." His published works include *The Mechanical Bride, Understanding Media, The Medium is the Message* and *War and Peace in the Global Village*.

M.G. (Vassanji) Born Moyez Vassanji in Africa, this writer moved to Toronto at the age of 30. His novels include *The Gunny Sack*, *Uhuru Street*, *The Book of Secrets*, *Amriika*, *No New Land* and *The In-Between World of Vikram Lall*.

Michael (Ondaatje) Born in Sri Lanka, lives in Toronto. Award-winning author of international best-sellers like *Anil's Ghost*, *The English Patient*, *Coming Through Slaughter* and *In the Skin of a Lion*.

Michel (Tremblay) Montreal, Québec. French Canadian playwright Tremblay is most famous for writing *Les Belles-Soeurs*, *La Duchesse de Langeais*, *La Duchesse et le Roturier*, *Des Nouvelles d'Édouard* and *La Maison Suspendue*.

Mordecai (Richler) Montreal, Québec. Multiple literary award winner, Richler has written books for both adults and children. His works include *The Acrobats*, *Barney's Version*, *Joshua Then and Now*, *Solomon Gursky Was Here*, *Cocksure*, *Home Sweet Home*, *Jacob Two-Two Meets the Hooded Fang* and *Jacob Two-Two and the Dinosaur*.

Nino (Ricci) Leamington, Ontario. Ricci has won numerous awards, including the Governor General's Award, the Trillium Award and the Betty Trask Award, for novels like *Lives of the Saints*, *In A Glass House*, *Where She Has Gone* and *Testament*.

Peter (Cumming) Brampton, Ontario. A children's author, director, playwright and journalist, Cumming wrote *Out on the Ice in the Middle of the Bay*, *Mogul and Me*, *A Horse Called Farmer*, *Ti-Jean* and *Snowdreams*.

Pierre (Berton) Whitehorse, Yukon. A companion of the Order of Canada and winner of three Governor General's Awards, this history-lover wrote numerous books, including *Klondike*, *The Promised Land*, *Pioneers of the North*, *Starting Out* and *The Invasion of Canada*.

Ralph (Connor) Glengarry, Ontario. Born Charles William Gordon, Connor wrote in the late nineteenth and early twentieth centuries. Among his novels are *Treading the Winepress*, *The Friendly Four*, *The Runner*, *The Man From Glengarry* and *The Arm of Gold*.

Robert W. (Service) Born in England, poet and novelist Robert William Service moved to Canada at the age of 20. Some of his best-known works include *The Shooting of Dan McGrew*, *The Law of the Yukon*, *The Cremation of Sam McGee* and *The House of Fear*.

Robertson (Davies) Thamesville, Ontario. Born William Robertson, Davies is most famous for his book *Fifth Business*. He also wrote *What's Bred in the Bone*, *The Manticore* and *World of Wonders*.

Robin (Blaser) Born in the States, Blaser moved to Canada at the age of 41. His published works include *The Moth Poem*, *Syntax*, *The Faerie Queene & The Park*, *Honestas*, *Pell Mell* and *The Holy Forest*.

Roch (Carrier) Sainte-Justine-de-Dorchester, Québec. Perhaps best known as the author of childrens' fave *The Hockey Sweater*, this Québecois author also penned *Prayers of a Very Wise Child*, *La Guerre, Yes Sir!* and *Il Est Par là, le Soleil*.

Rohinton (Mistry) Born in Bombay, Mistry immigrated to Toronto in the mid-70s. A master story-teller, Mistry has won multiple awards, including the Governor General's Award, Giller Prize and Commonwealth writers prize. His novels include *A Fine Balance*, *Such a Long Journey* and *Family Matters*.

Saul (Bellow) Lachine, Québec. Winner of a Nobel Prize, Bellow wrote plays and novels such as *Dangling Man*, *Herzog*, *The Last Analysis* and *The Bellarosa Connection*.

Stephen (Leacock) Born in England, Leacock was raised in Sutton, Ontario, and later attended Upper Canada College in Toronto. Leacock is best known for his humorous novels *Literary Lapses*, *Sunshine Sketches of a Little Town*, *Arcadian Adventures with the Idle Rich* and *My Discovery of England*.

Timothy (Findley) Toronto, Ontario. One of Canada's most prolific writers, Findley won numerous awards, including a Governor General's Award and Canadian Authors Association Award. He was also presented with the Order of Ontario and was named an Officer of The Order of Canada. His novels include *The Wars*, *The Last of the Crazy People*, *Famous Last Words*, *Not Wanted on the Voyage*, *Headhunter* and *The Piano Man's Daughter*.

William (Gibson) Born in the U.S. but raised and settled in Vancouver, Gibson is the science fiction novelist of such works as *Neuromancer, Count Zero, Idoru, All Tomorrow's Parties* and *Pattern Recognition.*

W.O. (Mitchell) Weyburn, Saskatchewan. William Ormond Mitchell wrote numerous short stories, novels and plays. Among his best are *Who Has Seen the Wind, Jake and the Kid, The Kite, The Vanishing Point* and *Roses Are Difficult Here.*

W.P. (Kinsella) Edmonton, Alberta. Born William Patrick, Kinsella writes mainly about his passion—baseball. His many novels include *Shoeless Joe, Field of Dreams* and *Dance Me Outside.*

Yann (Martel) Born in Spain, Martel spent much of his youth traveling. He's lived in Alaska, British Columbia, Ontario and Costa Rica, just to name a few places. He currently resides in Montreal and has written award-winning novels like *The Facts Behind the Helsinki Roccamatios, Self* and Booker prize-winning *The Life of Pi.*

Female Authors' Names

Alice (Munro) Wingham, Ontario. Three-time Governor General's Award Winner, Munro is best known for books like *The Lives of Girls and Women, The Love of a Good Woman* and *Runaway.* Many of her short stories are set in rural Ontario.

Anne (Hébert) Sainte-Catherine-de-Fossambault, Québec. Winner of a Governor General's Award for her poetry, this French writer is known for collections such as *Les songes en équilibres, Le Torrent* and *Le Tombeau des Rois.*

Ann-Marie (MacDonald) Born in West Germany, MacDonald lives in Toronto, Ontario. This actor, playwright and novelist has penned *Good Night Desdemona (Good Morning Juliet), The Arab's Mouth, Fall on Your Knees* and *The Way the Crow Flies.*

Antonine (Maillet) Bouctouche, New Brunswick. One of Acadia's most accomplished writers, Maillet's works include *Pointes-aux-Coques, La Sagouine, Don L'Original* and *Cent Ans Dans Les Bois.*

Aritha (Van Herk) Wetaskiwin, Alberta. The feminist author of *Judith, The Tent Peg, No Fixed Address, In Visible Ink, A Frozen Tongue* and *Mavericks: An Incorrigible History of Alberta.*

Blanche (Howard) Vancouver, British Columbia. Among Howard's novels are *Pretty Lady, The Manipulator, The Immortal Soul of Edwin Carlysle* and *Penelope's Way.* Howard also coauthored *A Celibate Season* with Carol Shields.

Bonnie (Stern) Toronto, Ontario. Canada's premiere cooking teacher, author, television host and columnist, Stern has published 12 cookbooks, including *Simply HeartSmart Cooking* and the award-winning *Essentials of Home Cooking.*

Carol (Shields) Born in Chicago, Shields moved to Canada at the age of 22 and spent much of her time in Winnipeg, Manitoba. She was a multiple award winner, scooping up prizes such as the Pulitzer, Governor General's Award and the Order of Canada. Her novels, short story collections and plays include *The Stone Diaries, Larry's Party, The Orange Fish, Swann, Small Ceremonies, Not Another Anniversary, Women Waiting* and *Unless.*

Charlotte (Gray) Born in England, Gray made Canada her home in 1979. She is the author of *Mrs. King: The Life and Times of Isabel Mackenzie King* and *Sisters in the Wilderness: The Lives of Susanna Moodie* and *Catharine Parr Traill.*

Di (Brandt) Winkler, Manitoba. Winner of a Governor General's Award for *Questions I Asked My Mother*, Brandt's poetic works include *Agnes in the Sky, Mother, Not Mother* and *Jerusalem, Beloved.*

Dionne (Brand) Born in Trinidad, Brand moved to Canada at 17. Her books and poetry, which deal primarily with racism and black women's history, include *Land to Light On, At the Full Change of the Moon* and *What We All Long For.*

Elizabeth (Smart) Ottawa, Ontario. A novelist and poet, Smart wrote *By Grand Central Station I Sat Down and Wept, A Bonus* and *The Assumption of Rogues and Rascals.*

Gabrielle (Roy) St. Boniface, Manitoba. Winner of two Governor General's Awards and France's Prix Femina, Roy authored *Bonheur* *d'Occasion, Alexandre Chenevert, Cet Été Qui Chantait, Ces Enfants de ma Vie* and *Rue Deschambault.*

Helen (Fogwill Porter) St. John's, Newfoundland. Fogwill Porter has been writing for almost 35 years. *Below the Bridge, January, February, June or July* and *A Long and Lonely Ride* are among her published works.

Ingeborg (Boyens) Born in Germany, Boyens lives in Winnipeg, Manitoba. A successful journalist, she also published the book *Unnatural Harvest: How Corporate Science is Secretly Altering our Food.*

Isabel (Huggan) Kitchener, Ontario. Huggan is the author of *The Elizabeth Stories, You Never Know* and *Belonging.*

Jacqueline (McLeod Rogers) Winnipeg, Manitoba. McLeod Rogers is the author of *Aspects of the Female Novel* and *Two Sides to a Story.*

Jane (Urquhart) Little Long Lac, Ontario. Best known for her novels *The Underpainter, The Stone Carvers, The Whirlpool, Changing Heaven* and *Away*, Urquhart has also published three books of poetry and a collection of short stories.

Jeannette (Armstrong) Okanagan Reserve, British Columbia. The Native American author of such works as *Breath Tracks, How Food Was Given, How Names Were Given, Enwhisteetkwa: Walk in Water* and *How Turtle Set the Animals Free.*

Josey (Vogels) Newtonville, Ontario. A sex columnist and relationship expert, Vogels is the author of five books, including *Dating: A Survival Guide From the Frontlines, The Secret Language of Girls* and *Bedside Manners: Sex Etiquette Made Easy.*

Joy (Kogawa) Vancouver, British Columbia. A poet, novelist and children's book author, Kogawa's works include *The Splintered Moon, A Choice of Dreams, Jericho Road, Six Poems, Obasan, Naomi's Road, Itsuka* and *A Song of Lilith.*

June (Callwood) Chatham, Ontario. A journalist and author of close to 30 books, Callwood wrote *The Man Who Lost Himself, Trial Without End* and *The Sleepwalker.*

Katherine (Govier) Edmonton, Alberta. This journalist loves to write novels and short stories in addition to her articles. Her works include *The Truth Teller*, *Angel Walk*, *The Immaculate Conception Photography Gallery*, *Before and After*, *Hearts of Flame* and *Creation*.

Leslie (Beck) Vancouver, British Columbia. Television expert, columnist, nutritionist and author, Beck has published numerous helpful books, including *Leslie Beck's 10 Steps to Healthy Eating*, *Leslie Beck's Nutrition Guide to Menopause*, *Leslie Beck's Nutrition Encyclopedia* and *Leslie Beck's Nutrition Guide to a Healthy Pregnancy*.

Linda (Rogers) Vancouver, British Columbia. An award-winning poet, novelist and children's author, Rogers's works include *Say My Name*, *The Memoirs of Charlie Louie*, *The Half Life of Radium*, *Hard Candy*, *Worm Sandwich*, *Queens of the Next Hot Star*, *Witness*, *Singing Rib*, *Love in the Rainforest* and *Heaven Cake*.

Lorna (Crozier) Swift Current, Saskatchewan. This Canadian poet has published *Inside Is the Sky*, *Crow's Black Joy*, *Everything Arrives at the Light*, *A Saving Grace: The Collected Poems of Mrs. Bentley* and *What the Living Won't Let Go*.

Lucy Maud (Montgomery) New London, Prince Edward Island. One of Canada's most internationally acclaimed authors, Montgomery wrote *Anne of Green Gables*, *Anne of Avonlea*, *Emily of New Moon*, *Emily's Quest* and *Jane of Lantern Hill*, among many others.

Margaret (Atwood) Ottawa, Ontario. One of Canada's most celebrated authors, Atwood has crafted numerous poems and novels, including *The Handmaid's Tale*, *Life Before Man*, *Wilderness Tips*, *The Robber Bride*, *Surfacing*, *Bluebeard's Egg*, *Alias Grace* and *Oryx and Crake*. Another famous Canadian author with this name is **Margaret Laurence**. Born in Neepawa, Manitoba, Laurence was famous for writing beautifully about life in Africa and Western Canada. Some of her best-known works include *The Stone Angel*, *The Diviners*, *Heart of a Stranger* and *A Jest of God*.

Marianne (Bluger) Ottawa, Ontario. Bluger is the author of eight books of poetry, including *Gathering Wild, Summer Grass, Tamarack & Clearcut: Haiku, Gusts, Early Evening Pieces* and *Scissor, Paper, Woman*.

Marilyn (Bowering) Winnipeg, Manitoba. Raised in Victoria, British Columbia, poet Bowering has written numerous books, such as *The Liberation of Newfoundland, One Who Became Lost, The Killing Room, Sleeping With Lambs, Love as it is, Visible Worlds* and *Anyone Can See I Love You*.

Marni (Jackson) Toronto, Ontario. A magazine journalist and author of *The Mother Zone* and *Pain: The Fifth Vital Sign*.

Martha (Brooks) Manitoba Sanatorium, Manitoba. A celebrated playwright and novelist, Brooks's works include, *Being With Henry, Bone Dance, Travelling on Into the Light and Other Stories, The Moons in August, Andrew's Tree* and *I Met a Bully on the Hill*.

Mavis (Gallant) Montreal, Québec. A poet, novelist and playwright, Gallant is the author of *Green Water, Green Sky, A Fairly Good Time, The Other Paris, My Heart Is Broken, From the Fifteenth District, Home Truths* and *In Transit*.

Nicole (Brossard) Montreal, Québec. Among her many novels, essays and poems, Brossard has published, *French Kiss, Lovhers, The Aerial Letter, Mauve Desert*, and *Baroque at Dawn*.

Nina Lee (Colwill) Gaspé, Québec. A self-proclaimed lover of laundry and writing, Colwill has authored numerous poems. Her work has also appeared in *Dropped Threads*.

Pauline (Johnson) Six Nations Indian Reserve near Brantford, Ontario. A poet in the late nineteenth century, Johnson's published works include *The Cattle Thief, And He Said Fight On, The Corn Husker* and *The Trail to Lillooet*.

Rose (Reisman) Toronto, Ontario. Author of many healthy cookbooks, Reisman has published numerous books including *The Art of Living Well, Divine Indulgences, Rose Reisman Brings Home Light Pasta* and *Rose Reisman Brings Home Light Cooking*.

Sandra (Birdsell) Hamiota, Manitoba. A winner of many awards for her writing, Birdsell's novels include *Katya, The Russländer, The Town That Floated Away, The Two-Headed Calf, The Chrome Suite,* and *The Missing Child.*

Sandy Frances (Duncan) Vancouver, British Columbia. This Canadian author has written numerous books, including *Dragonhunt, Pattern Makers, Listen to Me Grace Kelly, Cariboo Runaway, The Toothpaste Genie* and *British Columbia: Its Land, Mineral and Water Resources.*

Sharon (Thesen) Tisdale, Saskatchewan. Canadian poet and author of *Artemis Hates Romance, Holding the Prose, The Beginning of the Long Dash, The Pangs of Sunday: Poems* and *Aurora.*

Stephanie (Bolster) Vancouver, British Columbia. Poet Bolster is the author of *White Stone: The Alice Poems* and *Two Bowls of Milk,* both of which won multiple awards.

Susan (Musgrave) Vancouver Island, British Columbia. This poet and novelist's works include *Dreams Are More Real Than Bathtubs, Forcing the Narcissus* and *Musgrave Landing: Musings on the Writing Life.*

Character Names

Can't find an author's name that you like? Why not join the trend and label your child after a famous character? Whether it's someone from a book you read and loved or a name you simply like the sound of, here are a few choices to help with your search.

Male Characters' Names

Alexander The orthodontist and narrator of Alistair MacLeod's *No Great Mischief.*

Almásy A charming explorer and protagonist of Michael Ondaatje's *The English Patient.*

Austin The selfish painter and narrator of Jane Urquhart's *The Underpainter.*

AUTHORS' NAMES

Award-winning cookbook author Bonnie Stern has always liked her name. "It's very straightforward," she says, "and it's nice and friendly." As a child, Stern was lucky enough to avoid name teasing, but she does remember being sent home by a teacher to find out what her real name was. "[The teacher said] Bonnie is just a nickname," she explains. Although most people call her B, Bon, Bon-Bon or Bonnie Cuisine, Stern doesn't mind. On the other hand, she really doesn't like being referred to by her initials (BS), which fortunately doesn't happen often!

"I like my full name, Josephine, even though I don't really use it," explains sex and relationship author Josey Vogels. "It's a classic name that looks and sounds pleasing...[and] it has the right combination of hard and soft that I think I have as well." Named after her Uncle Sjef, whose Dutch name was translated to Joseph and ultimately to Jeff in Canada, Vogels says she often wishes her parents hadn't spelled her nickname, Josey, with an "ey" at the end. The reason: she's always correcting people who want to spell it with an "ie" and often feels like people think she's trying to be trendy with the spelling, even though she's not.

When healthy-cookbook author Rose Reisman thinks of her name, she's full of pride. "It is my identity," she says. "[And] Rose always brings a happy expression to people's faces. The flower is a beautiful image." Named after her grandmother, however, Rose often wished her name didn't sound so old-fashioned. As a child, she says she would have loved to be called by something trendy, like Chloe, instead.

Of all the characters that award-winning novelist Jane Urquhart has invented, Archangel Gstir from *The Stone Carvers* has her favourite name. While researching the history of an Ontario church to use as the main backdrop for her novel, Urquhart discovered that the church had once employed a priest named Archangel Gstir. "Because Archangel Gstir seemed in some ways to be a mythical saint-like character, the combination of the angel and the star [Gstir is German for star] seemed to, in essence, sum up his character," she says.

Awasin An adventurous Cree boy in Farley Mowat's *Lost in the Barrens*.

Barney A nostalgic television producer who had little luck with marriage in *Barney's Version* by Mordecai Richler.

Brian A troubled, small-town boy in W.O. Mitchell's *Who Has Seen the Wind*.

Buddy A self-destructive musician in *Coming Through Slaughter* by Michael Ondaatje.

Carlyle A once hopeful, widowed teacher in *Vanishing Point* by W.O. Mitchell.

Crake The brilliant man who tries to create a new race of people in Margaret Atwood's *Oryx and Crake*.

Duddy A lying bruiser who learns about love and life in *The Apprenticeship of Duddy Kravitz* by Mordecai Richler.

Dunstan A modest school teacher in *Fifth Business* by Robertson Davies.

Exodus A wonderful man of mixed Native blood in *Away* by Jane Urquhart.

Francis A keeper of secrets in *What's Bred in the Bone* by Robertson Davies.

Frederic A grumpy but kind journalist and publisher in *Swann* by Carol Shields.

Gamini A hard-working field doctor in Michael Ondaatje's *Anil's Ghost*.

Gustad An honest bank clerk and dedicated family man who finds himself unwittingly drawn into corruption in *Such a Long Journey* by Rohinton Mistry.

Henry The play-by-the-rules captain in *Creation* by Katherine Govier.

Homer The loveable orphan in John Irving's *The Cider House Rules*.

Ishvar A down-on-his-luck tailor in Rohinton Mistry's *A Fine Balance*.

Jack An unsure historian in *Happenstance* by Carol Shields.

Jake A storyteller and farm worker in W.O. Mitchell's *Jake and the Kid*.

Jal A spineless yet pleasant man in Rohinton Mistry's *Family Matters*.

John James A bird lover and artist in Katherine Govier's novel, *Creation*.

 KIDS' KORNER

Mohinder likes his name most because it represents a famous cricket player. Named by his grandfather, the 12-year-old says he doesn't like his nickname, "Mo," and sometimes wishes he could be called Kevin "because it's [only] five letters."

Although she wishes her name wasn't so boring and "weird-sounding," 13-year-old Kayla says there are a few things she likes about it. "It's short, doesn't take forever to spell and it's simple," she says. But she still wishes she could be called Monique instead. The reason? "Because it's different and fun and sounds way cooler," she explains.

Taylor's parents found her name in a baby name book and liked it so much that they gave it to her. Despite the fact that she doesn't like having a boy's name, the 10-year-old says she's pretty happy with their choice overall. "I like that it's not too long and it's easy to write," she says.

Francis (pronounced Franceese) has never really liked his name because no one says it properly. "I'm probably the only Francis in Ontario," says the 15-year-old. "I like Cis better because it isn't as weird. But one of my teachers thought I was Russian when she first heard it."

When you ask Melody Grace if she likes her name, the three-year-old says "yes" with great enthusiasm. And there isn't one little thing that she would change about it.

Laker A 17-year-old drifter who finds friendship in the most unsuspecting place in *Being with Henry* by Martha Brooks.

Larry An average man searching for the meaning of a happy marriage in *Larry's Party* by Carol Shields.

Liam A level-headed Irish Canadian farmer in Jane Urquhart's *Away*.

Lonny A young man plagued with guilt and bad memories. He finds love, friendship and understanding in *Bone Dance* by Martha Brooks.

Maneck An enlightened college student in Rohinton Mistry's *A Fine Balance*.

Matthew The kind, shy and wonderful adopted father of Anne in L.M. Montgomery's *Anne of Green Gables*.

Lyle A son who struggles to understand his father's kind and innocent ways in *Mercy Among the Children* by David Adams Richards.

Nariman An elderly man suffering from Parkinson's in *Family Matters* by Rohinton Mistry.

Om A tailor trying to flee tough times in Rohinton Mistry's *A Fine Balance*.

Owen The inspiring and unforgettable main character in *A Prayer for Owen Meany* by John Irving.

Patrick A grief-stricken 12-year-old boy who finally learns to heal after his younger brother's death in *Andrew's Tree* by Martha Brooks.

Percy The lazy, friendly and romantic police sergeant in Austin Clarke's *The Polished Hoe*.

Pi An exceptionally intelligent young man thrown into an unexpected adventure in Yann Martel's *The Life of Pi*.

Robert A young Canadian soldier who is misunderstood for the crimes he committed in Timothy Findley's *The Wars*.

Sarath A quiet archeologist in Michael Ondaatje's *Anil's Ghost*.

Sidney A kind and gentle outcast in *Mercy Among the Children* by David Adams Richards.

Simon The sympathetic American doctor who tries to help discover the truth behind two murders in Margaret Atwood's *Alias Grace*.

Tilman A talented woodcarver in Jane Urquhart's *The Stone Carvers*.

Vikram The corrupt yet sensitive protagonist of *The In-Between World of Vikram Lall* by M.G. Vassanji.

Vittorio An Italian child who grapples with losing his innocence in Nino Ricci's *The Book of Saints*.

Wilberforce The illegitimate but highly successful doctor in Austin Clarke's *The Polished Hoe*.

Female Characters' Names

Anil A curious forensic anthropologist in Michael Ondaatje's *Anil's Ghost*.

Anne The lovable do-gooder heroine of L.M. Montgomery's *Anne of Green Gables*.

Arachne A traveling underwear saleswoman in Aritha Van Herk's *No Fixed Address: An Amorous Journey*.

Autumn A gifted woman protected by her brother in *Mercy Among the Children* by David Adams Richards.

 FUN FACTS

A.A. Milne's famous character Winnie the Pooh was based on a Canadian bear named Winnie, short for Winnipeg.

Author Stephen Leacock's middle name was Butler, after his mother's maiden name.

Best-selling novelist John Irving was born John Wallace Blunt Jr.

Bola A young girl who escapes a mass suicide planned by her mother and goes on to have nine children of her own in *At the Full and Change of the Moon* by Dionne Brand.

Charis A troubled woman who falls under the spell of the cruel Zenia in *The Robber Bride* by Margaret Atwood.

Christine The observant narrator of and a writer in Gabrielle Roy's *Street of Riches*.

Coomy A cruel and heartless daughter in Rohinton Mistry's *Family Matters*.

Cordelia A mysterious and powerful girl in Margaret Atwood's *Cat's Eye*.

Daisy A heroine who's determined to understand her role in life in *The Stone Diaries* by Carol Shields.

Del A girl who grows to understand womanhood in Alice Munro's *Lives of Girls and Women*.

Dina An industrious Indian widow in Rohinton Mistry's *A Fine Balance*.

Elaine A lonely and controversial Canadian artist in *Cat's Eye* by Margaret Atwood.

Elly A beautiful wife and mother in *Mercy Among the Children* by David Adams Richards.

Fern A sensuous and lustful woman in *Lives of Girls and Women* by Alice Munro.

Fleda An eccentric woman who spends most of her time reading in Jane Urquhart's *The Whirlpool*.

Frances The lying rebel in *Fall on Your Knees* by Ann-Marie MacDonald.

Grace A young servant locked up for two murders she says she can't remember in Margaret Atwood's *Alias Grace*.

Hagar The memorable, determined main character from Margaret Laurence's *The Stone Angel*.

Iris The witty and often pessimistic part-time narrator of *The Blind Assassin* by Margaret Atwood.

Jilly An abused girl who learns to take control of her life in Charles De Lint's *The Onion Girl*.

JL An inspired cook in an all-male camp in *The Tent Peg* by Aritha Van Herk. JL's name was derived from the Biblical Jael, a heroine who killed her tormentor with a stake.

Judith The strong and independent lead character in Aritha Van Herk's novel *Judith*.

Juliet A young woman who grows up in *Runaway* by Alice Munro.

Katharine An emotional lover and principal character in Michael Ondaatje's *The English Patient*.

Kathleen The beauty with a wonderful voice in Ann-Marie MacDonald's *Fall on Your Knees*.

Klara A romantic historian and woodcarver in Jane Urquhart's *The Stone Carvers*.

Lily The innocent, truth-seeking invalid in *Fall on Your Knees* by Ann-Marie MacDonald.

Madeline An innocent child who is forced to grow up too quickly in Ann-Marie MacDonald's *The Way the Crow Flies*.

Marian The confused protagonist who suddenly can't eat after getting engaged in *The Edible Woman* by Margaret Atwood.

Marie-Ursule Leader of a secret slave society in Dionne Brand's *At the Full and Change of the Moon*.

Marilla Anne's hard-on-the-outside, mushy-in-the-middle adopted mother in L.M. Montgomery's *Anne of Green Gables*.

Mary-Mathilda A guilty but well-respected woman in Austin Clarke's *The Polished Hoe*.

Materia The Lebanese mother of four daughters in *Fall on your Knees* by Ann-Marie MacDonald.

Maude A woman who becomes obsessed with a book in Nicole Brossard's *Mauve Desert*.

Mélanie A determined young teenager who sets off on an adventure of her own in *Mauve Desert* by Nicole Brossard.

Mercedes A protective, devout Catholic in Ann-Marie MacDonald's *Fall on Your Knees*.

Moira A strong and independent lesbian, Moira was the best friend of Offred in Margaret Atwood's *The Handmaid's Tale*.

Offred The intelligent narrator and protagonist of Margaret Atwood's *The Handmaid's Tale*.

Ofglen A feminist handmaid and resistance fighter in Margaret Atwood's *The Handmaid's Tale*.

Oryx A young Asian girl sold into the sex trade by her parents in Margaret Atwood's *Oryx and Crake*.

Raylene An angry and abused woman in Charles De Lint's *The Onion Girl*.

Reta A loving wife and mother who lived with true happiness in *Unless* by Carol Shields.

Roxana A kind and compassionate daughter willing to undergo hardship to take care of her ailing father in *Family Matters* by Rohinton Mistry.

Ruth The difficult and not always kind protagonist of John Irving's *A Widow for One Year*.

Serena The anti-feminist and jealous wife of the Commander in Margaret Atwood's *The Handmaid's Tale*.

Zenia A self-centred, manipulative and beautiful main character in *The Robber Bride* by Margaret Atwood.

 CANUCK TRIVIA

Manitobans' favourite names were Lisa and David in 1970.

The Inuit were originally called Eskimos, which means "eaters of raw meat," by British settlers.

Tainted Names

We all have names that we just don't like. For me, it's Deanna, the name of a girl who pushed me around on my first day of grade one. For my friend James, it's Roger, the name of a youth soccer coach who constantly yelled at his daughter and wouldn't let her play. My girlfriend Annabelle hates Alicia, the name of a bossy, condescending, apple-eating kid (this was in the day of Fruit Roll-Ups) she was forced to walk to school with. And for my husband Austin, it's Darla, the name his older brothers used when making fun of him for being skinny.

No matter the reason for our dislike, there's often nothing we or anyone else can do to change our mind. Even if we meet a hundred nice Deannas, for instance, it might still be impossible to make up for that one cruel girl from our childhood.

So, what do you do if your partner loves a name that you think is tainted? Well, if you're like me, you'll play the I'm-carrying-this-baby-and-going-through-labour-while-you-sleep-soundly-through-the-night card to trump his opinion. Otherwise, you might agree to disagree on the name or set up a mini conference to try and reach a compromise.

If you do end up caving in to your partner's wish, make sure you're ready to deal with the consequences. Here's the good news: if you agree to name your baby after someone on your tainted list, your child will likely create a new meaning for the name. Before you know it, you'll associate that name with the true love of your life— your child. And now for the bad news: no matter how much you love your little one, you may still be unable to get over your dislike of the name. Another problem: you may come to resent your mate for talking you into choosing a name you don't like.

The best advice I can give is to avoid tainted names like the plague. Because you can't guarantee that you'll get over your poor associations, it's probably safer to steer clear of them altogether. After all, you don't want to end up cringing every time you scream your child's name in the park.

Chapter 5

-☆-

Ethnic Names

The second most spacious country in the world, Canada barely leaves a mark on the world's population. With just over 32 million inhabitants, we're overshadowed by physically smaller countries like Germany (over 82 million) and the U.S. (just under 300 million) and dwarfed by population giants like India (with over one billion people) and China (over 1.3 billion). What makes Canadians unique, however, is the diverse makeup of our population. Over 20 million of us are immigrants of varying ethnic origins. And you know what that means—scrumptious food choices at every corner, hip fashion trends and a lot of compelling literature, music and artwork.

As opposed to the melting pot society found in the United States, Canadians live within a cultural mosaic. What's the difference, you ask? A mosaic consists of individual pieces held together by the same glue. In our case, that glue is made up of pride, compassion and patriotism – typical ingredients used to create a Canadian. A melting pot, on the other hand, involves the assimilation or melding together of various entities to combine one new, integrated society. In other words, much of the cultural eccentricity is lost.

Canada's largest groups of immigrants include the English, with close to six million, and French, with over four and a half million. Following are the Scottish (just over four million), Irish (close to four million), German (almost three million), Italian (just over one million) and Chinese (just over one million).

People from Poland, Israel, Russia, Hungary, Greece and numerous other countries have also chosen to make Canada their home. Given this cultural diversity, it's not surprising that most major Canadian cities boast a Chinatown, Greektown, Jewish area and Italian corridor, among others. Besides the fact that these areas rank among the best places to eat, each of these "towns" within our cities helps to preserve the original culture and traditions of each ethnicity. They help new immigrants to feel immediately at home, provide them with a built-in support system and offer wonderful opportunities for other Canadians to learn about and embrace a culture from a different land.

And so this book would not truly represent Canada without paying tribute to the names from the numerous cultures that make up our citizenship. With these diverse ethnicities come unique naming traditions and a glimpse into the history of each country. From land- and nature-inspired names in Africa to myth-based monikers from Greece, the meanings of each name can help you to visualize the people who originally created them.

Due to spacing issues, this chapter could not include lists of names from all of the ethnicities that impact Canadian culture. So I've chosen to represent a few of our nation's most substantial ethnic groups along with one or two whose names were just too interesting to pass up. Others, like French, Hebrew, Muslim, Hindu and First Nations, can be found within other chapters of the book.

Whether you're looking for a name to celebrate your heritage or want to find something with a distinct and meaningful edge, the names on these pages are sure to help bulk up your "maybe" list.

African Names
African Boys' Names

Abasi Stern; demanding.

Adwin An artist.

Asad A lion.

Bwana Gentleman.

Camara Teacher.

REAL NAMES

Twenty-eight-year-old Kulvir's name is traditional and charged with meaning. "When a child is born, our sacred Sikh scripture, the Guru Granth Sahib, is randomly opened to a page and the first letter of the first word is determined to be the first letter of the child's name," he explains. At his naming ceremony, the equivalent of an English "K" was revealed, which prompted his parents to name him Kulvir.

When people shorten Rosemary's name to Rose, she corrects them very quickly. Prime example: a grade six teacher who was fond of nicknames. "I went up to him after school one day and told him my name was Rosemary and that I would appreciate if he called me Rosemary," says the 40-year-old. They never had a problem after that.

Jane always loved it when her mother called her Lady Jane. And she was thankful that she wasn't born a Jean or June, which she thinks sound too old. Her favourite names, though are "Phoebe and Daphne because "I like weird names and because my brother used to call me by them when I was a kid," says the 62-year-old. "But I also like the names— first and last—that have all the vowel sounds in them," she adds. "I think it sounds good."

"Saying that my name is who I am seems overly dramatic," says Jilanna. "But it's a shortcut to my identity." Given a combination of her mother's favourite names, Jill and Christiana, this 29-year-old has never had to share her name with anyone. And although she hates when people misspell and mispronounce it, Jilanna loves the fact that her name "holds its own among the Joannas and Gillians of the world."

Although he had a tough time writing his name in kindergarten, 27-year-old Dwight seems to have gotten a grasp on the spelling and has learned to like his unique name. "I can always get e-mail addresses on the internet with my full name because there are so few Dwights out there," he remarks.

"I was christened Joseph Terrence St. John," explains Terry, "But for whatever reason, I go by Terry." Nowadays, this causes him a bit of frustration, mainly because his credit cards and official documents say Joseph while he's never been known by that name. When asked what his name means to him, the 63-year-old says, "It's not a guy thing to have thought about, but I think you expect a Terry to be a slightly aggressive Irish bruiser."

Andrew is more of a fan of his middle name, Bevan, than he is of his first. "I like the fact that my second name is a family tradition from the last four generations," says the 28-year-old. "And it will be passed down should I have a son."

The best part about being named after both of his grandfathers is the pride that Edward Newton feels at carrying on an important heirloom. And although he's always liked his name, which is most often shortened to Ted, the 70-year-old feels like he has a lot to live up to.

The main reason Ali doesn't like her full name, Alicia, is because it sounds too feminine. "I felt as though I was supposed to be girly and pretty," she says, "when for most of my childhood I felt the opposite." So she changed it to Ali, something that's short, to the point, and fits her perfectly. "To me, [Ali] is who I am, the identity that I can always know will be there and change only when I want it to," explains the 26-year-old.

Fifty-one-year-old Ramona was named after a waltz that was popular the year she was born. She and her husband even danced to the song at their wedding and she likes it almost as much as she does her actual name. "There are very few people with the same name," she says. "So it is really easy to identify myself." But she's glad that no one ever shortened it to Mona or Moaner, two names she's not so fond of.

Chaka A great king. *Shaka.*

Chike God's power.

Dakarai Happiness.

Daudi Loved; adored.

Desta Happiness.

Erasto A peaceful man.

Essien The sixth son.

Fela Combative; confrontational.

Gamba A warrior.

Ghedi A traveler.

Habib Loved; adored.

Hakim A medicine man; doctor.

Harith A farmer.

Issa The Messiah.

Jabari Courageous.

Jelani Great; mighty.

Kamau A quiet warrior.

Kashka Friendly; kind; sociable.

Kenyatta A musician.

Lebna Soul.

Mani One who comes from the mountain.

Masud Happy and lucky. *Masoud.*

Nadif Born between seasons.

Nassor Triumphant; victorious.

Negus A king; emperor; ruler.

Obi Heart.

Ohini A chief. *Ohene.*

Rafiki A friend; companion.

Runako Good-looking; handsome.

Salim Peace. *Salman.*

Simba A lion.

Sundiata A hungry lion. *Sundyata, Soundiata, Sunjata.*

Tamirat A miracle.

Uba Rich.

Ulan Firstborn of twins.

Yobachi To pray to God.

Zareb Guardian; protector.

African Girls' Names

Adhiambo Female born after sunset.

Amara Paradise.

Ayana A beautiful flower.

Bella A freed slave.

Binta Godly.

Bupe Generosity; hospitality.

Desta Joy; cheerfulness.

Ebere Mercy.

Eshe Life.

Faizah Victorious.

Gzifa To be at peace.

Habiba Adored; a darling.

Halima Gentle. *Halimah*.

Ifeoma Beautiful.

Iman Faith.

Jendayi To give thanks.

Kenya A mountain; from Kiinyaa, meaning white mountain.

Kesia Favourite.

Khadija Born early.

Lakeesha From Leticia, meaning joy.

Lateefah Gentle.

Makemba A goddess.

Malika A queen or princess.

Mapenzi Loved; adored. *Mpenzi.*

Nadifa Born between seasons.

Naki First born daughter.

Obax A flower.

Ola Valuable.

Radhiya Pleasant; agreeable.

Rashida Righteous.

Raziya Pleasant; agreeable.

Safiya Pure. *Safia, Safiyeh, Safiyyah.*

Saida Helpful. *Saada.*

Tapanga Unpredictable and kind.

Uchenna The will of God.

Urenna A father's pride.

Wub Attractive; pretty.

Zainabu Beautiful.

Zarina Golden.

Zawadi A gift.

Chinese Names
Chinese Boys' Names

Bo Priceless; precious.

Chan A common Chinese clan name.

Chen Great.

Cong Smart; clever.

Fai The start; beginning.

Hsin An ancient dynasty.

Kong Magnificent; splendid.

Kuan-Yin The Buddhist deity of mercy.

Jin Golden.

Lee A plum.

Lian An elegant, graceful willow.

Liang Fine; excellent.

Manchu Pure; untainted.

Ming A dynasty.

Park A cypress tree.

Shaiming Sunlight.

Shen Intense thinker; religious; devout.

Shing Triumph; conquest.

Sying A star.

Wen Cultured; refined; civilized.

Yuan Unique; the original.

Chinese Girls' Names

Bing Qing Clear as ice.

Bo Valuable; prized; precious.

Chan Juan Refined; ladylike.

Chang Free; limitless.

Feng A maple.

Jing Crystal; shining.

Juan Gorgeous; graceful.

Lei The bud of a flower.

Lian The sun's daughter.

Lien A lotus.

Lin Yao A treasure of jade.

Mei A plum.

Ming Ue The bright moon.

Park A cypress tree.

Ping Duckweed.

Qing Yuan A clean and clear spring.

Shan Coral.

Shuang Clear and open.

Wei Priceless; important.

Xia The glow found during sunrise and sunset.

English Names
English Boys' Names

Acton Town or settlement by oak trees.

Addison Son of Adam. *Adison.*

Aston Town in the East. *Asten, Astin.*

Barrett A surname, meaning strong as a bear. *Bar, Baret, Barrat, Barret, Barry.*

Baxter A baker. *Bax, Baxie, Baxty, Baxy.*

Bentley A surname, meaning one who lives in a grassy meadow. *Ben, Benny, Bentlea, Bentlee, Bentlie, Lee.*

Calder A book or stream.

Charlton From the village of free men. *Charlesten, Charleston, Charleton, Charlie, Charlotin.*

Chauncey A chancellor. *Chan, Chance, Chancey, Chaunce, Chauncie, Chauncy.*

Churchill From the church on a hill; name of famous British prime minister, Sir Winston Churchill. *Church.*

Clayton A town built on clay. *Clay, Clayten, Claytin.*

Dempster A judge. *Demster.*

Dixson Son of Richard. *Dickson, Dix.*

Eaton An estate by the river. *Eatton, Eton, Eyton.*

Elliott From Elijah, meaning the Lord is God. *Eliot, Eliott, Eliud, Eliut, Elyot, Elyott.*

Elston Farm of a noble person. *Ellston.*

Elton The old town. *Alton, Ellton.*

Fairfax One with beautiful or blond hair. *Fair, Fax.*

Falkner One who teaches or trains falcons. *Falconer, Faulconer, Faulkner.*

Farley A meadow of sheep or bulls. *Fairley, Far, Farlay, Farlee, Farleigh, Farlie, Farly, Farrley.*

Grayson Son of the baliff. *Greydon, Greyson.*

Hadley A meadow of heather. *Hadlea, Hadlee, Hadleigh, Hadly, Lee.*

Keane Form of Keene, meaning intelligent. *Kean.*

Kenton From Kent; from a royal manor. *Kent, Kenten, Kentin.*

Laidley From the meadow of water.

Lawton From a town on the hill. *Laughton, Law.*

Palmer A pilgrim who bears a palm. *Palmar, Pallmer.*

Pierson Peter's son. *Piersen.*

Ralston One who lives on Ralph's farm.

Ramsey Land of the ram. *Ram, Ramsay, Ramsy, Ramzee.*

Sawyer One who works with wood.

Seaton Place or town by the sea. *Seeton, Seton.*

Thatcher A roof-fixer. *Thacher, Thatch.*

Walton A walled town. *Walt.*

Watson Walter's son. *Wathson.*

English Girls' Names

Adria Feminine short form of Adrian, meaning wealthy. *Adrea.*

Afton A place and river name. *Aftan, Aften, Aftine, Aftyn.*

Aldercy A chief.

Blythe Content; happy. *Blithe.*

Brooke A small stream. *Brook.*

Careen Form of Carina, a form of Cora, meaning maiden, or Carleen, a form of Caroline, meaning small and feminine. *Carreen.*

Christabel A combination of Christa, a form of Christina, meaning Christian, and Belle, meaning beautiful. *Bella, Belle, Chris, Christa, Christabel, Christabella, Christabelle.*

Clementine Feminine form of Clement, meaning merciful. *Clemence, Clemencie, Clemency, Clementina, Tina.*

Dahlia A flower. *Dahlya, Dalia, Dalya.*

Darrene Feminine form of Darren, meaning great. *Darene.*

Earlene Feminine form of Earl, meaning a nobleman. *Earlean, Earleen, Earlena, Earlina, Earlinda, Earline, Erlene, Erlenne, Erlina, Erlinda, Erline.*

Ebony Dark wood. *Ebanee, Ebanie, Ebany, Ebbony, Ebonee, Eboney, Ebonie, Ebonnie, Ebonye.*

Ember Embers of a fire. *Embir, Embyr.*

Fairley A clearing in the forest. *Fairlea, Fairlee, Fairleigh, Fairlie.*

Faith Faith. *Faithe, Fayth, Faythe.*

Gail Short form of Abigail, meaning joy. *Gael, Gale, Galyn, Gayle.*

Gwendolyn One with a white brow. *Gwen, Gwenda, Gwendolin, Gwendoline, Gwendolynn, Gwenna, Wenda, Wendoline, Wendolyn, Wendy.*

Harley Meadow of the hares. *Harlee, Harleigh, Harlie, Harly.*

Harper A harp player. *Harp, Harpe, Harpo.*

Honour Honour; integrity; dignity; respect. *Honor, Honoria, Nora.*

Ivy A tree of ivy. *Ivee, Ivey, Ivie.*

Kendra Form of Kendrick, meaning Henry's son, or Kenda, meaning a water baby. *Kena, Kendre, Kenadrea, Kendria, Kenna, Kennisha, Kindra, Kinna, Kyndra.*

Lane A narrow road. *Lain, Laine, Lanie, Lany, Layne.*

Marley From a nice meadow. *Marlea, Marly, Marrley.*

Maxie Short for Maxine, meaning greatest. *Maxee, Maxey, Maxi, Maxy.*

Misty Cloaked or covered by mist. *Mistee, Mistey, Misti, Mistie, Mystee, Mysti, Mystie.*

Rowena A famous friend; red-haired. *Ronni, Row, Rowan, Rowe, Roweena, Rowina, Winnie.*

Ryesen Rye. *Ryeson, Rysen, Rysin, Ryson.*

Tatum Happy; cheerful; joyful. *Tate, Tatumn.*

Tawny One with a brownish-yellow tan. *Tawni, Tawnie.*

Vanetta Form of Vanessa, meaning a butterfly. *Vaneta, Vanita, Vanneta, Vannetta, Venetta.*

German Names
German Boys' Names

Adal Noble. *Adel, Edel.*

Adalrich A noble ruler. *Adal, Adel, Adelrich, Alaric, Alarich, Alarick, Alarik, Aurick, Aurik, Uadalrich, Ullric, Ulrich.*

Arnold Eagle ruler. *Arnald, Arnaldo, Arnall, Arnaud, Arne, Arnell, Arnet, Arnett, Arnie, Arnoll, Arnot, Arnott.*

Baldwin Form of Baldewin, meaning brave friend. *Balduin, Baldwyn.*

Berend From Berinhard, meaning strong or brave as a bear. *Bernd.*

Bernhard From Berinhard, meaning strong or brave as a bear. *Barnard, Berend, Berinhard, Barnard, Bern, Bernardyn, Bernd, Bernon, Bernot.*

Bruno Having brown hair or brown skin. *Brunon.*

Claus Short for Nicolaus, a form of Nicholas, meaning victorious people. *Claas, Claes, Clause. Klaus.*

Eginhard Strong end of the sword. *Einhard, Enno.*

Gerhard Form of Gerard, meaning brave spearman. *Gary, Garrick, Gary, Gerrit.*

Gregor Form of Gregory, meaning an attentive watchman. *Greg, Grigor.*

Günther Warrior; army. *Guenter, Guenther, Gun, Gunnar, Guntar, Gunter, Gunthar.*

Heinrich Form of Henry, meaning household ruler. *Harro, Heike, Hein, Heine, Heinecke, Heinz, Henke, Hinrich.*

Helmut Brave; courageous. *Helmuth, Helmutt.*

Karl Form of Charles, meaning a farmer; strong and masculine. *Carl, Kaarle, Karlus.*

Kaspar Form of Casper, meaning imperial. *Kasper.*

Lothar Form of Luther, meaning famed warrior. *Loring, Lotaire, Lothair, Lothaire, Lotharing.*

Ludwig Form of Louis, meaning renowned in war. *Ludovic, Ludovico, Ludvig, Ludvik, Ludwik, Luki, Lutz.*

Meinhard Firm; strong; powerful. *Maynard, Meinke, Meino, Meinyard.*

Meinrad A strong counselor or advisor. *Meinke, Meino.*

Nicolaus Form of Nicholas, meaning victorious people. *Claas, Claus, Klaas, Klaus, Niklaas, Nikolas, Nikolaus, Nilo.*

Otto Wealthy. *Odo, Otek, Otello, Oto.*

Rainer A counselor. *Rainar, Rainey, Rainor, Reiner.*

Reinhard Brave counselor. *Rainart, Rainhard, Rainhart, Reineke, Rainhard, Reinhart, Renke, Renz, Reynard.*

Wolfgang Quarrel between wolves; a traveling wolf. *Wolf, Wolfe, Wolfie, Wolfgans, Wolfganz.*

Wolfrik Ruler of wolves. *Wolf, Wolfe, Wolfric, Wolfrick, Wulf, Wulfric, Wulfrick.*

Looking for French names? Check out the Acadian, Métis and French Canadian sections of the "Truly Canadian" chapter.

German Girls' Names

Adalheid One who is noble. *Ada, Adda, Addie, Adelaide, Adelheid, Aleida, Aleit, Alke, Heidi.*

Agnethe Form of Agnes, meaning pure; chaste. *Agatha, Aggie, Agneth.*

Aloisia A renowned warrior. *Aloisa, Aloysia.*

Benedikta Form of Benedicta, meaning blessed. *Benea, Benedetta, Benicia, Benna, Bennie, Bennicia.*

Brunhilde An armed warrior. *Brunhild, Brunhilda, Brünhilde, Brünnhilde.*

Clotilda A heroine; famed warrior. *Clotilde, Tilda.*

Conradina Feminine form of Conrad, meaning a brave counselor. *Conradine.*

Constanze Form of Constance, meaning firm and constant. *Constanz, Constanza, Stanzi.*

Cordula Heart; a jewel of the sea.

Dagmar A joyous or splendid day. *Dagmara, Dagomar.*

Ebba Strong; return of the tide. *Eba.*

Gerlinde A soft spear. *Gerlind, Lind, Linde.*

Gretchen Form of Margaret, meaning pearl; child of the light. *Greta, Gretchin.*

Gretel Form of Greta, a form of Margaret, meaning pearl; child of the light. *Greatal, Greatel, Gretal, Grete.*

Haldis Reliable; focused. *Halda, Haldi, Haldisse.*

Ilse Short form of Elizabeth, meaning God's oath; devoted to God. *Ilsa, Ilsey, Ilsie.*

KIDS' KORNER

Nolan's parents found his name in a baby name book and boy is he glad they did. The five-year old really likes his name. The main reason: It has two "n"s in it instead of "l"s.

I like that a lot of queens were named Elizabeth, so my name is royal," boasts 13-year-old Elizabeth. But she always wished her name sounded more like Jen "because then at least it [would] rhyme with something," she says.

Although 12-year-old Alyssa likes having an original name, she says she wishes that it was a bit different. "I would prefer it to be spelled Allysa," she explains. If she was allowed to pick another name for herself, she'd choose "Jerri or Chrissy because they are very uncommon names."

"I like my name because it is like a fairy's name," says 10-year-old Felicity. She can't think of anything she doesn't like about being called Felicity, but says that her favourite names are Cory, Taylor and Jordan because they're tom-boyish.

Alexander's mom knew he'd be a tough guy, so she named him after Alexander the Great. "I like the way it sounds," 11-year-old Alexander says about his name. "But I like to be called Alex instead." If he had to choose another name, Alex says he'd pick Ron, after his favourite *Harry Potter* character.

Although Anisa thinks there are too many A's in her name, the 12-year-old says she likes it overall "because I think it suits me and goes with my [last] name." But she has a secret to share: her name was really supposed to be Amina, her middle name, but her dad said he liked Anisa better, so he changed it.

Daniel's parents gave him his name "because they both really like it." And he couldn't be happier with their choice. "It's cool and people can call me Danny," says the three-year-old. "I like that."

Nine-year-old Michaelya thinks her name is nice and pretty. Sometimes, though, she says it's too long to fit on a page. If she had to choose another name, she'd pick Myaa. Why? "Because I made it up and I always use it in games," she explains.

Jade's biggest pet peeve about her name is its mispronunciation. For some reason, she says, people don't get that it's French as in Jad (like mad) not Jade. Once people do understand, the 16-year-old says she really likes having a unique name. "People are like Jade this and Jade that and everyone knows who they're talking about," she explains. "I've never met anyone with my name."

Haytham's parents chose his name because it is Muslim and unusual. "I like my name because it is different and it means young falcon," says the seven-year-old. If he had to choose another name for himself, Haytham says he'd pick Jimmy "because it is a name of a TV show, *Jimmy Neutron*," he explains.

Anesty's parents named him after his grandfather, who died around the time that he was born. And this 13-year-old is certainly glad they did. "[I like that] it is unique," he says of his name. But he wishes it didn't translate into Andy in English.

Käethe Form of Kate, which is short for Katherine, meaning pure; chaste. *Katchen, Käte, Kath, Kathe.*

Karola Form of Carolina, a form of Caroline, meaning small and feminine; form of Karolina, a feminine form of Karl, meaning strong and masculine. *Karole.*

Liesel Form of Elizabeth, meaning God's oath; devoted to God. *Leesel, Leesl, Leezel, Liese, Liezel, Liezl, Lisel.*

Lorelei Tempting; luring. *Loralie, Loralyn, Lorilee, Lorilyn, Lura, Lurette, Lurleen, Lurline.*

Margarethe Form of Margaret, meaning pearl; child of the light. *Margaret, Margarete, Margit, Margrit, Margot, Greta, Gretal, Gretchen, Grete, Gretel, Marga, Meret.*

Minetta Form of Mina, which is short for Wilhelmina, meaning an unwavering, resolute guardian. *Mina, Minda, Minetta, Minette, Mindy, Minnie, Minny, Myna.*

Odette Form of Odilia, meaning rich; wealthy. *Oddette, Odet, Odete, Odetta.*

Orlanda Renowned; bright sun. *Orlande, Orlando.*

Ragnhild Smart in combat. *Ragna, Ragnelle, Ragnhilde, Ragnild, Reinheld, Renilda, Renilde.*

Roderica Form of Roderick, meaning a famous ruler. *Rica, Ricka, Rickie, Rika, Rodericka, Roderika, Rodreica, Rodreicka, Rodreika.*

Selda Short form of Griselda, meaning grey; a stone; a heroine. *Seldah, Selde, Sellda, Zelda.*

Ulla Determined; willful. *Ulli, Ullima.*

Wanda One who wanders. *Vanda, Vande, Wahnda, Wenda, Wendi, Wendie, Wendy, Wonda.*

Greek Names

Greek Boys' Names

Achilles A Greek hero during the Trojan War. *Achill, Achille, Akil, Akilles.*

Adeipho Brother.

Adōnis Attractive; handsome. The good-looking young man loved by mythological figure *Aphrodite. Adonis, Adonnis, Adonys.*

Attis An attractive boy.

Bastiaan Revered; respected. *Baste, Bastien.*

Cadmus From the east.

Calisto Supremely beautiful. *Cal.*

Cohn Triumphant; victorious. *Cohen, Cohne.*

Cyrano From the ancient city of Cyrene.

Demetrius Earth-lover; follower of Demeter, the Greek goddess of agriculture and fertility. *Dametrius, Demeitrius, Demetreus, Demetrias, Demetrio, Demetrious, Demetrium, Demetrois, Demetrus, Demitirus, Demitri, Demitrius, Dimitrios, Dimitrius.*

Erasmus Loveable; amiable. *Erasmios, Erasmo, Rasmus.*

Eryx A mythological Greek figure. *Ericks, Eriks, Erix.*

Hermes Zeus's messenger in Greek mythology.

Homer A pledge; a hostage. *Homere, Homero, Homeros, Homerus.*

Isidore The gift of Isis. *Isador, Isadore, Isidor, Isidoro, Isodore, Isodoro, Issy, Izidor, Izidore, Izzy.*

Kosmo Form of Cosmo, meaning orderly; harmonious. *Kosmy*.

Laertes A well-known Greek figure.

Layland Man's protector. *Lailand*.

Leonidas Form of Leonard, meaning with the courage of a lion. *Leonida*, *Leonides*.

Midas A mythological Greek king and lover of gold. *Mydas*.

Nieander Victorious man. *Neander*.

Orestes A man of the mountain. *Oreste*.

Orpheus A mythological Greek hero. *Orphius*.

Panos Form of Peter, meaning rock. *Pano*, *Petros*.

Rhodes Land of roses; a Greek island. *Rhoads*, *Rhodas*, *Rodas*, *Rodes*.

Soterios A saviour; deliverer.

Xenos A stranger; foreigner. *Xeno*, *Zenos*.

Zander Short form of Alexander, meaning man's defender. *Zandrae*, *Zandy*.

Zeth One who investigates or researches.

Zeus Living; father or ruler of the gods in Greek mythology.

Greek Girls' Names

Achilla Feminine form of Achilles, a Greek hero during the Trojan War. *Achille*.

Adonia Beautiful; feminine form of Adõnis, meaning attractive; handsome.

Aegea From the Aegean Sea; form of Aegeus, meaning shield; a mythological Greek king. *Agea*.

Aphrodite Greek goddess of love.

Ariadne Holy; King Minos's daughter in Greek mythology. *Ari*, *Aria*, *Ariana*, *Ariane*.

Cypria From Cyprus, a Greek island. *Cipria*, *Cipriana*, *Cypra*, *Cypris*.

Eleni Light; torch.

Erianthe One who loves flowers; sweet as flowers. *Eriantha, Erianthia.*

Eurydice Wife of Orpheus and a beautiful nymph in Greek mythology. *Euridice, Euridyce, Eurydyce.*

Gelasia Laughing.

Hypatia The highest; surpassing. *Hyapatia.*

Ianthe A purple or violet flower. *Iantha, Ianthia, Ianthina.*

Isadora The gift of Isis. *Dora, Dory, Isadore, Isidora.*

Kaethe Pure; chaste.

Kalika A rosebud. *Kalyca.*

Lena Short form of Eleanor, meaning light. *Lenah, Lenea, Lenee, Lenette, Leonne, Leonora, Leonore, Lenore, Lina, Linah.*

Macaria Daughter of Hercules in Greek mythology. *Macarya.*

Melanctha A black flower. *Melantha, Melantho.*

Nastasia Form of Anastasia, meaning rebirth. *Nastasha, Nastashia, Nastasja, Natassa, Nastassia, Nastassja, Nastassya, Nastasya, Nastazia.*

Nitsa Form of Helen, meaning bright one; light. *Nytsa.*

Nyssa The start; beginning. *Nissa.*

Obelia A pillar; needle. *Obelie.*

Pelagia From the sea. *Pelga, Pelage, Pelageia, Pelagie, Pelgia.*

Phyllis A leafy branch or bough. *Fillis, Fyllis, Phil, Phillis, Philis, Phyl, Phylis, Phyllys.*

Tekla Divine fame. *Tecla, Thekla.*

Thaddea Brave. *Thada, Thadea, Thadda.*

Thaleia Form of Talia, meaning to bloom or flourish. *Talia, Thalia, Thalie, Thalya.*

Thecla Divine fame. *Tecla, Tekla, Thekla.*

Titania A giant. *Tania, Tita, Titanna, Titanya, Titianna, Tytania.*

Xenia Hospitable; generous; welcoming. *Xeenia, Xena, Zena, Zene, Zenia, Zina.*

Zelena A Greek goddess.

Zelia Passionate; zealous.

Zenaide Someone who'd devoted her life to God. *Zenaida, Zenayda.*

Irish Names
Irish Boys' Names

Beacán Small; little one. *Becan.*

Beanón Good. *Beinean, Beineón, Benen, Binean.*

Calbhach Bald. *Calvagh, Callough, Charles, Kalbach.*

Colmán Peaceful; a dove. *Cole, Coleman, Colman.*

Conor Desired; lover of wolves. *Conner, Connor, Conny, Konnor.*

Darby A free person. *Dar, Darb, Darbee, Darbey, Darbie.*

Donnelly Dark. *Donel, Donell, Donellle, Donelly, Donielle.*

Fergus Strong; masculine. *Fearghas, Fearghus, Feargus, Ferg, Fergie, Ferguson.*

Finbar One with fair hair. *Barry, Fin, Finn, Finnbar.*

Finnegan Having fair skin. *Fin, Finegan, Finn.*

Gallagher An enthusiastic aide. *Gallagar.*

Galvin A sparrow. *Gal, Gallven, Gallvin, Galvan, Galven.*

Grady Noble; famous. *Gradea, Gradee, Gradey, Gradie, Graidy.*

Hogan Youth.

Hurley Tide of the sea. *Hurlee, Hurleigh.*

Kealan Slight; slender. *Kelan.*

Keegan Little; fierce, fiery. *Keagan, Keagen, Kegan, Keghan.*

Keeley Attractive; handsome. *Kealey, Kealy, Keelie, Keely.*

Keiran Dark-haired. *Kearn, Keeran, Keir, Keiren, Keiron, Kern, Kern, Kier, Kieran, Kieren.*

Moriarty A warrior of the sea. *Mauriarty, Maury, Mori, Mory.*

Niall Form of Neil, meaning champion. *Neal, Néill, Nial, Nyle.*

Oran Green. *Ora, Orane, Oren, Orran, Orren, Orrin.*

Phelan Small wolf. *Phelen, Phelin.*

Quigley The maternal side. *Quig, Quiglee, Quigly.*

Quinlan Athletic; well-formed. *Quin, Quindlan, Quinlen, Quinlin, Quinn, Quinnlan, Quinnlen.*

Rafferty Wealthy; prosperous. *Rafe, Raferty, Raffarty.*

Reardon A royal writer or poet. *Rearden, Riordan.*

Roarke A renowned ruler. *Roark, Rorke, Rourke.*

Seamus Form of the name James, meaning someone who replaces. *Seamas, Shama*s.

Shanley Son of the hero. *Shandley, Shanlee, Shanleigh, Shanly.*

Sloan A fighter; warrior. *Sloane.*

Teague A poet. *Teagan, Teagun, Teak, Teegue, Teigue, Tegan.*

Tiernan A lord. *Tiarnán, Tighearnán.*

Irish Girls' Names

Aoife Form of Eve, meaning life. *Aoiffe.*

Ashling A dream or vision. *Aisling, Ashlin, Ashlyn, Ashlyng.*

Briana Feminine form of Brian, meaning strong; virtuous. *Breana, Breanna, Bria, Brianna, Brie, Bryanna.*

Casey Brave; vigilant. *Casee, Kasey.*

Cassidy Clever; intelligent. *Casadee, Casadi, Casadie, Cass, Cassadi, Cassadie, Cassady, Cassi, Cassidee, Cassidi, Cassidie, Cassie.*

Ciara Black. *Ceara, Cearra, Cera, Ciarra, Cieara, Cierr, Ciera.*

Decla A form of Declan, meaning goodness; a saint. *Dekla.*

Deirdre One who is sad; sorrowful. *Dedra, Deerdra, Deerdre, Deidrea, Deidrie, Deidra, Diedra, Deirdree, Didre, Dierdre, Dierdrie.*

Eithne A small fire.

Ennis An Irish place name. *Ennys*.

Étáin Bright; shining. *Aideen, Etain*.

Finella White; fair. *Fenella, Finella, Finola, Fionnghuala, Fionnuala, Fionola*.

Grania Love. *Grainne, Granna*.

Inis Form of Ennis, an Irish place name.

Iseult Fair. *Hisolda, Isolda, Isolde, Yseult, Ysolte*.

Isibéal Form of Isabel, meaning holy; God-loving. *Sibéal*.

Keeley Beautiful. *Kealey, Kealy, Keelie, Keely*.

Keelin Slight and fair. *Caoilfhionn, Kealin*.

Keverne A saint. *Kaverne, Kevern*.

Liadan A grey lady. *Leadan*.

Maeve Intoxicating; joyful. *Maive, Mayve, Meave*.

Maille A pearl; form of Molly, which is a form of Mary, meaning bitter. *Maili*.

Mairead Form of Margaret, meaning pearl; child of the light.

Moira Form of Mary, meaning bitter. *Maura, Moyra*.

Niamh Bright. *Nehm*.

Noirin Form of Noreen, a form of Eleanor, meaning light.

Nollaig Form of Noelle, meaning Christmas.

Orla A golden woman. *Orlagh, Orlie*.

Paili A form of Polly, which is a form of Mary, meaning bitter. *Pails*.

Riona Like a queen. *Reeona, Reona, Reonagh*.

Sadhbh Sweet and good. *Sabha, Sabia, Sadbha, Sadhbha, Saidhbhe, Sarah, Sally, Sive, Sophia*.

Siany Healthy. *Seeany*.

Sinéad Form of Jane, meaning God is gracious. *Sine, Sinead*.

Siobhan Form of Joan, meaning God is gracious. *Shibahn, Shibhan, Shioban, Siobhan, Siobháinín, Siobhann, Siobhon, Siovhan*.

Italian Names

Italian Boys' names

Angelo An angel; divine messenger. *Angelito, Angelos.*

Antonio Form of Anthony, meaning praiseworthy; priceless; flourishing. *Antonello, Antoino, Antonino, Antonnio, Antonios, Antonius, Antonyio, Antonyo.*

Augusto Form of Augustus, meaning magnificent; exalted. *Agosto, Augustos.*

Basilio Form of Basil, meaning regal; king-like. *Basile, Basilios, Basillius, Bazylio.*

Benigno From Benignus, meaning good and kind. *Benignos, Benignus.*

Brizio Form of Brice, meaning ambitious; short for Fabrizio, meaning a craftsman.

Carlo Form of Charles, meaning strong and masculine. *Carlos, Carolo, Karlo.*

Claudio Form of Claudius, meaning lame.

Dominico Form of Dominic, meaning belonging to the Lord. *Demenico, Domenico, Dominic, Dominick.*

Donato Gift. *Donatello, Donatus.*

Emilio One who flatters. *Emillio, Emilios, Emilo.*

Fabrizio A craftsman. *Brizio.*

Fausto A form of Faustus, meaning lucky or fortunate.

Francesco Form of Francis, meaning free or from France.

Giovanni Form of John, meaning God is merciful. *Geovanni, Gianni, Giovani, Giovannie, Giovanno, Giovany, Giovonni.*

Giuseppe Form of Joseph, meaning God adds. *Giuseppino.*

Guido Form of Guy, meaning valley; warrior.

Ignazio Form of Ignatius, meaning zealous; fervent. *Ignacio.*

Innocenzio Innocent. *Innocenty, Innocenci, Innocencio, Inocenci, Inocencio, Inocente.*

Lorenzo Form of Laurence, meaning crowned with laurel. *Lerenzo, Lorenco, Lorencz, Loretto, Lorinzo, Lorrezo, Renzo.*

Luciano Form of Lucius, meaning light. *Lucca, Lucio.*

Luigi Form of Louis, meaning renowned warrior. *Lui, Luigino.*

Marcello Form of Marcellus, which is a form of Marcus, meaning warlike. *Marcelo, Marchello, Marsello.*

Marciano Form of Martin, meaning warlike. *Marci, Marcio, Marsiano.*

Mario Form of Marius, which is a form of Marin, meaning sailor. *Mariano, Marios, Marrio.*

Matteo Form of Matthew, meaning gift from God. *Mateo, Matteus.*

Maurizio Form of Maurice, meaning one with dark skin; a moor. *Mauricio.*

Nico Victorious. *Nicco, Niko.*

Nunzio A messenger. *Nuncio.*

Orazio Form of Horace, meaning time-keeper. *Oracio.*

Paolo Form of Paul, meaning little one; small. *Paulo.*

Pietro Form of Peter, meaning a rock. *Pero, Piero.*

Raimondo Form of Raymond, meaning wise defender. *Raimundo, Raymondo, Raymundo.*

Rinaldo Form of Reynold, meaning king's councellor. *Renaldo, Rinald.*

Salvatore Saviour; rescuer. *Sal, Salbatore, Salvator, Salvidor.*

Sergio Form of Serge, meaning an attendant. *Serg.*

Taddeo Form of Thaddeus, meaning brave; courageous. *Tadeo.*

Valentino Form of Valentinus, meaning strong and healthy.

Vincenzo Form of Vincentius, meaning conqueror. *Vincenz, Vincenzio.*

Italian Girls' Names

Adriana Form of Adrienne, meaning wealthy; dark. *Adrea, Adreana, Adria, Adrianna.*

Alonza Feminine form of Alonzo, meaning noble; enthusiastic. *Lon, Lonza.*

Bambina A baby or young girl. *Bambi.*

Benigna Good; kind.

Caprice Unpredictable. *Caprece, Capricia, Caprise.*

Carmela A vineyard. *Carmaletta, Carmalla, Carmella, Carmellina.*

Caterina Pure; chaste. *Cat, Catarina, Katarina, Katerina.*

Concetta Pure; immaculate conception. *Concettina, Conchetta.*

Dominica One who belongs to the Lord. *Domenica, Domenika, Domineca, Dominika, Domonica, Domonika.*

Donata A gift from God. *Donatha, Donatta.*

Donatella Feminine form of Donatello, meaning a gift. *Donetella, Donotella.*

Elisabetta Form of Elizabeth, meaning God's oath; devoted to God. *Betta, Betty, Elissa, Elizabetta.*

Emerenzia Merit; worth. *Emerencia.*

Enrica Feminine form of Enrico, which is a form of Henry, meaning ruler of the house. *Enrika, Enriqua, Rica, Rika.*

Fiammetta A glittering fire.

Francesca Feminine form of Francesco, which is a form of Frances, meaning free; from France. *Franceska, Francessca, Franchesca, Franciska, Franzetta.*

Gianna Form of Giovanna, meaning God is gracious. *Geona, Giana, Gianella, Gianetta, Giannetta, Giannina.*

Giovanna Form of Jane, meaning God is gracious. *Anna, Gian, Gianina, Giann, Gianna, Giannina, Giavanna, Giavonna, Giovana.*

Giuseppina Feminine form of Giuseppe, which is a form of Joseph, meaning God adds.

Immacolata Immaculate.

Laurenza Feminine form of Lorenzo, which is a form of Laurence, meaning crowned with laurel. *Laurenca.*

Lucia Feminine form of Lucius, meaning light. *Luciana.*

Luigina Feminine form of Luigi, which is a form of Louis, meaning renowned warrior.

Mafalda A form of Matilda, meaning powerful fighter.

Maria Form of Mary, meaning bitter. *Marya.*

Marietta Form of Mary, meaning bitter. *Marieta, Maryetta.*

Mercede Merciful. *Mercedes.*

Niccola Form of Nicole, meaning triumphant people. *Nacola, Necola, Nichola, Nicola, Nikola, Nykola.*

Nicia Form of Nicole, meaning triumphant people. *Necea, Necia, Nycia.*

Nunzia A messenger. *Nuncia, Nunzea.*

Ottavia Eighth born. *Octavia.*

Patrizia Form of Patricia, meaning noble-woman.

Riccarda Feminine form of Riccardo, a form of Richard, meaning strong ruler; brave. *Rica, Ricca, Ricarda.*

Rosalba Form of Rosa, meaning rose.

Rosalia Form of Rosalia, a form of Rosa, meaning rose.

Suzetta Form of Susan, meaning a lily. *Suse, Susetta, Susette, Suze, Suzette.*

Valentina Strong. *Val, Valantina, Valentin, Valentine, Valida, Valyntina, Velora.*

Zola A ball or piece of earth. *Zoela.*

Looking for Hebrew names? Try the "Traditional Names" chapter.

Japanese Names
Japanese Boys' Names

Akio A bright boy.

Akira An anchor; smart.

Botan A peony flower.

Daiki Radiance; joy.

Eiji The second son.

Gorō The fifth son.

Harō First son of the wild boar.

Haru Born during the spring.

Hideyoshi Extremely good luck.

Hiroshi Generous.

Jiro The second male; second born son.

Isoroku The number 56.

Kisho Someone who knows his own mind.

Kiyoshi Quiet.

Mamoru The earth.

Masahiro Wise.

Masakazu Masa's first son.

Naoko Child of Nao; honest.

Raidon God of thunder.

Ren A water lily; one who arranges.

Ringo Apple; peace.

Ryugi Dragon man.

Saburo Third son.

Sanyu Happiness; joy.

Shino Bamboo stem.

Takahiro Flourishing; prosperous.

Taro First born son.

Tomi Wealthy; prosperous.

Washi An eagle.

Yasahiro Wise; peaceful.

Yasuo Peaceful; calm.

Yogi One who practices yoga.

Yoshiko Child of Yoshi.

Yukako Child of Yuka.

Japanese Girls' Names

Aiko Love child.

Akahana A red flower.

Akira Clear; bright.

Aoi Blue; hollyhock.

Ayamē An iris.

Bachiko A happy child.

Chika Near.

Chiyo A thousand years.

Cho Butterfly.

Dai Great.

Etsu Delight; enjoyment.

Fujita A field.

Fuyu Winter.

Hanako A flower child.

Haruki To shine brightly.

Hiroko Magnanimus.

Iva Great gift from God; a yew tree.

Jin Gentle; tender.

Kaiya Forgiveness.

Keiko Adored; revered.

Masami Elegance and beauty.

Misaki A beautiful flower blossom.

Mitsu Light.

Mitsuki A beautiful moon.

Miyo A beautiful child.

Naoko An honest child.

Natsuko Child of Natsu; child of summer.

Reiko Gratitude; child of Rei.

Sachiko A happy child.

Sorano From the sky.

Suki Beloved.

Suzuki A bell tree.

Tamiko Child of Tami.

Wakana Young herbs.

Yoshe Beauty.

Yuki Snow.

Yukiko Child of the snow.

Polish Names
Polish Boys' Names

Andrzej Form of Andreas and Andrew, meaning strong; brave.

Antoni Praise-worthy.

Aurek Having golden hair.

Bialas A boy with white hair. *Bialy.*

Dobry Kind; good.

Eryk Form of Erik, meaning brave ruler.

Filip Horse lover. *Fil.*

Gerik A wealthy spearman.

Jacek Form of Jacenty, meaning hyacinth. *Jach, Jack.*

Jakób Form of Jacob, meaning the supplanter. *Jakub, Kuba, Kubú.*

Jan Form of John, meaning God is merciful. *Ivan, Janek, Janik, Janko, Janusz.*

Jędrej From Andrew, meaning strong; brave. *Jedrik.*

Jerzy Form of George, meaning a farmer of the earth. *Jerek.*

Józef Form of Joseph, meaning God adds. *Josef, Josep, Yusef.*

Karol Form of Charles, meaning strong and manly. *Karolek.*

Kasper A treasurer.

Konrad Form of Conrad, meaning a brave counselor. *Kurt.*

Kornel A horn. *Kornek, Kornelek, Korneli, Korneliusz.*

Krzysztof Form of Christopher, meaning bearer of Christ.

Lech The founder of Poland. *Lechoslaw, Leszek.*

Ludwik Famed warrior.

Mandek Soldier; army man.

Marcin Confrontational. *Marcinek.*

Marek Form of Marcus, meaning warlike.

Marian Form of Mary, meaning bitter.

Pavel Little.

Pawel Form of Paul, meaning little one; small. *Inek, Pawl, Pawelek.*

Piotr Form of Peter, meaning rock. *Pietrek, Piotrek.*

Stanislaw Glorious government. *Stach, Stanislav, Stas, Statsio.*

Stefan Form of Stephen, meaning crown. *Szczepan.*

Szymon Form of Simon, meaning a good listener.

Tanek Immortal.

Tytus Form of Titus, meaning giant.

Zygmunt From Sigmund, meaning triumphant protector.

Polish Girls' Names

Adelajda Form of Adelaide, meaning noble and kind. *Adela.*

Anna Gracious. *Ania, Anka, Anula, Anusia.*

Barbara Foreigner; stranger. *Basa, Basha, Basia.*

Boleslawa Feminine form of Boleslaw, meaning the great glory.

Brygid Strength. *Brygida, Brygita, Zytka.*

Celestyn Heaven; celestial. *Celestyna.*

Danuta Form of Dana, meaning from Denmark.

Dorota Form of Dorothea, a form of Dorothy, meaning God's gift.

Edyta Form of Edith, meaning an expensive gift.

Elżbieta Form of Elizabeth, meaning God's oath; devoted to God.

Estera Form of Esther, meaning star.

Ewa Form of Eva, a form of Eve, meaning life. *Ewka, Ewusia.*

Febe Form of Phoebe, meaning one who shines; bright one.

Felcia Feminine form of Felix, meaning lucky. *Fela, Felicia, Felicja, Felicya, Felka.*

Filipina A horse-lover. *Filipa.*

Franciszka Form of Francesca, a form of Frances, meaning from France.

Gizela Form of Giselle, meaning a pledge.

Henryka Feminine form of Heinrich, a form of Henry, meaning ruler of the house.

Jadwiga Form of Hedwig, meaning war; a fighter; a refuge during war. *Wisa.*

Jolanta Form of Jolanda, a form of Yolanda, meaning a violet flower.

Kamila Form of Camilla, meaning young. *Kamilka, Mila, Milla.*

Krystyna Form of Christina, meaning Christian.

Maria Form of Mary, meaning bitter. *Macia, Mani, Mania, Manka, Marika, Marja, Marusia, Maryla, Maryli, Marysi, Marysia, Masia.*

Miloslawa Lover of glory.

Olesia A form of Alexander, meaning man's defender. *Ola.*

Rasine A rose.

Reina Queen.

Rościslawa Glory in victory.

Truda Form of Gertruda, a form of Gertrude, meaning a beloved warrior. *Trudka.*

Walentya Strong and healthy.

Zofia Form of Sophia, meaning intelligence; wise. *Zofja.*

Russian Names
Russian Boys' Names

Akim Form of Joachim, meaning God will establish. *Ioakim, Iov, Kima, Yakim.*

Ambrossij From Ambrosios, meaning immortal.

Avel Form of Abel, meaning breath; child. *Awel.*

Borislav Greatness or glory in battle. *Slava.*

Denis Form of Dionysus, the Greek god of wine. *Denya, Dionisij.*

Dominik Form of Dominicus, meaning of the Lord.

Efrem Form of Efraim, meaning fruitful. *Efrasha, Rema.*

Egor Form of George, meaning farmer of the earth. *Egorka, Egunya, Gora, Gorya.*

Filip Form of Philip, meaning horse-lover.

Fyodor God's gift.

Gavriil Form of Gabriel, meaning God is my strength. *Ganya, Gavril, Gavrila, Gavrya.*

Grigori Form of Gregory, meaning a watchman. *Grigor, Grinya, Grisha.*

Iakov Form of Iakobos, a form of Jacob, meaning supplanter.

Ignati From Ignatius, meaning fiery. *Ignasha, Ignat.*

Igor Form of Ivor, meaning yew bow; archer. *Gorik, Gosha, Iga.*

Innokenti Innocent. *Kenya, Kesha.*

Isaak Form of Isaac, meaning laughter. *Eisaak, Isak.*

Jeremija Form of Jeremiah, meaning God will uplift. *Jeremej.*

Jevstachi A fruitful harvest.

Kliment Mild and merciful. *Klim, Klima, Klimenti.*

Kondrati Form of Conrad, meaning a brave counselor. *Kondrasha, Kondrat.*

Konstantin Unwavering; steadfast. *Kostya.*

Lev A lion.

Maksim Short for Maksimilian, a form of Maximilian, meaning greatest. *Maks, Sima.*

Matvei Form of Matthew, meaning gift from God. *Matfei, Motya.*

Mikhail Form of Michael, meaning who is like God. *Michej, Mika, Minya, Misha.*

Moisse Form of Moses, meaning appointed for special things; taken by water.

Naum One who comforts.

Nikolai Form of Nicholas, meaning the victorious people. *Koka, Kolya, Nika, Nil, Nilya.*

Oleg Holy one.

Osip God will add or increase.

Pavel Form of Paul, meaning little one; small. *Panya, Pasha, Pava, Pusha.*

Prokhop Plentiful; abundant. *Prokopi, Pronya, Prosha.*

Sasha Form of Alexander, meaning man's defender.

Savvel Form of Saul, meaning asked for. *Sava, Savel, Saveli.*

Sergei Form of Serge, meaning an attendant. *Serezha, Serguei, Serzh.*

Vladimir Peaceful ruler; famous ruler.

Russian Girls' Names

Amaliya Hard-working. *Amaliji.*

Antonina Feminine form of Anthony, meaning praiseworthy; priceless; flourishing. *Nina.*

Cyzarine From Catherine, meaning pure.

Duscha Happy. *Dusa, Duschinka, Dusica.*

Ekaterina From Catherine, meaning pure. *Katerina, Katya, Ketti, Ketya, Kitti, Koka.*

Evdokiya A good gift. *Avdosha, Avdota, Avdunya, Avdusya, Dotya, Dunya, Dusha, Dusya, Eudokhia, Eudokia.*

Evgeniya Form of Eugenia, meaning noble. *Evgenia, Geka, Genya, Jevginnia, Zheka, Zhenya.*

Inessa Form of Agnes, meaning lamb; pure; virginal.

Ivanna Feminine form of Ivan, meaning God is good and gracious.

Klavdiya Form of Claudia, meaning lame. *Klanya, Klasha, Klava, Klavdya.*

Kiska Pure.

Klementina Form of Clementine, meaning merciful. *Klima.*

Lara Cheerful; famous.

Mariya Form of Mary, meaning bitter. *Manya, Mara, Marisha, Marya, Masha, Meri, Munya, Mura, Musya.*

Marta Form of Martha, meaning a lady. *Marfa, Muta.*

Nika Short for Veronika, a form of Veronica, meaning true image.

Ninel An anagram for famed Communist leader Vladimir Lenin. *Nelli, Nelya.*

Oksana Glory be to God.

Olga Holy or blessed one. *Elga, Helga, Lelya, Lyalya, Lyusha, Lyusya, Olesya, Olya.*

Renata Born again. *Nata, Rena.*

Sasha Shortened, feminine form of Alexander, meaning man's defender.

Sashenka Defender of mankind.

Tatiana A fairy queen. *Tanya, Tasha, Tata, Tatia, Tatiann, Tatianna, Tatihanna, Tatjana, Tatyana, Tusya.*

Tekla Form of Thekla, meaning holy or divine glory. *Fekla, Tjokle.*

Vania God's gift.

Vanka In God's favour.

Spanish Names
Spanish Boys' Names

Adrián Form of Adrian, meaning wealthy; dark. *Adrain, Adreian, Adreyan, Adriano, Adrien, Adrion, Adryan.*

Alberto Form of Albert, meaning bright and noble. *Berto.*

Alejandro Form of Alexander, meaning man's defender. *Alejándro, Aléjo, Alexjándro.*

Álvaro Cautious; elf army. *Albar, Albaro, Alvarso, Alverio.*

Benedicto Form of Benedict, meaning blessed. *Bendito, Benedetto, Benedictae, Benedito, Beni, Benito, Bento.*

Berilo A pale or sea-green gem. *Barilio, Barilo, Berilio.*

Carlos Form of Charles, meaning strong and masculine.

Casimiro Form of Casimir, meaning famous destroyer of peace. *Casemiera, Casemiro, Casimaro, Casimere, Casimero, Casimiera.*

Damario Form of Damaris, meaning gentle; tame. *Damaro.*

Diego One who supplants.

Eberardo Form of Eberhard, meaning having the courage of a wild boar. *Eberedo, Evelardo, Everado, Everando, Everardo.*

Emilio One who flatters. *Aemilio, Emelio, Emielo, Emileo, Emiliano, Emilios, Emillio, Emilo, Hemilio, Imelio, Melo, Milo.*

Enrique Ruler of the estate. *Anrique, Enrico, Enrigque, Enrigue, Enriques, Enrrique, Henrico, Henriko, Inriques, Quique.*

Felipe Form of Philip, meaning horse-lover. *Felippe, Felippo, Felipo, Filip, Filipe, Filipo, Filippe, Philippo.*

Fidel Trustworthy; faithful. *Fedelio, Fedil, Fidal, Fidelio, Fidélix, Fidolo.*

Frederico Form of Frederick, meaning a peaceful, merciful ruler. *Federigo, Federío, Fredericlo, Frederiko, Fredico, Fredrico, Friderico, Rico.*

García A common last name. *Garcia, Garcisa.*

Hilario Happy; cheerful. *Helario, Hilarrio, Hilorio, Ilario, Illario, Ilaro.*

Horatio One who keeps the time. *Horacio, Oracio, Orasio.*

Jacinto A hyacinth.

Javier Form of Xavier, meaning bright; a new house. *Javeir, Jevier, Xabier, Xaverio, Zavier.*

Joaquín God will give strength; God will establish. *Jehoichin, Joachín, Joachin, Joachino, Joakín, Joaquin, Jocquin, Joquinn, Juaquin, Yoaquín.*

Juan Form of John, meaning God is merciful. *Juancito, Juanito, Juann.*

Luis Form of Louis, meaning renowned warrior. *Luiz.*

Macario Happy; blessed. *Macareo, Macarro, Maccario, Mackario, Marcario, Mecario.*

Miguel Form of Michael, meaning who is like God. *Migel, Migueo.*

Pablo Form of Paul, meaning little one; small. *Pablos, Paublo.*

Pedro Form of Peter, meaning rock. *Pedrín, Pedrin, Pedruco, Petronio, Peyo.*

Reinaldo Form of Reynold, meaning advisor to the king. *Naldo, Rainaldo, Ranaldo, Raynaldo, Renaldo, Reynaldo, Rinaldo.*

Renato Form of Renatus, meaning born again; reborn.

Ricardo Form of Richard, meaning strong ruler; brave. *Racardo, Riccardo, Ricciardo, Ricco.*

Salvador A saviour. *Salavador, Salbador, Salvado, Salvadore, Salvadro, Salvarado, Salvator, Salvodor.*

Santiago Form of James, meaning someone who replaces. *Antiago, Chago, Diego, Sandiago, Sandiego, Saniago, Santago, Santeago, Santi, Santiaco, Santiego, Santigo, Santiogo.*

Spanish Girls' Names

Alvera Feminine form of Alvaro, meaning cautious; elf army. *Alvira, Alvra.*

Esperanza Hope. *Esparansa, Esparanza, Espe, Esperance, Esperans, Esperanta, Esperanz, Esperenza, Espranza, Sperancia, Speranza.*

Estella A star. *Estela, Estelae, Estell, Estellia, Estilla.*

Generosa Generous.

Hermosa Beautiful; attractive.

Inéz Form of Agnes, meaning lamb; pure; virginal. *Ines, Inés, Inesa, Inesita, Inessa, Inez.*

Jacaranda A jacaranda tree.

Josefina Feminine form of Joseph, meaning God adds. *Josefa, Josephina.*

Juana Feminine form of Juan, which is a form of John, meaning God is merciful. *Juanna, Yuana, Yuanna.*

Juliana Form of Julia, meaning young. *Julianna, Julliana, Jullianna.*

Leya Faithful. *Leyla.*

Lolita Sorrow. *Lita, Lulita.*

Luz Light. *Lucelida, Lucila, Lusa, Luzana, Luzi, Luziga.*

Lynda Pretty; attractive. *Linda, Lynde, Lyndi, Lyndy.*

Maribel Form of Mary, meaning bitter, and Belle, meaning beautiful. *Marabel, Marabelle, Mariabella, Maribelle, Marybel, Marybelle.*

Marta Form of Martha, meaning a lady. *Martila, Martina.*

Milagros Miracles. *Mila, Milagritos, Milagro, Milagrosa.*

Mora A blueberry. *Morea, Moria.*

Neva Snow. *Neiva, Neve, Nevea, Nevia, Nevita, Nieve.*

Pilar A pillar. *Peelar, Pelar, Peleria, Pilár, Piliar, Pillar.*

Prudencia Prudent; sensible. *Pru, Prudence, Prudenciana, Prudintia, Prudy.*

Raquel Form of Rachel, meaning lamb. *Racaela, Racquel, Raechel, Rakel, Rakhil, Raquela, Raquelle, Raquia, Requel.*

Ria A river. *Rea, Rhea.*

Rosario A rosary.

Rosita Form of Rose, meaning a rose. *Roseeta, Roseta, Rozeta, Rozita.*

Santana A saint. *Ana, Santa, Santaniata, Santanna, Santanne, Santenna, Santina.*

Soledad Solitary. *Saledá, Saledad, Soladá, Sole, Soleda, Soleta, Solita.*

Vittoria Form of Victoria, meaning victorious; triumphant. *Vitoria.*

Zoraida An enchanting or captivating woman. *Soilla, Zaila, Zalia, Ziola, Zolla, Zoyla.*

Middle Names

Long ones, short ones, tongue-twisters and multiples, middle names come in all shapes and sizes. And the best part about them is there aren't many rules to follow when it comes to choosing one. Another bonus: if it's really horrible, no one ever has to know about it.

For some, a middle name can be a blessing. My brother never felt like his real first name, John, suited him. So he's been known by his second name, Lindsay, for decades. For others, a middle name is merely another option in case you get bored or decide you like another name better. Some families have a tradition of using a middle name instead of a first.

For me, a middle name is a term of endearment. My mother is the only one who's ever referred to me as Shandley Sue (and luckily, it wasn't always when I was stirring up trouble). Being number seven of eight children, this was one of the only things I alone shared with my mother, which made it extra special.

Whether you pick the name of an ancestor or exercise your creative side with a more unique choice, your child's middle name will help define her as a person. And you'll probably find yourself using it more than you thought you would; especially when yelling at her to clean up her room or stop covering her baby sister in Vaseline. So before you make your choice, read through these tips and suggestions for picking the perfect one.

Spell it out

Consider your child's initials. If his first name is to be David and last is Gordon, you should avoid a middle name that starts with O. Unless, of course, you don't mind people calling him Dog. Same goes for Ashley Sandra Sampson.

Be creative

Couldn't choose a unique first name for your child? Now's your chance to wax creative. Although you should still keep your last name in mind, a middle name is a great way to have some fun with naming traditions.

Keep it in the family

Think naming your son after grandpa Ernest sounds too old-fashioned for the twenty-first century? Why not honour your favourite ancestor (or a close friend) with a middle name instead? That way, you've done your duty without having to inflict him with a name that's way passé.

Honour thy baby's mother

A great way to celebrate your child's mother is by giving him her maiden name. This is especially practical if you've chosen to give your kid his father's last name. This way, mom can feel like she's part of her son forever, and can help carry on her own family's tradition.

Make it ethnic

If you've always wanted to give your child an ethnic name but are afraid of the constant misspellings and mispronunciations she'll get, stick it in the middle. That way, everyone who truly understands the importance and meaning of this name will be able to say it properly, and you won't have to deal with the headaches caused by oblivious foreigners.

Opt for multiples

Who says a child can only have one middle name? Choosing multiple middle names is a great way to honour family members or stick in those favourite names that you just couldn't give up. Just ask actor Keifer Sutherland. He's got five of them.

Chapter 6

-☆-

Through the Ages: Classical Names

L ooking for a name that will stand the test of time? One that will be as popular today as it will be 20 years from now? Then it's best to go the traditional route, especially if you're naming a boy. Let's take a look...

Over the past 80 years, trends have proven that it's established Biblical names, not trendy or unique ones, that have real staying power on the boys' baby naming circuit. Take John, for example. This moniker was among the top picks across the country every decade from 1920 to 1970. James, on the other hand, managed to stick it out a little longer, its top 10 reign lasting until the 80s. Today, Michael graces the upper level of our most popular lists, and it's been around since the 60s. And David, although no longer in the top 10, has remained popular since 1950.

For girls, things are a bit less straightforward. It seems that our relationship with names is similar to our relationship with hair—we need to update it frequently. The longest a girl's name has stayed on the top 10 list is 30 years, as opposed to David's 50-year rule. So which girls were the winners? Well, Jennifer topped the charts from 1970 to 1990 while Sarah and Jessica have hung on the scene since the 80s. Although we can't be sure how long they'll last, trends suggest that these chart-toppers will fall from the top rungs in the next 10 years or so. And who knows what they'll be replaced by.

Wondering how a name becomes popular? The process isn't much different from any other trend. Be it the must-have sweater of the season or the technological it-toy of the year, trends catch on because many people want to follow them. It helps them to fit in and avoid being noticed. Having a non-stylish product or name, on the other hand, could cause you to stand out from the crowd, drawing attention to yourself.

Not quite sure what I mean? Picture this: You're standing on a busy downtown street wearing a bright green coat. Everyone else is wearing taupe. Who's going to be stared at and judged for being different? It's the same with names. Tell people your child's name is Olivia and they'll probably say something like "Oh, how pretty. I know another Olivia who's just a doll." This name is familiar, something they can relate to and understand because so many other people have it. But inform them that you've chosen the name Aloisha, a name that's never made it onto a popular list, and they may well be stumped for a response.

Take a look at Canada's best-loved names. From 1920 to 2000, these lists include the top names in the country from the data that was available at the time of publication.

Top Names in 1920
Boys

John	George	Edward
William	Thomas	Donald
Robert	Charles	
James	Arthur	

☆ **JAMES**

Yet another popular Hebrew name, James means someone who replaces. In addition to being a star internationally, James has made the top 20 on Canadian lists since the 20s.

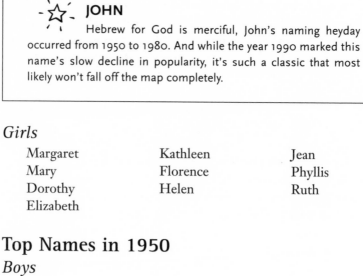

JOHN

Hebrew for God is merciful, John's naming heyday occurred from 1950 to 1980. And while the year 1990 marked this name's slow decline in popularity, it's such a classic that most likely won't fall off the map completely.

Girls

Margaret	Kathleen	Jean
Mary	Florence	Phyllis
Dorothy	Helen	Ruth
Elizabeth		

Top Names in 1950

Boys

William	Brian	Michael
John	Gary	Richard
David	Douglas	Robert
Donald	Joseph	Ronald
James	Kenneth	

Girls

Sharon	Donna	Mary
Barbara	Judith	Carol
Patricia	Susan	Sandra
Margaret	Elizabeth	Brenda
Linda	Deborah	

SUSAN

Hebrew for lily, Susan's popularity was seen mostly during the 50s, 60s and 70s. After that, it dropped off the top charts.

MICHAEL
    This name, which is of Hebrew origin, means who is like God. In terms of popularity, Michael jumped from being in the top 20 during 1950 to an ever-rising role amongst the top 10 from 1960 to today.

Top Names in 1960

Boys

William	Michael	Paul
Robert	Brian	Richard
David	Kevin	Joseph
James	Mark	Stephen
John	Kenneth	

Girls

Susan	Deborah	Margaret
Mary	Barbara	Brenda
Linda	Heather	Patricia
Karen	Darlene	Sandra
Donna	Catherine	

 DAVID
    An age-old naming superstar, David is of Hebrew origin and means beloved. It has been a mainstay on Canadian popularity charts since 1920, only recently dropping below the top 20.

REAL NAMES

"It means headaches for spelling and pronunciation problems," 33-year-old Leanne says about her name. A combination of Leah and Anne, the names of her two grandmothers, Leanne has always felt lucky to have her moniker. "My name is special to me because of its connection to my grandmothers," she says. "Since they have both passed away...they will always be a part of me."

"Unlike the 20 or so Jennifers I knew in school, my name wasn't very common where I grew up," says 32-year-old Gina. And that, she explains, was a blessing. "It always got very confusing with who was 'Jennifer' or 'Jenni' with an 'ie' or 'i' or 'y' at the end or just plain 'Jen,'" she says. Luckily, Gina didn't ever have to deal with that. The worst problems she ever experienced with her name involved strangers who would spell it as Jena or Geena. Oh, and there were those people who constantly asked her if it was short for Regina (it's not).

Carol never thinks about her name because she barely ever hears it. "I'm always called mom, honey or hey you," laughs the 67-year-old. But when she finally sat down to contemplate it, Carol said she actually prefers her middle name, Lyn. "I don't particularly like Carol because it has a hard sound," she says. "Lyn suggests softness and sweetness and all things nice."

While 41-year-old Cynthia hates being called Cindy, she's actually pleased with her name overall. "It's somewhat uncommon, not plain and means Moon Goddess," she explains. "And it feels like a strong, yet feminine name to me."

"I don't like it or hate it," 42-year-old Mark says of his name. "But I guess I would say that...[the other Marks] I know are pretty nice guys." Overall, Mark says his name feels powerful. "It allows me to keep my head held high." And he's a huge fan of his nickname, Marco. "It's a bit unexpected for a guy of French and Scottish descent," he explains.

ROBERT
Of English origin, the name Robert represents brilliance and fame. And according to Canada's baby name lists, it should mean über popular as well. Hitting the scene during the 20s, Robert maintained top 20 status until the 90s. It's just now starting to come down from its high.

Top Names in 1970

Boys

Robert	Christopher	Paul
Michael	Jason	William
John	Kevin	Scott
David	Mark	
James	Richard	

Girls

Tracy	Kimberly	Nicole
Tammy	Karen	Patricia
Michelle	Kelly	Shannon
Lisa	Mary	Susan
Jennifer	Christine	Cheryl
Angela		

 JENNIFER
Wow! Was this name ever popular in the 70s. And the amazing thing is, it's managed to stay in the top 10 (and now 20) ever since. What's it mean? It's Welsh for a white spirit.

KIDS' KORNER

Three-year-old Trent says his parents gave him his name because they liked him. Although he wouldn't want to change his moniker, Trent says he'd pick the name Doctor for himself if he had to. The reason: "Because that is what I want to be."

"I like my name because it's just mine and my parents picked it out," says nine-year-old Pamela. She dislikes the "ela" part at the end of it, though, and prefers to go by Pam. Anyone who calls her Pamela instead is bound to get a noogie.

"I like that it's really feminine and it's common so it's not weird like some random name," says 16-year-old Amanda about her name. Unfortunately, this commonality can be a bit of a problem. "I have at least one or two Amandas in each class," she complains.

One day, before he was born, Chad's father decided he didn't like Brandon, the name his mother had picked out for him. So he went to the bookshelf, took out an atlas and found the name Chad. And the 13-year-old couldn't be happier with his father's choice. "I'm named after a country [in Africa]," he boasts.

What's the best part about 12-year-old Tom's name? "It doesn't take long to spell and has the least syllables and letters," he says. But Tom does wish there weren't so many nicknames for people to choose from. From Tommy to Tomithy, he's heard them all.

Kayla's favourite name is Haylee, but since her sister already took that one, she's out of luck. "I am very jealous that she got it," says the 12-year-old of her sister's lucky moniker. But Kayla says she's still happy with her own name, especially since "it's really popular around the world."

 NICOLE

Meaning people of victory, this name is shared by both the Greek and the French. It's been popular (amongst the top 20 if not 10) on Canadian baby name lists since 1970.

Prime Ministers' Names

Always dreamed of raising the next leader of our country? Then you should probably give him a common name. With six former Prime Ministers named John (including Jean Chrétien), it seems the simpler and more traditional the name, the better when it comes to politics.

Now this isn't to say that an Eleutherios could never make it into our government's top seat, but judging by the common names—from Alexander to William—held by our leaders, it seems that a simple moniker may be a prerequisite for entering our political upper tier.

See for yourself. This complete list of our leaders (and the dates they held power) even includes their mostly traditional middle names.

John Alexander Macdonald (1867-1873, 1878-1891)

Alexander Mackenzie (1873-1878)

John Joseph Caldwell Abbott (1891-1892)

John Sparrow David Thompson (1892-1894)

Mackenzie Bowell (1894-1896)

Charles Tupper (1896-1896)

Wilfrid Laurier (1896-1911)

Robert Laird Borden (1911-1920)

Arthur Meighen (1920-1921, 1926-1926)

William Lyon Mackenzie King (1921-1926, 1926-1930, 1935-1948)

Richard Bedford Bennett (1930-1935)

Louis Stephen St-Laurent (1948-1957)

John George Diefenbaker (1957-1963)

Lester Bowles Pearson (1963-1968)

Pierre Elliott Trudeau (1968-1979, 1980-1984)

Charles Joseph (Joe) Clark (1979-1980)

John Napier Turner (1984-1984)

Martin Brian Mulroney (1984-1993)

Kim Campbell (1983-1983)

Jean Joseph Jacques Chrétien (1993-2003)

Paul Edgar Phillipe Martin (2003-)

Top Names in 1980

Boys

Robert	James	Joseph
Michael	Jason	Kevin
Christopher	Ryan	John
Matthew	Daniel	Adam
David		

Girls

Michelle	Sarah	Crystal
Amanda	Erin	Amy
Melissa	Tara	Nicole
Angela	Jessica	Heather
Lisa	Melanie	Shannon
Jennifer		

 FUN FACTS

Actor Jason Lee (*Almost Famous* and *Vanilla Sky*) named his son Pilot Inspektor Riesgraf.

Naming children after a deceased relative is a common tradition among Jewish people from Germany and Eastern Europe. In some cases, these names can be changed to reflect more recent times by creating a similar-sounding name, for instance changing Elsie to Kelsey.

In Japan, only members of the royal family have a middle name.

JESSICA
It wasn't until the mid-80s that this name really climbed the charts, reaching top 10 status in 1990. Now Jessica, which is Hebrew for wealthy and grace of God, has reached national acclaim, jumping into the top five nationwide.

Top Names in 1990

Boys

Ryan	Kyle	Tyler
Andrew	Jordan	James
Christopher	Joshua	David
Michael	Justin	Daniel
Matthew		

Girls

Samantha	Jennifer	Sarah
Amanda	Jessica	Megan
Ashley	Nicole	Kayla
Brittany	Stephanie	Melissa

Top Names in 2000

Boys

Matthew	Michael	Benjamin
Joshua	Alexander	Dylan
Nicholas	Jacob	Ethan
Tyler	William	Logan
Ryan	Andrew	

Girls

Sarah	Madison	Ashley
Jessica	Emily	Victoria
Hannah	Samantha	Haley
Emma	Olivia	Jasmine
Taylor	MacKenzie	

CANUCK TRIVIA

The most popular girls' names in Canada from 1700 to 1729 were Marie-Josèphe, Marie-Anne, Marie-Madeleine, Marie-Louise and Marie-Catherine.

Canadian jazz crooner Molly Johnson chose old-fashioned names for her two sons—Otis and Henry.

Movie Characters' Names

Whether it's because we want our child to embody the personality traits of a favourite character or because we simply love the sound of a name, many of us turn to the big screen for baby name inspiration. And there's nothing wrong with that.

Not only does Hollywood produce unique monikers, but the film industry often helps set baby naming trends. Don't believe me? Have you ever met a Rhett or Scarlett? Chances are their parents were huge fans of *Gone with the Wind*. And what about the ever-trendy Madison? It became popular in the early and mid-90s, shortly after the release of the hit flick *Splash*. Daryl Hannah played Madison to Tom Hanks's Allen in this blockbuster.

Can't think of any good character names? Here are a few original picks to help jog your memory.

Boys

Achilles *Troy*	**Hatch** *Hideaway*
Alexei *K-19: The Widowmaker*	**Igby** *Igby Goes Down*
Catcher *Down With Love*	**Indiana** *Indiana Jones* movies
Conrad *The Game*	**Jamal** *Finding Forrester*
Danger *Million Dollar Baby*	**Jerzy** *Welcome to Collinwood*
Dexter *The Tall Guy*	**Josef** *The Secret Life of Words*
Dillard *Crackers*	**Linus** *Ocean's Twelve*
Dirk *Boogie Nights*	**Logan** *X-Men*
Ellis *The Shawshank Redemption*	**Lowell** *The Insider*

Marciello *It's All About Love*
Maximus *Gladiator*
Melvin *The Big Hit*
Mickey *Snatch*
Monty *25th Hour*
Norther *Big Fish*
Obi-wan *Star Wars* movies
Oseary *The Life Aquatic with Steve Zissou*

Rafe *Pearl Harbour*
Rory *The Devil's Own*
Rubin *The Hurricane*
Quinn *Six Days Seven Nights*
Sheldon *Death to Smoochy*
Tobin *The Interpreter*
Tristan *Legends of the Fall*
Wendell *L.A. Confidential*
Woodrow *Mission to Mars*

Girls

Adele *The Legend of Bagger Vance*
Amelia *The Terminal*
Bitsey *The Life of David Gale*
Britt *The Life and Death of Peter Sellers*
Carlotta *The Phantom of the Opera*
Cassie *Murder by Numbers*
Clementine *Eternal Sunshine of the Spotless Mind*
Cosette *Les Misérables*
Desiree *Sunshine State*
Elle *Legally Blond*
Eustacia *The Return of the Native*
Faunia *The Human Stain*
Frannie *In the Cut*
Gilda *Head in the Clouds*
Gracie *Miss Congeniality*
Gwen *Men of Honour*

Illeana *Taking Lives*
Jojo *Moonlight Mile*
Kaela *Supernova*
Kiki *America's Sweethearts*
Lanie *Life or Something Like it*
Lavinia *The Banger Sisters*
Lola *Shark Tale*
Marina *Sinbad: Legend of the Seven Seas*
Nyah *Mission: Impossible II*
Olympias *Alexander*
Shandurai *Besieged*
Siddalee *Divine Secrets of the Ya-Ya Sisterhood*
Skylar *Good Will Hunting*
Sookie *Igby Goes Down*
Stella *The Italian Job*
Teena *Boys Don't Cry*
Tess *Ocean's Twelve*
Thelma *Thelma & Louise*
Velma *Chicago*

Chapter 7

-☆-

Celebrity Names

Mike Myers, Avril Lavigne, Donald Sutherland. These are just a few of the famous Canadian names we like to slip into conversation with visitors. Associating ourselves with the same country as these celebs helps elevate us to a level of quasi-stardom, if only for a second. Imagine how great we'd feel if we actually knew them, let alone shared their names?

Perhaps that's why so many Canadians are naming their kids after Hollywood's A-list—to give them a leg up from day one. Ethan (as in actor Ethan Hawke) ranks among the top 10 boys' names across the country. And Emma, the name of Jennifer Aniston's child on *Friends*, sits even higher. Other top 20 famous names include Alyssa (Milano), Julia (Roberts), Liam (Neeson), Samantha (a character on *Sex in the City*), Aidan (Quinn), Justin (Timberlake) and, of course, Jessica (Simpson). Or maybe it has nothing to do with celebs at all and Canadians are just fond of these recognizable names. No matter what the reason, I think they're all great choices.

Thinking of joining the masses to choose a silver screen name for your budding star? Before you rush off to welcome the next Sting or Madonna, here are a few things to keep in mind:

Avoid the Dramatic

Choose a distinctive celeb's name, such as Cher, if you're prepared for your child to be teased. If you intend to accompany her name with sequined, see-through outfits, the ridicule could possibly be unbearable. While you may love her music, there really is only room for one Cher on this planet.

Be Realistic

Don't expect your child to live up to the name you've given him. If you call him Leonardo with the hopes that he'll become a millions-of-dollars-earning, movie-making-machine and he wants to be something less famous (like, say, a doctor), you might find yourself disappointed. And he could be crushed by not being able to fulfill your dreams for him.

Choose Carefully

Unfortunately, certain stars have tarnished their names as well as their reputations. Take Paris Hilton, for example. Many now cringe at the sound of her name. It conjures up images of a spoiled socialite, sex video star and ditsy blond. Even if your daughter turns out to be Hilton's moral opposite, she'll probably be stereotyped as one and the same with her Hollywood counterpart.

Beware of the Mob

Love the name Marlon? To many, this moniker embodies images of mobsters, violence and theft—a result of Marlon Brando's famous role in *The Godfather* movies. Even though the actor himself wasn't a hitman, do you really want to give your little one an in to the seedy underground?

HEY BABY!

 REAL NAMES

Although 39-year-old Craig likes the fact that his name is "simple and basic, but not too common," he always wished for something a bit more unique and distinctive to suit his personality. Pretty much anything that's not based on an emotion (like Faith or Hope) and "non-weird names" (like Bruce Willis and Demi Moore's kids, Rumer, Scout and Tallulah) would suit him just fine.

When Walter was born 28 years ago, his parents named him after Walter Cronkite, the famous CBS newscaster they watched nightly upon immigrating to Canada. Besides feeling that his name is often associated with elderly men, Walter agrees with their decision. He's always enjoyed being one of the only young Walters around.

Ivy's parents thought her name was perfect because it was short and easy to spell. "Unbeknownst to them, I was the last person in kindergarten who could figure it out," says the 35-year-old. "I couldn't get the "y" quite right." Despite her spelling troubles, Ivy's always liked her name because she considered it a gift from her parents.

Marlee wouldn't change her name for anything. "It is original and unique, kind of like myself," says the 29-year-old. Although she was often called Bob (after reggae star Bob Marley) in her youth, Marlee's name has a much more meaningful origin. Her parents named her after her godmother, Mary-Lee, dropping the "y" and the hyphen to make it different—just how she likes it.

Janis likes that her name is "somewhat unique." The 35-year-old, however, does have one pet peeve. She can't stand it when people spell it wrong, with an "ice" at the end instead of an "is."

Celebrities' Names

Can't think of a celebrity name that you like? Here are a few of my favourites to help you decide.

Celebrity Boys' Names

Antonio (Banderas) This Spanish heartthrob has starred in *Desperado*, *Assassins*, *Original Sin*, *The Mask of Zorro*, *Frida* and *Femme Fatale*.

Ashton (Kutcher) No one screams 70s quite like Kutcher, who played Michael Kelso on *That 70s Show*. Kutcher has also performed in movies like *Dude, Where's My Car?*, *Just Married*, *My Boss's Daughter* and *Cheaper by the Dozen*.

Atom (Egoyan) Born Atom Yeghoyan in Cairo, Egypt. Egoyan's parents changed their surname upon moving to Victoria, British Columbia three years later. Egoyan is best known for his directing work on *Ararat, Exotica, Felicia's Journey* and *The Sweet Hereafter*.

Ben (Affleck) Once known as half of Bennifer (during his relationship with J-Lo), Affleck has acted in movies such as *Armageddon, Chasing Amy, Reindeer Games, Pearl Harbor, The Sum of All Fears* and *Paycheck*.

Bono Born Paul Hewson, this *U2* front man is now known as much for his political activism as he is for his sultry singing voice.

Brad (Pitt) Absolutely gorgeous and talented to boot! Pitt's best roles can be watched in *Meet Joe Black, Se7en, Thelma & Louise, Ocean's Eleven, Fight Club, Spy Game, Snatch, Troy* and *Ocean's Twelve*.

Bryan (Adams) Kingston, Ontario. Canada's answer to Bruce Springsteen, Adams is known the world over for his rockin' voice and fantastic photography.

Burt (Reynolds) Famous for his role as B.L. Stryker on the television show of the same name, Reynolds has had a lengthy and varied career, including performances in *Striptease, Deliverance, Lucky Lady, Hooper, Rent-A-Cop* and *Boogie Nights*.

Clint (Eastwood) The ultimate movie tough guy, Eastwood has gained fame as both an actor and director. Known for his roles in *Dirty Harry, Joe Kidd, Hang 'Em High, Sudden Impact, The Rookie, In the Line of Fire* and *Bridges of Madison County*, Eastwood won Oscars for his directing of *Unforgiven* and *Million Dollar Baby*.

Colm (Feore) Born in Massachusetts, Feore was raised in Ireland and Ottawa, Ontario. He's starred in tons of movies and

141

television miniseries, including *The Sum of All Fears*, *Chicago* and *The Chronicles of Riddick*.

Dan (Aykroyd) Ottawa, Ontario. The Blues Brother himself, Aykroyd has made audiences laugh for years on *Saturday Night Live* and in such films as *Ghostbusters*, *Caddyshack II*, *Dragnet* and *Tommy Boy*.

Dave (Foley) Toronto, Ontario. One of the original *Kids in the Hall*, Foley has also tried his hand at movies, playing roles in *My Boss's Daughter*, *Ham & Cheese* and *Childstar*.

David (Hewlett) Born in England but raised in Toronto, Hewlett played an unforgettable role in the Canadian television series *Traders*. He has also starred in films such as *Cube*, *Treed Murray* and *Nothing* and the television series *Stargate: Atlantis*.

Dennis (Quaid) Formerly married to actress Meg Ryan, Dennis has had quite a movie career of his own, including *The Rookie*, *Any Given Sunday*, *Great Balls of Fire!*, *Wyatt Earp*, *The Day After Tomorrow*, *Cold Creek Manor*, *The Alamo* and *In Good Company*.

Don (Cheadle) He's wowed us with exceptional talent in films like *Traffic* and *The Assassination of Richard Nixon*. He made us laugh in *Rush Hour 2*, *Ocean's Eleven* and *Ocean's Twelve*. But he stole our hearts in *Hotel Rwanda*.

Donald (Sutherland) St. John, New Brunswick. Father of Kiefer, Sutherland is best known for movies like *The Dirty Dozen*, *Kelly's Heroes*, *The Eagle Has Landed*, *Ordinary People*, *A Dry White Season*, *JFK*, *Space Cowboys*, *The Italian Job* and *Cold Mountain*.

Elias (Koteas) Montreal, Québec. Gemini Award-winning actor for his role in *Ararat*, Koteas also starred in *Exotica*, *Malick* and *Stander*.

Eric (McCormack) Toronto, Ontario. A Hollywood comedian best known for his portrayal of Will on television's hit show *Will & Grace*.

George (Clooney) What woman wouldn't want to name her son after this gorgeously hunky star of *Batman & Robin*, *Out of Sight*,

O Brother, Where Art Thou?, The Perfect Storm, Ocean's Eleven, Intolerable Cruelty and *Ocean's Twelve?*

Gord (Downie) Kingston, Ontario. Eccentric lead singer of Canadian rock band the *Tragically Hip*.

Harrison (Ford) Handsome and talented, Ford has starred in every Indiana Jones film as well as a ton of others, including *Patriot Games, The Fugitive, Regarding Henry, Presumed Innocent, Witness, Six Days Seven Nights* and *What Lies Beneath.*

Heath (Ledger) An Australian babe, this actor can be seen in *10 Things I Hate About You, The Patriot, Ned Kelly, Monster's Ball, The Four Feathers, The Order* and *A Knight's Tale.*

Henry (Czerny) Toronto, Ontario. This Canuck actor has appeared in big screen flicks like *Mission Impossible* and *The Pink Panther.*

Hume (Cronyn) London, Ontario. Married to actress Jessica Tandy, Cronyn starred in a long list of films, including *Sunrise at Campobello, Cocoon, Camilla* and *Twelve Angry Men.*

Jamie (Foxx) Although he appeared in films like *Any Given Sunday, Booty Call* and *Ali,* actor Jamie Foxx seemed to explode onto the Hollywood scene in 2004 with his performances in *Collateral* and *Ray.* A year later, he took home the Oscars' Best Actor award for his portrayal of Ray Charles.

Jarvis (Church) Formerly known as Gerald Eaton, Church was born in Jamaica but lives in Toronto. The former leader singer of Canadian band the Philosopher Kings, Church changed his name to better represent Toronto when he launched a solo career.

Jason (Priestly) Vancouver, British Columbia. Most famous for his role as Brandon Walsh on *Beverly Hills, 90210,* Priestly has also appeared in films such as *Eye of the Beholder* and *Darkness Falling.*

Jim (Carrey) Newmarket, Ontario. One of Hollywood's funniest comedians, Carrey has appeared in movies such as *Me, Myself & Irene, The Mask, The Majestic* and *Liar Liar.*

John (Candy) Toronto, Ontario. Once Canada's favourite funny man, Candy made audiences around the world laugh at his performances in *SCTV*, *Trains, Planes and Automobiles*, *Uncle Buck* and *Canadian Bacon*.

Joshua (Jackson) Vancouver, British Columbia. Star of television drama *Dawson's Creek* and movies such as *Cruel Intentions*, *Scream 2* and *The Skulls*.

Jude (Law) One of Hollywood's favourite leading men, Law can be seen in *The Talented Mr. Ripley*, *Road to Perdition*, *Artificial Intelligence: AI*, *Cold Mountain*, *Alfie*, *Closer*, and *The Aviator*.

Keanu (Reeves) In Hawaiian, this *Matrix* star's name means "cool breeze over the water." Although born in Beirut, Keanu spent the majority of his childhood in Toronto. Besides gaining international recognition for his role as Neo in the *Matrix* films, Reeves has also appeared in *Point Break*, *Dangerous Liaisons*, *Speed*, *The Devil's Advocate*, *Sweet November*, *Something's Gotta Give* and *Constantine*.

Kiefer (Sutherland) Born in London, England, Sutherland was raised by his actor father, Donald, and actress mother, Shirley Douglas, in Toronto. Now famous for his portrayal of terrorist-fighter Jack Bauer in the television show *24*, Sutherland had a bunch of hit movies, including *Stand by Me*, *Flatliners*, *Young Guns*, *A Few Good Men*, *A Time to Kill*, *At Close Range* and *Taking Lives*.

Leonard (Cohen) Montreal, Québec. Singer, songwriter and poet extraordinaire, Cohen's been an entertaining favourite for decades.

Leonardo (DiCaprio) Proof that working in television can lead to a successful movie career, DiCaprio has starred in numerous box office hits, including *What's Eating Gilbert Grape?*, *Romeo & Juliet*, *Titanic*, *Catch Me If You Can* and *The Aviator*.

Luke (Perry) An actor best known for his work on the 90s hit television series, *Beverly Hills, 90210*.

Mark-Paul (Gosselaar) Known for his roles as Detective John Clark, Jr., on *NYPD Blue* and Zack Morris on *Saved by the Bell*.

Matt (Craven) Port Colborne, Ontario. A talented actor with a seemingly unending list of films, including *The Statement, The Clearing, Dragonfly, The Life of David Gale* and *Assault on Precinct 13*. Another famous actor of the same name: **Matt Damon**.

Michael (Bublé) Burnaby, British Columbia. This handsome Sinatra-esque crooner released his first album in 2003 and is now a hit the world over. Actor **Michael J. Fox** of Edmonton, Alberta, also shares this name.

Mike (Myers) Toronto, Ontario. Comedian Myers definitely made it big on the silver screen. The *Austin Powers* films made him a household name while movies like *Wayne's World, So I Married an Axe Murderer* and *The Cat in the Hat* are popular with fans everywhere. Myers also gained fame for his voice work on the animated features *Shrek* and *Shrek 2*.

Morgan (Freeman) A classic actor who seems to have been around forever, Freeman finally won an Academy Award in 2005 for his performance in *Million Dollar Baby*. He's also appeared in *Lean on Me, Driving Miss Daisy, Glory, The Power of One, The Shawshank Redemption* and *The Sum of All Fears*.

Neil (Young) Toronto, Ontario. A hippie icon, Young is famous for chart-topping albums like *Ragged Glory, Harvest Moon* and *Mirror Ball*.

Norman (Jewison) Toronto, Ontario. The famed Hollywood director of films *The Statement, Dinner with Friends, The Hurricane* and *Moonstruck*.

Orlando (Bloom) This British heartthrob rose to fame with the Lord of the Rings flicks. He also stars in *Black Hawk Down, Pirates of the Caribbean: The Curse of the Black Pearl, Ned Kelly* and *Troy*.

Oscar (Peterson) Montreal, Québec. One of Canada's most famous jazz greats, Peterson plays the piano like no other.

Paul (Gross) Calgary, Alberta. Famous for his role as Constable Benton Fraser in the popular Canadian series *Due South*, Gross also acted in, wrote and directed the film *Men with Brooms*.

Rick (Mercer) Middle Cove, Newfoundland. Well known for his role in the television spoof *This Hour Has 22 Minutes*, Mercer also created, wrote and performed in his own sitcom called *Made in Canada*.

Robin (Williams) Perhaps one of the funniest comedians of our time, Williams has charmed audiences with his roles in *Mrs. Doubtfire*, *Good Morning Vietnam*, *Patch Adams*, *Awakenings*, *The Fisher King*, *Good Will Hunting* and *Dead Poets Society*.

Rod (Cameron) Calgary, Alberta. Once a stand-in for Fred McMurray, Cameron starred in movies such as *The Bounty Killer*, *Requiem for a Gunfighter* and *Passport to Treason*.

Ryan (Gosling) London, Ontario. A regular on the *Mickey Mouse Club*, Gosling soon made his way to the big screen with flicks *Remember the Titans*, *Murder by Numbers* and *The Notebook*.

Seán (Cullen) Peterborough, Ontario. Gemini Award-winner for his comedy, Cullen had his own television show in 2003 and appeared in films *Phil the Alien* and *Saint Ralph*.

Sting Born Gordon Matthew Sumner, super singer Sting's stage name came from friends who thought a striped sweater made him look like a bee.

Tobey (Maguire) The actor of *Spiderman* fame has also appeared in *Pleasantville*, *The Cider House Rules*, *Wonder Boys* and *Seabiscuit*.

Tom (Green) Pembroke, Ontario. Strangely unique funny man (kind of like a car wreck you just can't help but look at), Green was briefly married to Hollywood starlet Drew Barrymore. He's appeared in comedies *Road Trip*, *Freddy Got Fingered* and *Stealing Harvard*. Also sharing this name are Hollywood favourites **Tom Cruise** and **Tom Hanks**.

Will (Smith) 90s rapper turned Hollywood superhero, Smith has saved the world (or at least a few hot babes) in movies like *Independence Day*, *Enemy of the State*, *Men in Black*, *Bad Boys* and *I-Robot*.

Celebrity Girls' Names

Alanis (Morissette) Ottawa, Ontario. With four major albums and numerous awards to her name, Alanis is a Canadian singing great. Her most recent title: ordained minister. She took an online course so she can perform marriage ceremonies for her gay friends.

Angelina (Jolie) Perhaps Hollywood's most out-there star, Jolie's gorgeous lips have graced the screens of *Lara Croft Tomb Raider*, *Original Sin*, *Life or Something Like it*, *Gone in Sixty Seconds*, *Taking Lives* and *Mr. and Mrs. Smith*. Jolie also won an Oscar for her work in *Girl, Interrupted*.

Annette (Bening) Married to former womanizer Warren Beatty and star of films like *Postcards from the Edge*, *The Grifters*, *Regarding Henry*, *Love Affair*, *American Beauty* and *Being Julia*, Benning is definitely talented.

Arsinee (Khanjian) Born in Lebanon, Khanjian moved to Montreal, Québec, in 1975. She is married to Canadian director Atom Egoyan and has appeared in *Exotica*, *The Sweet Hereafter*, *Coldwater* and *Ararat*.

Avril (Lavigne) Napanee, Ontario. French for April, this teen singing sensation has rocked the world with her stick-it-to-you ballads like *Sk8er Boi* and *Under my Skin*.

Carrie-Anne (Moss) Vancouver, British Columbia. There's not a *Matrix* fan around who doesn't recognize the face of this Canadian beauty. The actress has also starred in films like *Chocolat* and *Red Planet*.

Cate (Blanchett) You'll be hard-pressed to find a film in which this Australian native isn't fabulous. From *Elizabeth* and *The Shipping News* to *Charlotte Gray* and an Oscar-winning performance in *The Aviator*, Blanchett is definitely worth watching.

Celine (Dion) Charlemagne, Québec. Possibly Canada's most famed and highly praised singing superstar.

Charlize (Theron) Oscar-winning Theron is famous for her roles in *Monster*, *The Italian Job*, *Sweet November*, *The Legend of Bagger Vance* and *Head in the Clouds*.

Claudia (Ferri) Montreal, Québec. You can see this actress in *Killing Time*, *Soother* and *Mambo Italiano*. Another famous woman of this name: supermodel **Claudia Schiffer**.

Courteney (Cox) Best known for her role as Monica on the television hit *Friends*, Cox has also appeared in films *Scream*, *3000 Miles to Graceland*, *Alien Love Triangle* and *November*.

Deborah (Cox) Toronto, Ontario. Pop singer and actress, Cox has starred in the film *Love Come Down* and the television series *Soul Food*.

Demi (Moore) Owner of that famous bod, Moore can be found in *St. Elmo's Fire*, *About Last Night*, *Ghost*, *A Few Good Men*, *G.I. Jane*, *Striptease* and *Charlie's Angels: Full Throttle*.

Drea (De Matteo) The sexy star of television series *The Sopranos* and *Joey*. De Matteo can also be found in films *Swordfish*, *Deuces Wild*, *Beacon Hill* and *Assault on Precinct 13*.

Elisha (Cuthbert) Calgary, Alberta. Both a model and an actress, Cuthbert shot to fame with her role as Jack Bauer's daughter on television series *24*. She has also appeared in films such as *Lucky Girl*, *Old School* and *The Girl Next Door*. Friends call her "Heesh."

Estella (Warren) Peterborough, Ontario. Once a national champion swimmer, Estella is now one of the modeling world's most gorgeous stars.

Evangeline (Lilly) Fort Saskatchewan, Alberta. This up-and-comer is best known for her role as Kate Ryan on television's popular series *Lost*.

Gwyneth (Paltrow) This Hollywood superstar knows how to make an old-fashioned name work. Winner of an Academy award for her performance in *Shakespeare in Love*, Paltrow can also be seen in *Sky Captain and the World of Tomorrow*, *Shallow Hal*, *View from the Top*, *The Royal Tenenbaums* and *Bounce*.

Halle (Berry) Sexy and talented, this Academy award winner can be seen in *Monster's Ball*, *Swordfish*, *X-Men*, *Die Another Day* and *Gothika*.

Hilary (Swank) Two-time Best Actress Oscar winner for her performances in *Boys Don't Cry* and *Million Dollar Baby*, Swank can definitely be labeled an acting genius. She can also be seen in *The Next Karate Kid*, *Heartwood*, *The Gift*, *The Affair of the Necklace* and *Insomnia*.

Jada (Pinkett-Smith) Wife of star Will Smith, Pinkett-Smith has appeared in numerous films, including *If These Walls Could Talk*, *Return to Paradise*, *Ali*, *The Matrix Reloaded* and *Collateral*.

Kate (Hudson) Daughter of actress Goldie Hawn, Kate's career got a jump start after her performance as Penny Lane in *Almost Famous*.

Kendall (Cross) Regina, Saskatchewan. A Canadian actress with roles in films such as *The New Beachcombers*, *Paycheck* and *The Butterfly Effect*.

Jann (Arden) Calgary, Alberta. Born Jann Arden Richards, this soulful musician sings from the heart on numerous albums, including *Time for Mercy* and *Blood Red Cherry*.

Jennifer (Tilly) Born Jennifer Chan in California, Tilly moved to Victoria, British Columbia, with her mother and siblings at age six. She's starred in films such as *Liar Liar*, *Bullets Over Broadway* and *Bride of Chucky*. This name was also made famous by former *Friend* **Jennifer Aniston**.

Jill (Hennessy) Edmonton, Alberta. Former star of *Law & Order*, Hennessy now stars in her own show, *Crossing Jordan*. On the big screen, she can be seen in *Autumn in New York*, *The Acting Class* and *Exit Wounds*.

Julia (Roberts) Ultra famous star of hits like *Pretty Woman*, *Ocean's Eleven*, *Ocean's Twelve* and *Notting Hill*. Roberts won an Oscar for her performance in *Erin Brockovich*.

Julianne (Moore) A graceful actress, Moore has starred in *Magnolia, Hannibal, Boogie Nights, Far From Heaven, The Shipping News, The Hours, Laws of Attraction* and *The Forgotten*.

Kylie (Minogue) Australian singing sensation now known popularly as Kylie, Minogue made a huge comeback with her album *Body Language* in 2003.

Linda (Evangelista) St. Catharines, Ontario. One of Canada's best-known faces, Evangelista is one of the world's top models.

Mady (Correl) Montreal, Québec. Although you may not remember her, Correl starred alongside Charlie Chaplin in the film *Monsieur Verdoux*.

Margot (Kidder) Yellowknife, Northwest Territories. You'll probably know her best as *Superman's* Lois Lane, but Kidder has appeared in numerous films since then, including *Maverick, Angel Blade* and *Crime and Punishment*.

Mary-Louise (Parker) A lover of the stage, this actress also dabbled in film, starring in movies like *Grand Canyon, Fried Green Tomatoes, Bullets over Broadway* and *Red Dragon*.

Meg (Ryan) A true Hollywood sweetheart, Ryan has starred in *When Harry Met Sally, Sleepless in Seattle, Courage Under Fire, You've Got Mail, City of Angels, Proof of Life* and *In the Cut*.

Megan (Follows) Toronto, Ontario. Canada's very recognizable *Anne of Green Gables*.

Michelle (Pfeiffer) Sultry and sexy, actress Pfeiffer has starred in *The Fabulous Baker Boys, Up Close & Personal, The Age of Innocence, The Deep End of the Ocean, What Lies Beneath, White Oleander* and *I Am Sam*.

Mimi (Kuzyk) Winnipeg, Manitoba. A television actress known for her roles in *Hill Street Blues* and *Blue Murder*, Kuzyk also starred in films like *Lost and Delirious, The Final Cut, The Human Stain* and *The Day After Tomorrow*.

Naomi (Watts) Raised in Australia, this stunning actress has appeared in *The Ring, Le Divorce, I Heart Huckabees, 21 Grams* and *Ned Kelly*.

Natalie (Portman) Portman seemed to jump to fame with *Star Wars: Episode 1—The Phantom Menace*. From there, she proved her worth with stellar roles in *Anywhere but Here*, *Where the Heart Is*, *Cold Mountain* and *Closer*.

Natasha (Henstridge) Springdale, Newfoundland. A gorgeous actress who's starred in movies such as *Species*, *Bounce* and *The Whole Nine Yards*.

Nelly (Furtado) Victoria, British Columbia. An ultra popular singer with a genre all her own—a mix of pop, rock, Portuguese and R&B music. Her best selling albums include *Whoa, Nelly!* and *Folklore*.

Neve (Campbell) Guelph, Ontario. Her main claim to fame was the hit television series *Party of Five*. That's before she started starring in popular movies such as *Wild Things*, *Scream*, *Three to Tango* and *The Company*, that is.

Nia (Vardalos) Winnipeg, Manitoba. Nominated for an Oscar for her work on the hit film *My Big, Fat Greek Wedding*, Vardalos has also starred in *Meet Prince Charming* and *Connie and Carla*.

Nicole (Kidman) Tom Cruise's ex has made a huge career from films like *Moulin Rouge!*, *The Human Stain*, *Cold Mountain*, *Dogville*, *The Stepford Wives* and *Birth*.

Pamela (Anderson) Ladysmith, British Columbia. From Labatt Blue Girl to Playboy playmate, this sexy Canadian didn't take long to steam up Hollywood. You might remember seeing her bouncing along the beach in TV's *Baywatch*.

Pascale (Bussieres) Montreal, Québec. One of Québec's favourite actresses, Bussieres has appeared in *La Turbulance des Fluides*, *The Blue Butterfly* and *Petites Coupures*. She is also well known for her role on the 1993 television series *Blanche*.

Penélope (Cruz) This Spanish sweetie stars in *All the Pretty Horses*, *Vanilla Sky*, *Captain Corelli's Mandolin* and *Head in the Clouds*.

Rachel (Blanchard) Toronto, Ontario. Best known for her role as Cher on TV's *Clueless*, Blanchard has graced movie screens in such films as *Without a Paddle*, *Road Trip* and *Where the Truth Lies*.

Salma (Hayek) The Mexican bombshell starring in *Desperado, Fools Rush In, The Faculty, Dogma, Chain of Fools, Traffic, Hotel, Frida, Once Upon a Time in Mexico* and *After the Sunset.*

Sarah (McLachlan) Halifax, Nova Scotia. She of the shiver-producing smooth voice has sold over 22 million records worldwide. This name is also shared by actresses **Sarah Chalke** of Ottawa, Ontario (television series *Roseanne* and *Scrubs*) and **Sarah Polley** of Toronto, Ontario (star of films like *The Sweet Hereafter, Exotica, The Life Before This* and *My Life Without Me*).

Shania (Twain) Timmins, Ontario. Born Eileen Edwards, Twain changed her name to Shania, which is Ojibway for "I'm on my way." Renowned across the globe for her catchy country pop songs, Shania is a mainstay on the international music scene.

Susan (Clark) Sarnia, Ontario. This actress is best known for her role as Webster's mom on the 80s television series *Webster.*

Tyra (Banks) Voluptuous supermodel turned actress, Banks has appeared in *Love & Basketball, Coyote Ugly, Larceny* and *Halloween: The Homecoming.*

Uma (Thurman) An actress, writer and producer, Thurman has starred in *Dangerous Liaisons, Pulp Fiction, Gattaca, Beautiful Girls, The Truth About Cats & Dogs* and *Kill Bill.*

Celebrities' Kids' Names

Celebrities are always competing for something. Be it making the best fashion statement, winning a Golden Globe or being voted the most romantic couple, the stars never seem to tire of trying to one-up each other. The latest in their competitive craze is baby names. From Audio Science to Zola, Hollywood's elite are going all out to create unique names for their kids. Here's a sampling of some of their faves.

Sons of Celebrities

Audio Although actress Shannyn Sossamon (*A Knight's Tale*) thought it would be acceptable to name her son Audio Science, I'm not too sure how well he's going to like it when he hits school.

KIDS' KORNER

When asked what she likes best about her name, 12-year-old Nisha replies, "Nisha means night and I love the night time, so my name reflects me." That and the fact that it's unique and sounds nice make her name a definite keeper.

Dennis loves the fact that he shares his name with a famous basketball player. But that's not where he got his moniker, explains the 13-year-old. "I looked like my uncle Dennis," he says, so his parents decided to give him that name.

Three-year-old Ethan is proud of his first name. "I like my name because it starts with an 'e,'" he says. But his favourite name of all time is Barney, which could have something to do with the three stuffed Barneys he sleeps with every night.

"My mom liked the actor Aidan Quinn, so she decided that would be a good name for me," says nine-year-old Ayden. And even though she spelled it differently to make it more unique, Ayden likes that he's one of the only people he knows with his name. "I think it means that I'm creative," he says. And that's just fine with him.

When asked why her parents named her Kara, the four-year-old says, "because I wanted that name." She likes it mostly because it's short but hates when people think it's Tara. If she had to choose another one, she'd pick Cinderella because she likes princesses.

Beckett Finn Second son of Dixie Chick Natalie Maines and actor hubby Adrian Pasdar (*Secondhand Lions*).

Blanket The ultra weird and unfortunate name given to one of Michael Jackson's sons.

Braeden Cooper Eldest son of former *Hercules* star Kevin Sorbo and his wife Sam.

Brooklyn Victoria and David Beckham's son was named in tribute to the American place in which he was conceived.

Casper First child of supermodel Claudia Schiffer and director husband Matthew Vaughn.

Charlie Twin son of CNN anchor Soledad O'Brien and husband Brad Raymond.

Cruz The youngest son of Victoria and David Beckham, Cruz is traditionally a girl's name in Spanish.

Dashiell Uniquely named son of talented actress Cate Blanchett and husband Andrew Upton.

Dante Amadeo Son of television star Christopher Meloni (*Law & Order: Special Victims Unit*) and wife Sherman.

Finley Arthur Born to *Charmed* star Holly Marie Combs and husband David Donoho.

Griffin Arthur The first born for actors Brendan (*School Ties* and *Bedazzled*) and Afton (*George of the Jungle* and *Reality Bites*) Fraser.

Holden Fletcher Youngest son of actors Brendan and Afton Fraser.

Hudson Actor Harvey Keitel's son with California potter Lisa Karmazin.

Indiana The first son for actors Casey Affleck and Summer Phoenix.

Jackson Slade Eldest son of Dixie Chick superstar Natalie Maines and her actor husband Adrian Pasdar. Jackson was also the name chosen by *CNN* anchor Soledad O'Brien and husband Brad Raymond for one of their twin sons.

Jacob Hurley Son of singer Jon Bon Jovi and wife Dorothea.

James Wilke It's been said that Sarah Jessica Parker and Matthew Broderick's son was named after his late father, James, and her favourite author, Wilkie Collins.

Jesse James Louis No relation to the tough guy of the same name, this Jesse James is the eldest son of Jon Bon Jovi and wife Dorothea.

Kaiis Steven Twin son of actress Geena Davis and her dentist husband Reza Jarrahy.

Kian William Actress Geena Davis and husband Reza Jarrahy welcomed twin son Kian in May, 2004.

Magnus Son of famed funny man Will Ferrell and wife Viveca Paulin.

Marco Son of Canadian actress and star of *Crossing Jordan*, Jill Hennessy, and husband Paolo Mastropietro.

Maxwell Born to former *NYPD Blue* cast member Charlotte Ross and her manager husband Michael Goldman.

Michael Charles Traditionally named son of actor Mark-Paul and wife Lisa Gosselaar.

Milo First son of actress Liv Tyler and rocker hubby Royston Langdon.

Nathan Thomas Son of comedian Jon Stewart and his graphic designer wife Tracey.

Phinnaeus Walter Twin son of academy award-winning actress Julia Roberts and husband Daniel Moder.

Prince Michael Talk about taking egoism to an extreme, this name was chosen for another of Michael Jackson's sons.

Rafferty A cool name for the son of actors Jude Law and Sadie Frost.

Rene-Charles Famed in vitro son of Canadian super singer Celine Dion and manager husband Rene Angelil.

Roman Walker Son of *Will & Grace* star Debra Messing and her college sweetheart Daniel Zelman. The name Roman was also chosen by actress Cate Blanchett and husband Andrew Upton.

Romeo A popular choice for celebrities' kids, this name was bestowed upon the sons of Jon Bon Jovi and wife Dorothea and David and Victoria Beckham.

Ryder Russell Big screen sweetie Kate Hudson's first son with Black Crows lead singer Chris Robinson.

Satchel Although it sounds like a book bag, Woody Allen and Mia Farrow thought this name best suited their little guy.

Seven Not a fan of traditional names, Erykah Badu and then-boyfriend Andre Benjamin (a.k.a. Andre 3000) of the group OutKast gave this numerical name to their son.

Shane Haaken Son of Kevin Sorbo, star of *Gene Roddenberry's Andromeda*, and wife Sam.

Theo The progeny of director Steven Spielberg and wife Kate Capshaw.

Vance The only son of Wilson Phillips singer Chynna Phillips and actor husband Billy Baldwin.

William Atticus Son of actors Mary-Louise Parker and Billy Crudup.

Wyatt The only child born to unmarried Hollywood couple Kurt Russell and Goldie Hawn.

Zen Scott Sure to be a well-balanced kid, Zen was named by his parents, actor Corey Feldman and wife Susie.

Daughters of Celebrities

Agatha Marie Daughter of actor Thomas Gibson (*Far and Away*, *Eyes Wide Shut*) and wife Cristina.

Apple Blythe Named after the fruit, this daughter was born to the much-adored actress Gwyneth Paltrow and her rocker husband Chris Martin of Coldplay.

Ava Twin daughter of Peri Gilpin, star of *Frasier*, and her husband Christian Vincent. Other celebs who were fond of this name include actress Susan Sarandon and Tim Robbins, Reese Witherspoon and actor husband Ryan Phillippe, Heather Locklear and musician hubby Richie Sambora, Aidan Quinn, tennis star John McEnroe and Tatum O'Neal and U2 drummer Larry Mullen Jr.

Barbara A traditional, family name for this Bush twin, daughter of President George and First Lady Laura, of course.

Bria A beautiful name for the daughter of comedian Eddie Murphy and his ex-wife Nicole.

Brooke Michelle The third child of actor Billy Baldwin and wife Chynna Phillips, former singer with pop trio Wilson Phillips.

Carys Zeta Michael Douglas and Catherine Zeta Jones picked this fun name for their daughter.

Catherine Rose Daughter of *Curb Your Enthusiasm* actress Cheryl Hines and husband Paul Young.

Chelsea Who other than Bill and Hilary's daughter?

Clementine Another fruity name, this time chosen by super-model Claudia Schiffer and director husband Matthew Vaughn.

Coco Riley Who could forget the yummy-sounding name of Courteney Cox and David Arquette's daughter? Think this means she's already wearing Chanel?

Deva Daughter born to actors Monica Bellucci (*The Passion of the Christ*) and Vincent Cassel (*Ocean's Twelve*).

Eulala Grace Eldest daughter of actress Marcia Gay Harden (*Mystic River* and *Pollock*) and hubby Thaddeus Scheel.

Eva Ruth Twin daughter of Dixie Chick Martie and husband Gareth Maguire.

Gracie Daughter of country singing super couple Faith Hill and Tim McGraw.

Hazel Patricia Twin daughter of Academy award-winning actress Julia Roberts and husband Daniel Moder.

FUN FACTS

U2 lead singer Bono named his son Elijah Bob Patricus Guggi Q Hewson. Guess he couldn't decide on a name.

Uma Thurman's middle name is Karuna, which means compassion.

Actor Keifer Sutherland was given six names by his parents: Kiefer William Frederick Dempsey George Rufus Sutherland. Now that's a mouthful.

India Ann Sushil Daughter of Canadian singer Sarah McLachlan and her drummer husband Ashwin Sood.

Ivanka The Donald's (Trump, that is) daughter with ex-wife Ivana.

Jameson Definitely given a unisex name, Jameson is the eldest daughter of Chynna Phillips and husband Billy Baldwin.

Jane Erin Daughter of Canadian comedian Jim Carrey and first wife Melissa Womer.

Jenna One of the newsworthy twins of President George and First Lady Laura Bush.

Julitta Dee Twin daughter of actress Marcia Gay Harden (*Welcome to Mooseport* and *Mona Lisa Smile*) and husband Thaddeus Scheel.

Kathleen Emilie Twin daughter of country singer Martie Maguire of the Dixie Chicks and her husband Gareth.

Leni Gorgeous daughter of supermodel Heidi Klum and ex-boyfriend Flavio Briatore.

Lovelace Famed television chef Emeril Lagasse and his wife Alden chose this interesting name for their daughter.

Makena Lei Gordon Daughter of film star Helen Hunt and partner Matthew Carnahan.

Marina First daughter for Matt LeBlanc of *Friends* fame and wife Melissa.

Mattea Angel Actress Mira Sorvino and husband Chris Backus welcomed their daughter in November, 2004.

Phoebe Daughter of *ER*'s Dr. Susan Lewis (a.k.a. Sherry Stringfield) and journalist hubby Larry Joseph.

Puma Believe it or not, soulful singer Erykah Badu gave this brand name to her child. Wonder if she'll get free shoes?

Rumer Glenn Actress Demi Moore and then-husband Bruce Willis chose this name for one of their daughters.

Sailor Christie Brinkley and Peter Cook's daughter. They must really like boating.

Sam A popular unisex name for the daughter of actor Charlie Sheen and actress Denise Richards.

Scout LaRue Daughter of Hollywood celebs Demi Moore and Bruce Willis.

Sofia Bella Actors Leah Remini (*King of Queens*) and Angelo Pagan (*Swordfish* and *Dance with Me*) welcomed Sofia in June, 2004.

Sophia Eva Pietra Television star Christopher Meloni (*Law & Order: Special Victims Unit*) and wife Sherman's first child.

Stella Twin daughter of *Frasier* star Peri Gilpin and artist husband Christian Vincent.

Stephanie Rose First born for Jon Bon Jovi and wife Dorothea.

Tallulah Belle Eldest daughter of Bruce Willis and Demi Moore.

Tu The poorly named daughter of actor Robert Morrow, star of *Northern Exposure*, and wife Debbon Ayer. Put her first and last name together and you get Tu Morrow. Now that's just mean.

Zahara Adopted daughter of gorgeous actress Angelina Jolie.

Zahra Savannah Daughter of out-there comedian Chris Rock and wife Malaak.

Zola Funny man Eddie Murphy and ex-wife Nicole chose this name for their daughter.

 CANUCK TRIVIA

Group of Seven painter A.Y. Jackson's full name was Alexander Young.

The most popular boys' names in Canada from 1700 to 1729 were Jean-Baptiste, Joseph, Pierre, François and Louis.

Royal Names

Although they seem to be merely symbolic, the Royal family still plays a role in Canadian culture. From tabloids to literature, they're everywhere. And many of us live for the next scandal at Buckingham Palace. No matter how badly they mess up their lives, however, the Royals still manage to make at least their names seem regal.

Royal boys' names:

Alexander	David	Nicholas
Andrew	Edward	Peter
Antony	Frederick	Philip
Arthur	George	Richard
Cassius	Harry	Samuel
Charles	Henry	Teackle
Christian	James	William
Columbus	John	
Daniel	Michael	

Royal girls' names:

Alexandra	Eugenie	Rose
Alice	Flora	Sarah
Amelia	Gabriella	Serena
Anne	Helen	Sophie
Birgitte	Katharine	Sylvana
Davina	Louise	Wallis
Diana	Margaret	Windsor
Elizabeth	Margarita	Victoria
Eloise	Marina	Zenouska
Estella	Mary	

Chapter 8

-☆-

Around the World

L et's play a game. It's called "Guess which two names are the
    most popular worldwide" (or at least in the countries that I
mention in this chapter). If you said Emma and Daniel, give yourself
a hefty pat on the back, or a small one on your growing belly, because
you guessed it! Unfortunately I can't give out prizes for this one so
you'll just have to be satisfied with the pat and the knowledge that
you were, once again, correct.

Want some more? The next most popular names across the globe
include Laura, Sarah, Julia and Sophie for girls and David, James and
Jack for boys. Amazing, isn't it, that they're so similar and traditional?
It appears that these typically English names are so popular that
they've managed to sneak onto the top 10 lists for countries like
Germany, France, Norway, Spain and Switzerland, where the majority
of names are influenced by the native language. Whether it's due
to the shrinking global village, an increasing influence of English-
speakers or the just plain irresistible nature of these names, old-
fashioned English monikers are storming the world stage and they
seem to be there to stay.

In this chapter, I list the most popular baby names found in 19
different countries, including Canada. From the unique options in
Iceland to the traditional ones used in Australia, no one country

shares all of its names with another. By merely looking through these lists, you can clearly identify each country's culture. For instance, the Japanese, Polish and Italians seem to have a strong connection with their distinct identities—none of their names are repeated on the other countries' lists. Canada, Australia, England, Ireland, Austria and the U.S., on the other hand, have many similarities, especially in terms of the names they're most fond of.

Whether you're curious about the naming differences between our nation and others or simply want to catch a glimpse of what's happening in different cultures, you've come to the right place. Not only will the following lists give you more ideas for unique names, but they'll also help you to figure out if any of your favourite choices are popular (or maybe too popular) across the globe.

Australia

Boys

Joshua	Thomas	Liam
Lachlan	Samuel	Matthew
Jack	James	William
Ethan		

Girls

Emily	Georgia	Olivia
Ella	Charlotte	Isabella
Sophie	Chloe	Emma
Jessica		

 EMMA

Emma, which means complete in German, is one of the most popular girls' names in the world. A relative newcomer to the popularity scene, Emma has graced Canada's top 10 baby name lists since 1999.

DANIEL
Hebrew, meaning the Lord is my judge, Daniel is one of the world's most popular name choices for baby boys. It has appeared among the top 20 baby names in various Canadian provinces and territories consistently since 1950.

Austria

Boys

Lukas	Alexander	Julian
Florian	Fabian	Daniel
Tobias	Michael	Simon
David		

Girls

Sarah	Lena	Katharina
Anna	Hannah	Leonie
Julia	Lisa	Vanessa
Laura		

REAL NAMES
Laura loves the way her name sounds, especially when pronounced in Italian. But this wasn't always the case. Throughout her 29 years, Laura has often wished for something a little less common. "I always thought it would be fun to have a unique name," she says.

Marilyn, 45, was born Mary; her parents began calling her by her middle name because they liked it better. But she's not so fond of the idea. "It's just [not a name] I would choose for myself," she says. "It's not all that feminine." If she could pick her own name, Marilyn says she'd choose Lyn. "To me, Lyn is very feminine," she explains.

- ☆ - **MOHAMMED**

While Mohammed didn't make it onto the international lists in this chapter, that doesn't mean it isn't a popular choice around the globe. Rather, those countries where it's most popular aren't easy places to gather baby-name statistics.

A Muslim moniker meaning highly praised, Mohammed was the name of a famed prophet. And it is often placed before a Muslim given name in parts of Singapore and Malaysia, among others. After the given name comes the prefix "bin" followed by the father's name. Mohammed's popularity has grown so wide that it now sits on the top 20 list in Britain and Wales.

Canada

Boys

Matthew
Joshua
Jacob
Ryan
Alexander

Nicholas
Michael
Logan
Ethan

Tyler, Connor, Andrew, Benjamin and Liam (tied)

Girls

Sarah
Olivia
Hannah
Emma

Emily
Madison
Megan

Jessica
Samantha
Grace

Denmark

Boys

Mikkel
Frederik
Mathias
Mads

Rasmus
Emil
Oliver

Christian
Magnus
Lucas

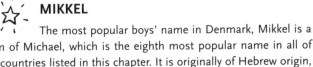

MIKKEL
The most popular boys' name in Denmark, Mikkel is a form of Michael, which is the eighth most popular name in all of the countries listed in this chapter. It is originally of Hebrew origin, meaning who is like God.

Girls

Emma	Laura	Ida
Julie	Caroline	Sarah
Mathilde	Cecilie	Freja
Sofia		

England

Boys

Jack	Daniel	Samuel
Joshua	Oliver	William
Thomas	Benjamin	Joseph
James		

Girls

Emily	Sophie	Olivia
Ellie	Megan	Charlotte
Chloe	Lucy	Hannah
Jessica		

LAURA
Of Latin origin, Laura means a laurel. It, too, is one of the world's most popular baby names for girls. Although it hasn't made a recent appearance on Canada's top 10 lists, it has appeared amongst the top 20 choices in BC and the Yukon from 1980 to 1993.

165

KIDS' KORNER

Aaron's parents chose his name "because they figured it would be good for me," says the 12-year-old. When asked what he likes best about their choice, Aaron replies, "that it's the name of a person that abolished slavery."

"My parents are religious, so when my mom was pregnant with me, God gave her a dream telling her to give me a name with 'k' and 'r' in it," 13-year-old Krystal explains when describing the origin of her name. And though she wishes she was called Kristian, because it's more original, she thinks her name suits her well overall.

Finland

Boys

Niko	Lauri	Aleksi
Eetu	Leevi	Arttu
Juho	Joona	Ville
Veeti		

Girls

Ella	Sara	Viivi
Emma	Venla	Nea
Anni	Iida	Veera
Siiri		

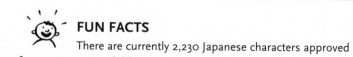

FUN FACTS

There are currently 2,230 Japanese characters approved for use in naming children.

Singer Seal's real name is Sealhenry Samuel.

The word Métis, meaning "mixed," is used to describe Aboriginal peoples of both French and Indian origins.

CANUCK TRIVIA
In Inuktitut, the name Inuit means "the people."
Over 60 per cent of children born in Nunavut are given their mother's surname.

France

Boys

Thomas	Maxime	Clément
Lucas	Antoine	Alexandre
Théo	Quentin	Nicholas
Hugo		

Girls

Léa	Emma	Marie
Manon	Océane	Laura
Chloé	Sarah	Julie
Camille		

Germany

Boys

Alexander	Lukas	David
Maximillian	Jonas	Niklas
Paul	Tim	Luca
Leon		

Girls

Marie	Laura	Sarah
Sophie	Lea	Julia
Maria	Katharina	Lena
Anna/Anne (a tie)		

-☆- **JACK**
Although Jack hasn't appeared on the most popular lists in Canada, it has stood up well on the international scene. A Hebrew form of John, meaning God is gracious, this name also means supplanter.

Iceland
Boys

Sigurður	Ólafur	Kristján
Guðmundur	Magnús	Björn
Jón	Einar	Bjarni
Gunnar		

Girls

Guðrún	Margarét	Jóhanna
Sigríður	Ingibjörg	Anna
Kristín	Sigrún	Ragnheiður

Ireland
Boys

Sean	James	Cian
Jack	Daniel	David
Adam	Michael	Dylan
Conor		

Girls

Emma	Katie	Chloe
Sarah	Sophie	Amy
Aoife	Rachel	Leah
Ciara		

MISAKI

Misaki is the number one girls' name in Japan. When translated into English, it means beautiful flower blossom.

Italy
Boys

Giuseppe	Luigi	Vincenzo
Giovanni	Francesco	Pietro
Antonio	Angelo	Salvatore
Mario		

Girls

Maria	Angela	Lucia
Anna	Giovanna	Carmela
Giuseppina	Teresa	Caterina
Rosa		

Japan
Boys

Shun	Shouta	Kenta
Takumi	Souta	Daiki
Shou	Kaito	Yuu
Ren		

Girls

Misaki	Riko	Yuuka
Aoi	Miyu	Rin
Nanami	Moe	Ai
Miu	Mitsuki	

PIOTR

In Poland, Piotr is the number one name choice for parents of baby boys. It is a form of Peter, which is of Latin and Greek origin, meaning rock. While Peter is not found on any of the top 10 lists for countries mentioned in this chapter, an Italian version, Pietro, does appear.

Norway
Boys

Mathias	Kristian	Sander
Tobias	Jonas	Kristoffer
Andreas	Markus	Daniel
Martin		

Girls

Emma	Julia	Maria
Ida	Nora	Ingrid
Thea	Emilie	Hanna
Sara		

Poland
Boys

Piotr	Stanislaw	Józef
Jan	Tomasz	Marcin
Andrzej	Pawel	Marek
Krzysztof		

Girls

Anna	Agnieszka	Ewa
Maria	Krystyna	Elżeibeta
Katarzyna	Barbara	Zofia
Malgorzata		

Spelling Bee

Love the name Emily but hate how popular it is? Why not change the spelling to make it more unique? One of the easiest ways to change an ultra-popular name is by replacing one letter with another, for instance, swapping an "i" with a "y," would make it Emyly. Or, try adding another letter so you have Ehmily, Emmily or Emilly instead. Another tip: change the first letter if you really like the sound of the name but want to make it a bit different—i.e. Vanessa becomes Danessa or Janessa. Just be careful. You don't want to make the name so hard to spell that your little one has trouble, or so strange that she's teased by other kids. Here's a list of a few common names with untraditional spellings. See if you can figure out what the original was.

Boys

Adham	Isack	Paddrick
Aleksander	Jachob	Phillp
Allastair	Jaeson	Rafaele
Bartholomieu	Jaymie	Richart
Bearnard	Kalvin	Rhyan
Blayne	Kennith	Simeon
Camiron	Konnor	Steevan
Christepher	Lewes	Theodor
Daemean	Mackenzy	Tomas
Earwin	Marc	Vernen
Edouard	Mathieu	Viktor
Evered	Michail	Wallas
Frantz	Naethan	Warrin
Gaberial	Nealle	Weslee
Gerart	Nikolas	Xaiver
Henery	Olliver	Zachari
Ibrahim	Ostin	

Girls

Abbigale	Hana	Pricilla
Aleksandra	Holley	Racheal
Alyce	Isobel	Rebeckah
Bethanee	Jacklyn	Sarrah
Brittainey	Kaitlan	Shantell
Caeleigh	Kandas	Staicy
Cascy	Leea	Taenya
Darlean	Leighanne	Teresea
Eadith	Lynda	Traicey
Elanor	Mackensi	Ursala
Eryca	Margarette	Valarie
Ferne	Melanney	Venesa
Franncis	Michaella	Yasimine
Gavrielle	Natalea	Zabrina
Genaveve	Ondrea	Zoie
Giorgia	Patriceia	
Haillee	Pennelopi	

Scotland

Boys

Jack	James	Matthew
Lewis	Jamie	Ross
Cameron	Liam	Callum
Ryan		

Girls

Chloe	Erin	Lauren
Sophie	Ellie	Megan
Emma	Rachel	Hannah
Amy		

Spain

Boys

Alejandro	Javier	Sergio
Daniel	Adrián	Carlos
Pablo	Álvaro	Hugo
David		

Girls

Lucía	Marta	Sara
María	Andrea	Claudia
Paula	Alba	Ana
Laura		

Sweden

Boys

William	Erik	Alexander
Filip	Emil	Viktor
Oscar	Isak	Anton
Lucas		

Girls

Emma	Julia	Alva
Maja	Linnéa	Wilma
Ida	Hanna	Klara
Elin		

Switzerland (German-speaking only)

Boys

Luca	Lukas	Marco
Jan	David	Noah
Simon	Fabian	Jonas
Joel		

Girls

Laura	Julia	Celine
Michelle	Jasmin	Nina
Sarah	Vanessa	Sara
Leas		

United States

Boys

Jacob	Andrew	Daniel
Michael	Joseph	Christopher
Joshua	Ethan	Anthony
Matthew		

Girls

Emily	Olivia	Ashley
Emma	Abigail	Elizabeth
Madison	Alexis	Samantha
Hannah		

Fashionista Names

There's no doubt about it, fashion has an impact on everyone's life. Whether you're a fan of designer duds or Wal-Mart steals, you have to wear something when you leave the house. What better way to cover up a lack of fashion know-how than by giving your child a hot industry name? Or, if you're lucky enough to have great fashion sense, one of these monikers could help you to celebrate your love of all things chic.

Famous designers

Boys

Adolfo Sardina	Calvin Klein	Clements
Andrew Marc	Christian	Ribeiro
Arthur Mendonca	Lacroix	Cole Haan

Dan Caten
David Dixon
Dean Caten
Domenico Dolce
Emanuel Ungaro
Emilio Pucci
Gianfranco Ferre
Gianni Versace
Giorgio Armani
Guccio Gucci
Guy Laroche

Hugo Boss
James Mischka
Jean-Paul Gaultier
Joeffer Caoc
Karl Lagerfeld
Kenneth Cole
Levi Strauss
Louis Vuitton
Marc Jacobs
Mark Badgley
Michael Kors

Naoki Takizawa
Oscar de la Renta
Paul Frank
Perry Ellis
Ralph Lauren
Roberto Cavalli
Salvatore Farragamo
Stefano Gabbana
Tommy Hilfiger
Valentino Garavani

Girls

Agnes B
Anne Klein
Betsey Johnson
Catherine
Malandrino
Coco Chanel
Cynthia Rowley

Dana Buchman
Diane von Furstenberg
Donatella Versace
Donna Karan
Jeanne Lottie
Judith Leiber
Kate Spade

Liz Claiborne
Nicole Miller
Shelly Segal
Stella McCartney
Vera Wang
Vivian Westwood

Fashion houses

Azzaro
Blamain
Burberry
Cardin
Carven
Celine
Cerruti
Chanel
Chloé
Dior

Escada
Fendi
Givenchy
Gucci
Exte
Halston
Hermes
Herrera
Krizia
Lacoste

Moschino
Mulberry
Prada
Pucci
Rochas
Valentino
Versace
Vionnet
Yves Saint Laurent

Chapter 9

☆

What's In a Name?

From affecting the way they interact with others to determining their personality, names have a tremendous impact on children's lives. And all it takes is an unfortunate one like Dunce to force others to jump to conclusions about who your child really is. That's why it's so important to think of everything—spelling, meaning, pronunciation and popularity—before settling on a name for your new bundle.

Today, we're lucky to live in a less formal society. With the exception of the school system, people rarely refer to colleagues or peers by their last names. Instead, you can call your boss Frank or Donna and your in-laws Sid and Judy. Since the last name is rarely used, people have to rely on their first to make an overall impression. So we're seeing a new trend: a smaller percentage of kids are being given popular names while more and more are being named distinctively.

In an age when technology changes daily, it seems strange that people could be weirded out by an unusual name. Unfortunately, this sentiment is pretty common in today's society. From pink hair to eyebrow piercings, a great many of us frown upon the unusual, feeling out of place when confronted with originality. The same goes for first names. While we may turn our noses up at yet another Jennifer or Matthew, mocking their over-popularity and their parents' lack of imagination, we contradict ourselves by making fun of the name Moondog, for instance, or for being shocked by the first Shalishka we meet.

Being raised as the only Shandley I know, I must admit that I'm partial to the unique and creative, especially when it comes to names. And being one of only two kids in my class with an original name certainly gave me first hand experience with the pros and cons of opting for an unusual moniker.

Having a unique name has its benefits—everyone knows who people are referring to when they mention you; it's a great conversation starter (especially if there's a good story behind its creation) and an unusual name can help you stand out above the crowd of seemingly endless Hannahs and Jasons. Another bonus of having an original name is that no one will have a preconceived stereotype about it. It's pretty unlikely that they'll have met another Shandley they didn't like. Plus, the more original the name, the harder it is to create a derogatory nickname. The worst I ever got was "chandelier."

Now for the downside of living with a different name. First of all, no one besides my family ever pronounces it properly (they always leave out the "d"). Next, barely anyone spells it right the first time. Also, many people assume I'm a man and I have to repeat myself at least twice when being introduced to someone new. And, what I considered to be the most horrific as a child, you will never, ever find it on personalized mirrors, pencils, erasers or hairbrushes.

So, if you're planning on choosing an unusual name for your child, make sure to weigh the pros and cons. And think about just how unique you want it to be. Having a name like Apple may be OK for celebrities' kids, for instance. They're popular from the moment they're born simply because of who their parents are. But imagine an Apple in a grade six class in White Horse, British Columbia? She'd likely be laughed out of the room. And this embarrassment could have lasting damage to her psyche.

In addition to lowering a child's self-esteem, being stuck with a name that's too weird, hard to spell or easy to make fun of could cause your child to be less socially desirable, according to a study by the Department of Physology at the University of North Alabama. It could cause your child to become an introvert who chooses to spend time playing by himself rather than risk altercations with other kids. A bad name could also instill fear and unnecessary stress in little ones who are constantly teased or misunderstood. And for some, these feelings and insecurities can last until adulthood.

REAL NAMES

Although 33-year-old Ashk is proud of his unique name now, this wasn't always the case. "Growing up in the U.S. and Canada, everyone else had common names like Bill and Mike," he says. "Mine was different and as a child you want to fit in more than be different." So for a while during high school, he used his middle name, Nissan (pronounced Nason) instead. Since he didn't feel that this name suited him, Ashk returned to the original and has stuck with it ever since.

Twenty-six-year-old Ingrie was given a Canadianized version of her Finnish grandmother's name, Ingkari. "[My grandmother's name] was changed to Ingrie when she moved here as a little girl so others could spell and pronounce it," she explains. Although she wished for a name common enough to be found on personalized pencils, mirrors and brushes as a kid, Ingrie is now thrilled with being unique. "My name means being different, which I am in other ways—biracial and feminist—and being proud of being different."

Still Want to Choose an Unusual Name?

You understand the potential downfalls but just can't bear to give up your favourite made-up name. Here are a few tips to help tone down or slightly alter an unusual name to help your child avoid some potentially embarrassing moments.

Spell Well

If you're creating a name, remember to make it as easy to spell as possible. The last thing you want is for your child to constantly have to correct people, let alone for him to be confused about it himself.

Use a Nickname

Use a more familiar-sounding nickname to help your child ease into the social routine. As a kid, I was known as Shan, which was easier for young friends to remember and less of a mouthful for people to pronounce.

KIDS' KORNER

Rhea's aunt gets credit for her well-loved name. "[She] suggested it and my parents thought it would be nice," explains the 12-year-old. Although Rhea likes having the same name as a Greek goddess, she's sick of hearing people mispronounce it and says she hates having to share it with "a really ugly bird" of the same name.

Nine-year-old Khayman's parents named him after the Cayman Islands "because that was where they were when they thought of me," he says. And he's extremely happy with their choice since he's never met anyone else with his name. If he had to pick another name for himself, Khayman says he'd choose Joe Billy Bob Frank Junior because, although it's a mouthful, that's what his older brother and sister always call him.

Choose an Easy Middle Name

Give your kid a more traditional middle name like Jane or Dan. That way if she gets sick of being teased about her first name, she has another option.

Consider Your Last Name

Avoid combining a unique, hard-to-spell or ultra long first name with a distinct last one. It'll be hard enough for others to accept a Checheshawna, let alone a Checheshawna Trebolinka.

Be Consistent

If choosing an unusual name for one child, make sure it flows with your other kids' names. Poor little Ashktlyn will feel completely left out if her sisters are named Anne, Mary and Sue.

Living Up to Expectations

Sometimes the name you give your child can be harder to live up to than your own expectations of him. Imagine trying to match the accomplishments of Albert Einstein just because you share his name?

Before you decide on an established name, read this advice to help avoid setting your kid up for future disappointment or humiliation.

Don't Do It

No matter how much you like the name Shakespeare or Picasso, just say no. Trust me, your kid will thank you for it. These names are too distinct, meaning everyone will automatically think of the famous predecessor when they hear it. You don't want your child to be embarrassed if he's a horrible musician named Bach, for instance.

Choose Wisely

Avoid giving kids the full name of a famous explorer, athlete or inventor. If your last name's Columbus, for instance, don't name your child Christopher. First of all, your child will almost definitely be teased for having the exact name of someone famous. And secondly, young Shaquille O'Neal may feel let down when he discovers that he's better at debating than he is at basketball.

Do Your Research

Before naming your child after a celebrity, think long and hard about what you're doing. Research the person and the meaning of his name to find out all his good and bad points before making your decision. While lauded for talents on the basketball court, for instance, the highly tattooed and pierced Dennis Rodman is also known as a temperamental showman who conducts stunts (like wearing a wedding dress to a book signing) to garner attention. He's got a lengthy police record and is an ultimate bad guy. Do you really want your child to have to live up to that stigma?

Just for Laughs

Think naming your child Charlie Brown or Justin Case is just plain cute? Think again. Any name that could cause your kid to be the butt of playground jokes isn't endearing, it's cruel.

I once worked in an office where people made fun of a woman named Sandi Beach. Although Sandi seemed quite content with her name, and has such a wonderful personality that you instantly forget how unusual it is, she was plagued by snickers and looks of disbelief pretty much everywhere she went. And in the U.S. last year, there were two boys named ESPN. What do you call them for short? E? Plus, how's a teacher supposed to pronounce that? Like espen or e-s-p-n?

There are many downsides to having a joke name. Your child will be subject to endless bouts of teasing that will most likely last from grade school all the way past the board room. No matter how hard she tries to establish herself as her own person, she'll always be the one with the embarrassingly bad name. The result: low self-confidence, resentment, anxiety and possibly depression.

Giving your child a humorous name also shows that you didn't have enough respect for him to think of anything more serious or distinguished. You put your own sense of humour above your child's psychological welfare, which could prove to him that you don't value his own opinion as much as you do your own. Is it really worth it for a short-lived laugh at your child's expense?

 FUN FACTS

Like blue jeans? So did the parents of seven American boys. In fact, they liked them so much that they named their unsuspecting sons Denim.

In the U.S., parents are beginning to name their children after food. Names like Gouda, Almond, Veal and Bologna are a few of note.

In Austria, it is forbidden to invent a name. If you want to choose something unique, you have to prove that it existed for another person.

 CANUCK TRIVIA

Québec is the only province with considerably different names on its most popular lists.

The "B" in former Prime Minister Lester B. Pearson's name stands for Bowles.

Names to Avoid at all Costs

While I'm all for unusual names, there are some that should just never be used—unless you want to pay years of therapy bills, that is. Take the name Nimrod, for example. Although this is a valid name that's been used across the globe for decades, it has a negative stigma attached to it on this side of the world. Case in point: I tested peoples' reactions to this name by using it to place an order at a favourite burger joint. Each person who saw the name, from the cashier to the line chef, laughed and asked me if I was serious. Since I actually know of someone named Nimrod, I couldn't believe how horribly people responded to his name.

Imagine having people laugh at you each time they heard or saw your name because they thought it was a joke? For the sake of poorly named children everywhere, I urge you to save your own child from humiliation by avoiding all of the following:

Adolf	Euridyce	Osama
Almond	Fagan	Poem
Banjo	Fashion	Precious
Barbie	Female	Prince
Blanket	Flea	Purity
Bologna	Flirt	Queenie
Boo	Free	Rambo
Car	Gouda	Rebel
Cloud	Happy	Saddam
Danger	Hateya	Schmoopie
Dork	Kiwi	Spontaneous
Dude	Lady	Sweetpea
Dumb	Lattice	Tater
Dunce	Napoleon	Tree
Easy	Nazi (pronounced	Unique
Ecstasy	Naazeee)	Veal
Elmo	Nerd	Vixen
Englebert	Nimrod	Welcome

Chapter 10

☆

Popular Names

No matter how much we may hate to admit it, there's something kind of hip about having a popular name. It's easy to spell, people understand it and teachers don't get tripped up by it. Plus, imagine how cool it would have felt to share the same name as your best friend in elementary school.

Another bonus to popular names is the fact that many of them are innately cool. Whether it's because they're frequently found in movies or because they've been made cool by a well-liked person, there's just something about popular names that makes them fashionable. It's kind of like when you were in grade school. (You remember—all it took to be cool was having the same pen or backpack as another kid.) Today, naming your child the same as thousands of others gives you a VIP pass to the popular lounge. Basically, it tells people that you were with it enough to realize which name was "in."

Problem is, this level of coolness could drop dramatically when your kid enters school. Somehow being known as Ethan C. doesn't have the same effect as it would if he were just plain Ethan. Instead of being hip, he's now one of the crowd—a little guy who blends into the group instead of standing above it. All of a sudden, the "special" feeling he had over his name is gone. Instead of believing that you gave him a unique gift, he'll realize that he has to share it with three other kids in his grade. It's kind of like giving him a birthday present and then presenting his siblings or friends with the exact same thing. It quickly loses its novelty.

Another downside to common names is the rate at which they drop off the charts. Just like the latest fashion craze, popular names are fickle and short-lived. While they'll probably be deemed stylish for longer than one season, it could take a mere five to 10 years for your kid's name to be booted off the most-popular list. And once that happens, it can be a quick trip down to the Island of Misfit Names. Take popular 1920s names like Marjorie, Violet and Norman, for example. Once they dropped off the top chart, they never made it back. And you can just imagine how well an old-fashioned name like these would go over today.

So exactly who's choosing names from the popular list? A heck of a lot of people—from parents who want their kids to be hip to those who were oblivious to the name's popularity. And there's absolutely nothing wrong with that, especially if you really like the name. Some people, however, cringe at the thought of their child having to share her name with a bunch of others. If you can relate to this feeling, you may want to forgo names on this list in favour of a less common one found in other chapters.

 REAL NAMES

As a child and young teenager, 32-year-old Tracy was plagued with the problem of many popularly named kids—she was one of many Tracys in her class. All grown up and out in the work force, Tracy says she's grown to like her name and shed the feeling that it's too common. "Now that I'm not in school and live and work around people of different ages, there are no other Tracys in my life," she beams.

Otto VI just welcomed his first son, Otto Owen VII, a.k.a OO7. "It wasn't planned," he says of the nickname. "It just happened to work out that way." Named after generations of Ottos, the 36-year-old thinks keeping a name in the family is a special tradition. "I enjoyed it tremendously while growing up" he says of being Otto VI. Now that he's passed the torch onto OO7, "it's up to him to carry it on," he says.

Karen's mother always hated having a nickname, so she decided to give her daughter a short name that couldn't be turned into a diminutive. Although the 36-year-old is mostly happy with her mother's choice, she does wish that her name wasn't so common. "There were always at least two other girls named Karen in my class," she says. "So I grew up thinking my name was Karen S."

"It starts with a 'Y' and so few people have that," remarks 32-year-old Yvonne of her name. If she absolutely had to choose another moniker, which she wouldn't want to do, she says she'd choose Michelle. The reason: it's her real first name that she doesn't use.

As a child, Sidney (who goes by Sid) sometimes wished he had a more macho-sounding name. "It was not as masculine a name as some others," says the 72-year-old; especially since Sydney is now a popular choice for baby girls. But overall, Sid says, "my name was never an issue and it was rather good to have a distinctive one." And even though he never met his namesake, a paternal grandfather, Sid feels honoured to have part of his family's history with him every day.

Only Tory's father ever calls her by her real name, Victoria. And that only happens when he's really mad. With the exception of official documents like her birth certificate, passport and driver's license, Tory has been known as Tory since day one. "But sometimes it's annoying," admits the 28-year-old. "I have two signatures. One for Tory and one for Victoria."

Summer never wanted another name, even when kids teased her as a child. "My mom always told me they were just jealous," the 29-year-old says of the experience. Besides, with a name she describes as "unique, beautiful and memorable," who would want anything different? When talking about names for her own future children, Summer says, "I think it is important to try to give a child a special identity and naming them something interesting and beautiful is a great way to do that. Names like Jen, John, Sarah and Mike will not happen with me."

"I love my name because almost no one else has it," says 51-year-old Georgina. Plus, she adds, "it has a masculine touch, which gives me more of an edge." Known by most as George or Georgie, she was named after her maternal grandmother. Her only qualm about the name: people used to call her Georgy Porgy as a kid.

Popular Names

From number one chart toppers to names favoured by numerous people in each province, this list contains popular picks from across the country.

Popular Boys' Names

Aaron (Hebrew, Arabic) Exalted; a messenger. *Aahron, Aaran, Aarao, Aaren, Aareon, Aarin, Aarone, Aaronn, Aarron, Aaryn, Aeron, Aharon, Ahran, Ahren, Ahron, Arek, Aren, Arin, Aron, Aronek, Aronne, Arran, Arrin, Arron.*

Adrian (Greek, Latin) Rick; dark one. *Adarian, Addie, Ade, Adrain, Adrean, Adreeyan, Adreian, Adren, Adreyan, Adri, Adriane, Adriann, Adriano, Adrien, Adrion, Adron, Adryan, Adryon, Aydrien, Aydrienne, Hadrian, Hadrianus.*

Aidan (Gaelic) Fire. *Aden, Adin, Aiden, Aydan, Ayden, Aydin.*

Alex (Greek) A short form of Alexander, meaning man's defender. *Alax, Alecs, Alix, Allax, Allex, Elek.*

Alexander (Greek) Man's defender. *Al, Alasdair, Alastair, Alaster, Alec, Alecsandar, Alejandro, Alejo, Aleksandar, Aleksander, Aleksei, Aleksey, Alessandro, Alex, Alexandar, Alexandor, Alexandr, Alexandre, Alexandros, Alexis, Alexsander, Alexxander, Alexzander, Alick, Alik, Alisander, Alixander, Alixandre, Alsandare, Sacha, Sander, Sanders, Sandie, Sandor, Sandro, Sandy, Sasha, Xander.*

Alexandre (French) Another form of Alexander, meaning man's defender. *Alec, Alek, Alex, Alexander.*

Alexis (Greek) A short form of Alexander. *Alexace, Alexei, Alexes, Alexey, Alexi, Alexie, Alexio, Alexios, Alexius, Alexiz, Alexy, Lex.*

Andrew (Greek) Manly; courageous. *Anders, Andie, Andonis, Andor, Andre, Andreas, Andrei, Andres, Andrews, Andrey, Andries, Andros, Andru, Andrys, Andy, Drew.*

Angus (Scottish) Excellent. *Aeneas, Aengus, Ange, Angos, Aonghas.*

Antonio (Spanish) Praiseworthy. *Antone, Antonioh, Antonyo, Toni, Tony.*

Arjun (Hindu) White; one of the Pandavas. *Arj.*

Armaan (Muslim) Hope; desire. *Arman.*

Ashton (English) A place of ash trees. *Ashteen, Ashten, Ashtin, Ashtone.*

Austin (Latin) Majestic; a city in Texas. *Aust, Austen, Auston, Austy, Austyn.*

Ayden (Gaelic) A form of Aidan, meaning fire. *Aiden, Aydan, Aydin, Aydon.*

Benjamin (Hebrew) Son of the right hand. *Behnjamin, Bejamin, Ben, Benermain, Benjamaim, Benjaman, Benjamen, Benjamine, Benjamino, Benjamon, Benjamyn, Benjemin, Benji, Benjie, Benjiman, Benjimen, Benjjmen, Benjy, Benni, Bennie, Benny, Benyamin, Benyamino.*

Blake (Old English) Pale. *Blaike, Blakely, Blakeman, Blakey, Blakie, Blanco, Blayke.*

Bradley (Old English) A broad or wide meadow. *Brad, Braden, Bradie, Bradlay, Bradlea, Bradlee, Bradleigh, Bradlie, Bradly, Bradney, Brady, Braeden, Braedon.*

Brady (Irish, English) Full of spirit; broad. *Brade, Bradee, Bradey, Braidy.*

Brandon (English) Sword; a fiery hill. *Bran, Brand, Brandan, Branden, Brandin, Brandone, Brandonn, Brandyn, Branndan, Branndon, Branny.*

Brayden (English) Brave. *Braedan, Braedon, Braydon, Braydun, Brayton.*

Brendan (Irish, German) A small raven; sword. *Breandan, Bren, Brend, Brenden, Brendie, Brendin, Brendon, Brenn, Brennan, Brenndan, Bryn.*

Brody (Gaelic) A ditch. *Brodee, Broden, Broderic, Broderick, Brodey, Brodi, Brodie, Broedy.*

Bryan (Irish) Strong; a form of Brian, meaning honourable. *Bry, Bryant, Brye, Bryen.*

Bryce (Celtic) Quick; a form of Brice. *Brise, Bry, Brycen, Bryceton, Brye, Bryse, Bryson, Bryston.*

Callum (Irish) A dove. *Callam, Callim, Calum, Calym.*

Cameron (Scottish) Bent or crooked nose. *Cam, Camar, Camaron, Cameran, Camerohn, Camerson, Cami, Camiren, Camm, Cammie, Camron.*

Carson (Swedish, Scandinavian) Son of Carr. *Carr, Carrson, Cars, Carsan, Carsen, Karsen.*

Carter (English) A cart driver. *Cart, Cartah, Cartie.*

Chase (French) A hunter. *Chace, Chaise, Chason, Chass.*

Christian (Latin, English) Follower of Christ; appointed. *Chresta, Chretien, Chris, Christain, Christen, Christiaan, Christiane, Christianos, Christyan, Chrystian, Cris, Cristian, Kris, Kriss, Krist, Kristian.*

Christopher (Greek) Bearer of Christ. *Chris, Chrisopherson, Christafer, Christepher, Christhoper, Christifer, Christipher, Christof, Christofer, Christoff, Christoper, Christophe, Christopherr, Christos, Christpher, Cris, Cristobal, Cristobel, Cristoforo, Kester, Kit, Kitt, Kris, Kristofer, Kristof, Kristopher .*

Cody (Celtic, English) An assistant; a cushion. *Coday, Code, Codee, Codey, Codi, Codiak, Codie, Coedy, Coty, Kodey, Kodie, Kody.*

Colby (English) A coal town. *Colbey, Colbi, Colbie, Cole, Colie, Collby, Kolby.*

Cole (Greek, English) The peoples' victory; coal; short for Coleman, meaning a coal miner. *Coal, Colet, Coley, Colie, Kohl, Kole, Nicholas.*

Colin (Irish) Youth; victorious. *Colan, Cole, Colen, Collin, Collyn, Colyn.*

Colton (English) A coal town. *Cole, Collton, Colston, Colt, Coltan, Coltawn, Colten, Coltrane, Kol, Kole, Kolton.*

Connor (Irish) Lover of wolves; wanted. *Con, Conn, Connee, Conner, Conor, Kon, Konnor.*

Cooper (English) A barrel maker. *Coop, Coup, Couper, Koop, Kooper, Kouper.*

Cyrus (Persian) The sun. *Ciro, Cy, Cyris, Syrus.*

Dakota (Native American) Tribal name; friend. *Dac, Dack, Dacoda, Dak, Dakodah, Dakotah, Dekoda, Dekota, Dekotes, Kota.*

Damien (Greek) Form of Damian, meaning sweet; one who tames. *Daemien, Daimien, Dame, Dameon, Dami, Damie, Damyen, Damyon, Damyun.*

Dante (Latin) Long-lasting. *Dan, Danatay, Danne, Dant, Danté, Dantey, Dauntay, Daunté, Dayntay, Dontae, Dontay, Donté.*

Darius (Greek, Persian) Rich; a king. *Dare, Dareas, Dareus, Darian, Darien, Darieus, Dario, Darrius.*

Darren (Irish, English) Great; a rocky hill. *Daran, Dare, Daren, Darin, Daron, Darran, Darrian, Darrien, Darrience, Darrin, Darrion, Darron, Darryn, Darun, Daryn, Dearron, Deren, Dereon, Derren, Derron, Derry.*

Dawson (English) The son of David. *Dawsan, Dawse, Dawsen, Dawsin.*

Dayton (English) A bright town. *Daeton, Daiton, Day, Daye, Daytawn, Deytawn, Deyton.*

Declan (Irish) Goodness; a saint. *Deaclan, Dec, Deck, Dek, Deklan, Deklon.*

Devin (Irish) A poet. *Deavin, Delvin, Dev, Devan, Deven, Devlen, Devlyn, Devon, Devonn, Devvy, Devyn.*

Devon (English) Defender. *Deavon, Deivon, Deivone, Dev, Devin, Devoen, Devohn, Devohne, Devond, Devone, Devonn, Devonne, Devontaine, Devy, Devyn.*

Dominic (Latin) Of the Lord. *Deco, Demenico, Dom, Domaic, Domeka, Domenic, Domenico, Domingo, Domini, Dominick, Dominie, Dominique, Dominy, Domonic, Nick.*

Dylan (Welsh) Son of the sea. *Dill, Dillan, Dillon, Dilloyn, Dilon, Dyl, Dylahn, Dylen, Dylin, Dyllan, Dyllon, Dylon.*

Eli (Hebrew) Elevated. *El, Elie, Elier, Eloi, Eloy, Ely.*

Elias (Greek) Another form of Elijah. *El, Eli, Elia, Eliace, Eliasz, Elice, Ellice, Ellis, Elyas.*

Eric (Scandinavian) Always powerful. *Ehrich, Ehrick, Erek, Erich, Erick, Erickson, Erico, Ericson, Erik, Erric, Eryc, Eryk, Eryke, Rick.*

Ethan (Hebrew, Latin) Strong; firm. *Eathan, Eitan, Etan, Eth, Ethe, Ethen, Ethin, Ethon.*

Evan (Irish, Scottish, Welsh) A youthful warrior; right handed; God is good. *Eoin, Ev, Evann, Evans, Even, Evens, Evin, Evyn, Ewan, Ewen.*

Felix (Latin) Happy. *Fee, Felic, Felice, Felicio, Felike, Felixce, Felo, Felizio, Filix, Phelix, Philix.*

Gabriel (Hebrew) God is my strength. *Gab, Gabby, Gabe, Gabi, Gabko, Gable, Gabo, Gabor, Gabrail, Gabreal, Gabrel, Gabriele, Gabriell, Gabrielli, Gabriello, Gabris, Gabryel, Gabys, Gavi, Gavriel, Gavril, Gebereal, Ghabriel, Riel.*

Gage (French) A pledge. *Gager.*

Garrett (Irish) Courageous; one who watches. *Gar, Gareth, Garett, Garitt, Garrad, Garrat, Garret, Garritt, Gary, Gerret, Gerrett, Gerrot, Gerry.*

Gavin (Welsh) A white hawk. *Gav, Gavan, Gaven, Gavinn, Gavino, Gavon, Gavvin, Gavyn, Gavynn, Gawain, Gawaine, Gawayn, Gawayne, Gawen.*

Graham (English) A great house; warlike. *Graeham, Graeme, Grahame, Gram, Grame.*

Grayson (English) Son of a gray-haired man; son of a bailiff. *Gracen, Gracyn, Gray, Graydon, Grey, Greydon, Greyson.*

Griffin (Latin) Having a hooked nose. *Greffen, Grifee, Griff, Griffen, Griffey, Griffon, Griffy, Gryphon.*

Harrison (English) The son of Harry. *Harrey, Harrie, Harris, Harrisan, Harrisen, Harry.*

Hayden (English) A hill of heather. *Aidan, Haddan, Haddon, Haden, Hadon, Hadyn, Haidyn, Hay, Haydan, Haydn, Haydon, Haydyn.*

Hudson (English) The son of Hugh. *Hud, Hudsan, Hudsen, Hudsin, Hudsyn.*

Hunter (English) A hunter. *Hunt.*

Isaac (Hebrew) Laughter. *Icek, Ike, Ikey, Ikie, Isaak, Isacco, Isack, Isak, Ishaq, Isiacc, Isiak, Itzak, Ixaka, Izak, Izaak, Ize, Izek, Izzy.*

Ivan (Russian) God is good; a form of John, meaning God is gracious. *Ivahn, Ivanchik, Ivanek, Ivanicheck, Ivano, Ivas, Ive, Ivey, Ivie, Vanya.*

Jack (English, Hebrew) Grace of God; supplanter; from John, meaning God is gracious. *Jackee, Jackie, Jacko, Jackub, Jacky, Jacque, Jak, Jaki, Jax, Jock.*

Jackson (English) The son of Jack. *Jackee, Jacks, Jacsen, Jacson, Jakson, Jax, Jaxen, Jaxon.*

Jaden (Hebrew) God heard; form of Jadon, meaning God listens. *Jacdon, Jadin, Jaeden, Jaedon, Jaiden, Jaydon.*

Jake (Hebrew) Short for Jacob. *Jaik, Jakee, Jakey, Jakie, Jayk, Jayke.*

Jakob (Hebrew) A form of Jacob. *Jakab, Jake, Jakeb, Jakey, Jakie, Jakiv, Jakobe, Jakov, Jakovian, Jakub, Jakubek, Jekebs.*

Jared (Hebrew) A descendant. *Jahred, Jaired, Jarad, Jarid, Jarod, Jarode, Jarrad, Jarred, Jarret, Jarryd, Jerad, Jered, Jerod, Jerrad, Jerrod, Jerryd, Yarden, Yared.*

Jason (Greek) A healer. *Jace, Jacen, Jacey, Jaeson, Jahson, Jaisen, Jaison, Jase, Jasen, Jasey, Jasin, Jasten, Jasun, Jasyn, Jay, Jayce, Jaycen, Jaysen, Jayson, Jaysun.*

Jasper (English, Persian) A semi-precious gem; a treasurer. *Jas, Jasp, Jaspar, Jaspur, Jaspy, Jaspyr, Jaz, Jazper, Jazz, Jazzper, Jespar, Jesper.*

Jayden (English) Form of Jaden, meaning God heard. *Jade, Jaide, Jaiden, Jaidi, Jaidie, Jaidon, Jayde, Jaydey, Jaydon, Jaydun, Jaydy.*

Jeffrey (English, German) The peace of God. *Geoff, Geoffrey, Geoffry, Gioffredo, Jeff, Jefferies, Jefferey, Jeffery, Jeffree, Jeffrery, Jeffrie, Jeffries, Jeffry, Jeffy, Jefry.*

Jeremiah (Hebrew) A prophet of the Lord. *Geremiah, Gerry, Jaramia, Jemeriah, Jeramiah, Jere, Jeremaya, Jeremi, Jeremia, Jeremias, Jeremija, Jeremy, Jerimiah, Jerimiha, Jerimya, Jermiah, Jerry.*

Jeremy (Hebrew) Uplifted by God. *Jaramie, Jaremay, Jaremi, Jaremy, Jem, Jemmie, Jemmy, Jerahmy, Jeramee, Jeramey, Jeramie, Jeramy, Jere, Jeremah, Jereme, Jeremey, Jeremia, Jeremiah, Jeremias, Jeremyah, Jereomy, Jerime, Jerimiah, Jerimias, Jerimy, Jermey, Jerome, Jeromy, Jerr, Jerremy, Jerrey, Jerrie, Jerry.*

Jesse (Hebrew) Rich. *Jesee, Jesi, Jesiah, Jesie, Jess, Jessee, Jessey, Jessi, Jessie, Jessy, Jessye.*

Joel (Hebrew) God is willing. *Joe, Joël, Joelie, Joell, Joely, Jole, Joly, Yoel.*

Jonah (Hebrew) A dove; peace. *Gionah, Jona, Jonas, Joneh, Yonah, Yonas, Yunus.*

Jonathan (Hebrew) A form of Johnathan, meaning God's gift. *Janathan, Johnathon, Jon, Jonatan, Jonate, Jonatha, Jonathen, Jonathon, Jonnathan, Jonni, Jonnie, Jonny, Jonothan.*

Jordan (Hebrew) To descend. *Jared, Jordaan, Jodae, Jordain, Jordaine, Jordany, Jorden, Jordenn, Jordi, Jordie, Jordin, Jordon, Jordy, Jordyn, Jori, Jorrdan, Jorrin, Jory, Jourdain, Jourdan.*

Julian (Greek, Latin) Form of Julius; youthful. *Jolyon, Juliaan, Juliane, Juliano, Julien, Julion, Jullian, Julyan, Julyon, Julyun.*

Justin (Latin) Just; fair. *Jestin, Just, Justain, Justan, Justas, Justen, Justice, Justinas, Justine, Justinian, Justinius, Justinn, Justino, Justins, Justinus, Justo, Juston, Justton, Justun, Justyn, Justyne.*

Kaden (American, Arabic) A fighter; from the name Kadin, meaning companion. *Cade, Caden, Caiden, Kadan, Kade, Kadon, Kadyn, Kaiden.*

Kai (Hawaiian) The sea.

Kaleb (Hebrew) A form of Caleb, meaning faithful. *Kal, Kalab, Kalb, Kale, Kalib, Kilab.*

Keegan (Irish) Fiery; small and fierce. *Kaegan, Keagan, Keagin, Keegen, Kegan, Kege, Keghan, Keghun, Kegun.*

Keenan (Irish) Little one. *Keanan, Keanen, Keenen, Keenon, Kenan, Kienan, Kienen, Kienon.*

Kevin (Celtic) Handsome; gentle. *Kavan, Keevin, Keevon, Kev, Kevahngn, Kevan, Keven, Keveon, Kevon, Kevron, Kevvie, Kevvy, Kevyn.*

Kieran (Irish) Little and dark. *Keiran, Keiren, Keiron, Kern, Kernan, Kier, Kieren, Kierin, Kiernan, Kieron, Kiers, Kyran.*

Lachlan (Scottish) From the land of lakes. *Lachlann, Lacklan, Lackland, Lakelan, Laughlin, Lock, Locklan.*

Landon (English) A long hill. *Land, Landan, Landen, Landin.*

Levi (Hebrew) United; harmonious. *Leavi, Leevi, Lev, Levey, Levie, Levin, Levitis, Levon, Levy.*

Liam (Irish) A protector; form of William, meaning a resolute guardian. *Leam, Leeam, Leeum.*

Logan (Irish) A meadow. *Logen, Login, Loggy, Logun.*

Lucas (Latin) A form of Lucius, meaning light. *Loucas, Luc, Lucca, Luces, Luk, Luka, Lukas, Luke, Lukes, Lukus.*

Luis (Spanish) Form of Louis, meaning an accomplished warrior. *Luez, Luiz.*

Malcolm (Celtic) Follower of the dove or Saint Columba. *Mal, Malc, Malcolum, Malcom, Malcum, Malk, Malkelm, Malkolm.*

Marcus (Latin) Warlike. *Marc, Marcas, Marcellus, Marcio, Marckus, Marco, Marcos, Marcous, Marek, Mark, Markov, Markus, Marky.*

Markus (Latin) A form of Marcus, meaning warlike. *Mark, Markas, Markus, Marky.*

Marshall (French) A care-giver for horses. *Marschal, Marsh, Marshal, Marshel, Marshell, Marsy.*

Martin (Latin) Warlike; aggressive. *Maartin, Marciano, Marcin, Marinos, Marius, Mart, Martan, Martel, Marten, Martey, Marti,*

Martie, Martinas, Martine, Martinez, Martinho, Martiniano, Martino, Martinos, Martins, Marto, Marton, Marts, Marty, Martyn, Mertin.

Mason (French) One who works with stones. *Mace, Maison, Mase, Masson, Sonny.*

Mathieu (French) Form of Matthew, meaning a gift from God. *Mathie, Mathieux, Mathiew, Matthieu, Matthiew, Mattieu, Mattieux.*

Mathis (French) Form of Mathias or Matthew, meaning a gift from God. *Maitias, Mathi, Mathia, Mathis, Mathus, Matthia, Matthis, Matus.*

Max (Latin) Greatest; short for Maximilian and Maxwell. *Mac, Mack, Maks, Maksim, Massimiliano, Maxa, Maxey, Maxfield, Maxie, Maxim, Maximiliano, Maximilien, Maximino, Maximo, Maximus.*

Maxwell (English) From the well of Marcus. *Max, Maxe, Maxie, Maxwel, Maxwill, Maxy.*

Michael (Hebrew) Who is like God. *Machael, Machas, Mahail, Maichail, Maikal, Makael, Makal, Makell, Makis, Meikel, Mekal, Micah, Micha, Michail, Michak, Michal, Michalek, Michau, Micheal, Michel, Michele, Mick, Mickel, Mickey, Mickie, Micky, Miguel, Mihail, Mihailo, Mihkel, Mikaek, Mikael, Mikala, Mike, Mikeal, Mikel, Mikelis, Mikell, Mikey, Mikhail, Mikhalis, Mikhos, Mikiee, Mikkel, Mikko, Miko, Mischa, Misha, Mitch, Mitchell, Mychal, Mykal.*

Mitchell (English) A form of Michael, meaning who is like God. *Mitch, Mitchael, Mitchall, Mitchel, Mitchele, Mitchelle, Mitchem, Mitchie, Mitchill, Mitchy, Mitshell, Mytch, Mytchell, Mytchil.*

Nathan (Hebrew) Short for Nathaniel, meaning God's gift. *Naethan, Nat, Natan, Nataniele, Nate, Nathanial, Nathann, Nathean, Nathen, Nathian, Nathin, Nathon, Natthan, Natthaen, Natthen, Natty, Naythan.*

Nathaniel (Hebrew) God's gift. *Nat, Natanael, Nataniel, Nate, Nathan, Nathanael, Nathanal, Nathaneal, Nathaneil, Nathanel, Nathanial, Nathanie, Nathanuel, Nathanyal, Nathanyel, Nathe, Natheal, Nathel, Nathenial, Natheniel, Nathinel, Nethaniel, Thaniel.*

Nicholas (Greek) The victorious people. *Nic, Nicanor, Niccolo, Nichalas, Nichelas, Nichlas, Nichlos, Nichol, Nicholus, Nick, Nickee,*

Nickie, Nicklus, Nickolas, Nickolaus, Nicky, Nicol, Nicolaas, Nicolai, Nicolas, Nikki, Nikky, Niklas, Niklos, Niko, Nikolai, Nikolais, Nikolas, Nikolaus, Nikolo, Nikolos, Nikos, Nioclás, Niocol, Nyck, Nykolas.

Nicolas (Greek) Short for Nicholas, meaning the victorious people. *Nic, Nico, Nicolus, Nick, Nickolas, Nikolas, Nikolo, Nyck, Nykolas.*

Nolan (Irish) Noble. *Noland, Nole, Nolen, Nolin, Nollan, Nolline, Nolun, Nolyn, Nowlan, Nuallan.*

Olivier (French) Form of Oliver, meaning olive tree. *Nollie, Oliiero, Oliwa, Ollie, Olliver, Ollivor.*

Owen (Welsh) Well-born. *Owain, Owan, Owens, Owin, Owon, Owwen.*

Parker (English) Keeper of the park. *Park, Parke, Parkes, Parkey, Parkley, Parks.*

Patrick (English) A nobleman. *Paddey, Paddie, Paddy, Padraic, Pat, Patek, Patric, Patrice, Patricio, Patricius, Patrik, Patrique, Patrizio, Patrizius, Patryk, Pats, Patsy.*

Quinn (Irish) Wise; short for Quinton, Quincy and Quinlan. *Quin.*

Riley (Irish) Brave; courageous. *Reilly, Rilley, Rilye, Rylee, Ryley, Rylie, Ryly.*

Rowan (Gaelic, English) Red; rugged. *Roan, Rohan, Rowe, Rowen, Rowney.*

Ryan (Irish) Little ruler or king. *Rhine, Rhyan, Rhyne, Rian, Ryane, Ryann, Ryen, Ryne, Ryon, Ryun.*

Rylan (English) The land of rye. *Rycroft, Rye, Ryeland, Ryland, Rylin, Rylund, Ryman, Ryton.*

Sean (Hebrew, Irish) The grace of God. *Seaghan, Séan, Seán, Seanán, Seane, Seann, Shaan, Shaine, Shane, Shaughn, Shaun, Shaune, Shawn, Shayne, Shone.*

Sebastian (Latin) Respected; honoured. *Bastian, Bastien, Sabastian, Sabastien, Seb, Sebashun, Sebastiano, Sebastien, Sebastin, Sebastion, Sebastuan, Sebbie, Sebestyén, Sebo, Sepasetiano.*

Simon (Hebrew) A good listener. *Saimon, Samien, Semjén, Semon, Shimon, Si, Sim, Siman, Simao, Simen, Simeon, Simion, Simm, Simmon, Simmonds, Simmons, Simms, Simmy, Simonas, Simone, Simson, Simyon, Siomonn, Sye, Symon, Syms.*

Spencer (English) A giver; provider. *Spence, Spencey, Spencre, Spense, Spenser, Spensor, Spensy.*

Steven (Greek) From Stephen, meaning crown. *Steave, Steeve, Stevie, Stevy.*

Tanner (English) A leather tanner. *Tan, Tanier, Tann, Tannar, Tanne, Tanney, Tannie, Tannor, Tanny.*

Taylor (English) A tailor. *Tailer, Tailor, Talor, Tay, Tayler, Tayley, Taylour, Teyle, Tier.*

Travis (English, French) A form of Travers, meaning a crossing or crossroads. *Travais, Traver, Traves, Travess, Traveus, Travey, Travious, Traviss, Travus, Travuss, Travys, Trevais, Trever.*

Trevor (Celtic) Vigilant. *Trefor, Trev, Trevar, Trevaris, Trevarus, Trever, Trevis, Trevoris, Trevorus, Trevur, Treve, Treyvor.*

Tristan (Welsh) Noisy. *Trestan, Treston, Trestyn, Tris, Trisan, Trist, Tristano, Tristen, Tristian, Tristin, Triston, Tristram, Tristy, Tristyn, Trystan.*

Ty (English) Short for Tyler, meaning a roofer or tile maker. Also short for Tyrone, meaning king. *Ti, Tie, Tye.*

Tyler (English) A roofer or tile maker. *Tile, Tiler, Ty, Tye, Tyel, Tylar, Tyle, Tyle, Tylee, Tylere, Tylir, Tyller, Tylor.*

Tyson (French) The son of Ty. *Tieson, Tison, Tiszon, Tyce, Tyeson, Tyse, Tysen, Tysone, Tysson, Tysy.*

Vincent (Latin) Conqueror. *Vencent, Vikent, Vikenti, Vikesha, Vin, Vince, Vincence, Vincens, Vincente, Vincentius, Vincents, Vincenty, Vincenz, Vincenzio, Vincenzo, Vinci, Vinciente, Vinco, Vinko, Vinn, Vinnie, Vinny.*

Wesley (English) The west meadow. *Wes, Weslee, Wesleyan, Weslie, Wesly, Wess, Wessley, Westleigh, Westley.*

Wyatt (French) Little warrior. *Wiatt, Wy, Wyat, Wyatte, Wye, Wyeth.*

Xander (Greek) Short for Alexander, meaning protector. *Xan, Xande, Xandere, Xandre.*

Xavier (Arabic, Basque) Bright; a new house. *Giaffar, Jaffar, Javier, Saverio, Xabier, Xaiver, Xaver, Xavian, Xavon, Xever, Xzaiver, Xzavaier, Xzaver, Xzavier, Xzavion, Zavey, Zavier.*

Zachary (Hebrew) Remembered by God; a form of Zachariah. *Zacary, Zaccary, Zacchary, Zach, Zacha, Zacharey, Zachari, Zacharia, Zacharie, Zachaury, Zachery, Zachry, Zack, Zachar, Zacharie, Zackary, Zackery, Zak, Zakari, Zakary, Zakri, Zakrie, Zakry, Zeke.*

Popular Girls' Names

Aaliyah (Hebrew) Advancing; to ascend. *Aalia, Aalliya, Alia, Aliya, Aliyah.*

Abby (Hebrew) Short for Abigail, meaning joy. *Abbe, Abbee, Abbey, Abbie, Abbye.*

Abigail (Hebrew) A father's joy. *Abagael, Abagail, Abagale, Abagil, Abbegail, Abbegale, Abbegayle, Abbey, Abbie, Abbigail, Abbigale, Abby, Abbygale, Abbygayle, Abegail, Abey, Abigal, Abigayle, Avigail, Gail, Gayle.*

Alexa (Greek) Short for Alexandra, meaning protector of mankind; female version of Alexander. *Alecksa, Alekia, Aleksa, Aleksah, Alex, Alexia.*

Alexandra (Greek) Protector of mankind. *Alandra, Aleix, Alejandra, Aleka, Aleks, Alex, Alexsandra.*

Alexis (Greek) Short for Alexandra, meaning protector of mankind. *Aleksus, Alex, Alexcis, Alexes, Alexi, Alexiou, Alexisia, Alexius, Alexsia, Alexus, Alexx, Alexxis, Alexys, Alexyss, Lexie, Lexis, Lexus.*

Alicia (German, Greek, English) Female; delicate; noble. *Alecia, Alesha, Alesia, Alica, Alikah, Alisha, Alissa, Allicea, Alycia, Alysha, Alyshia, Alysia, Ilysa, Ilysha.*

Allison (German, English) Noble; a form of Alice. *Ali, Alicen, Alicyn, Alisann, Alisanne, Alisen, Alison, Alisoun, Alisson, Alisun, Alisyn, Allcen, Allcenne, Alles, Allesse, Allicen, Allicenne, Allie, Allis, Allise, Allix, Allsun, Ally, Alysann, Alysanne, Alysin, Alyson, Alysun.*

Alyssa (Greek) Rational; logical. *Alissa, Allissa, Allissaie, Allyssa, Ilyssa, Illyssah, Lissa, Lyssa, Lyssah, Lyssy.*

Amanda (Latin) Lovable. *Amada, Amanada, Amand, Amandah, Amandalee, Amandi, Amandie, Amandine, Amandy, Amata, Manda, Mandaline, Mandee, Mandi, Mandie, Mandy.*

Amber (Arabic, French) Semi-precious, yellow-brown gem. *Ambar, Ameretta, Amberia, Amberre, Ambreise, Amberly, Ambur, Amburr.*

Amelia (Latin, German) A hard worker. *Aimee, Amalea, Amalee, Amalia, Amalie, Amaliya, Amaylyuh, Ameila, Amelcia, Ameldy, Amele, Ameley, Ameleah, Ameli, Amelie, Amelina, Amelinda, Amelita, Amella, Amelya, Amilia, Amilina, Amilisa, Amilita, Amillia, Amilyn, Amity, Amylia, Emele, Emelia.*

Amy (Latin) Beloved. *Aimee, Aimie, Amata, Ame, Amey, Ami, Amia, Amice, Amie, Amii, Amiiee, Amil, Amiko, Amio, Ammie, Ammy, Amye, Amylyn.*

Andrea (Greek) Courageous; feminine. *Aindrea, Andee, Andera, Anderea, Andra, Andrah, Andraia, Andree, Andi, Andie, Andra, Andrae, Andraya, Andre, Andreah, Andrean, Andreana, Andreane, Andreanna, Andreanne, Andreea, Andreena, Andreia, Andreja, Andreka, Andrel, Andrelle, Andrena, Andrene, Andressa, Andrette, Andreya, Andri, Andria, Andriana, Andriea, Andrienne, Andrietta, Andrina, Andris.*

Angela (Greek) Divine messenger; angel. *Aingeal, Angala, Anganita, Ange, Angel, Angele, Angelea, Angeleah, Angelee, Angeleigh, Angelene, Angeles, Angelia, Angelic, Angelica, Angelika, Angelina, Angeline, Angelique, Angelita, Angell, Angella, Angie, Angiola, Anglea, Anjela, Anjelica, Anngilla.*

Angelina (Latin) Angel; a form of Angela. *Angalena, Angalina, Ange, Angeleen, Angelena, Angelene, Angeliana, Angellina, Angelyn, Angelyna, Angelyne, Angelynn, Angie, Anhelina, Anje, Anjelina, Anjie.*

Annika (Scandinavian, Hebrew) Form of Anne, meaning gracious. *Aneka, Anekah, Anica, Anika, Annica, Nica, Nika, Nikky.*

Ariana (Greek) The holy one. *Ari, Ariane, Arianie, Ariann, Arianna, Arianne, Aryann, Aryanne.*

Ariane (French) Holy. *Aeriann, Airiann, Ari, Arianie, Ariann, Arianne, Arieanne, Arien, Arienne, Aryane, Aryanne.*

Ashley (English) An ash tree. *Ash, Ashalee, Ashalei, Ashaley, Ashby, Ashe, Ashelee, Ashelei, Asheleigh, Asheley, Ashely, Ashla, Ashlan, Ashlea, Ashlee, Ashlei, Ashleigh, Ashli, Ashlie, Ashlin, Ashling, Ashly, Ashlye.*

Audrey (English) Noble and strong. *Aude, Audery, Audey, Audi, Audie, Audra, Audray, Audre, Audree, Audreen, Audreye, Audri, Audria, Audrianna, Audrianne, Audrie, Audrina, Audriya, Audry, Audrye, Audy.*

Autumn (Latin) Autumn; the fall season. *Autom, Autum.*

Ava (German) A bird. *Aualee, Avada, Avae, Avah, Avaset, Ave, Aveen, Avelyn, Avia, Aviana, Aviance, Avilina, Avis, Aviva, Eva.*

Avery (English) Elf ruler. *Avary, Ave, Averee, Averi, Averie, Aves.*

Bailey (English) A bailiff. *Bailee, Bailley, Baillie, Baily, Bali, Baylee, Bayley, Bayli, Baylie.*

Breanna (Irish) Strong. *Bre-Ann, Bre-Anna, Breanda, Breana, Breann, Breanne, Breawna, Bree, Breean, Breeana, Breeana, Breiana, Breiann, Brianna, Brie.*

Brianna (Irish) Strong; female version of Brian. *Brana, Breana, Breann, Breanna, Bria, Briahna, Brianda, Briannah, Brianne, Brianni, Briauna, Brina, Bryanna, Bryna.*

Brittany (Latin) From England. *Brinnee, Brit, Brita, Britanee, Britannia, Britanny, Britany, Briteny, Britley, Britlyn, Britney, Britni, Britt, Britta, Brittan, Brittaney, Brittani, Brittania, Brittanie, Brittannia, Britteny, Brittni, Brittnie, Brittny.*

Brooke (English) A brook or stream. *Brook, Brookey, Brookie, Brooky.*

Brooklyn (English, American) A place name and combination of Brook and Lynn. *Brookellen, Brookelyn, Brooklin, Brooklynn, Brooklynne.*

Caitlin (Irish) Pure; virginal. *Caeley, Cailey, Cailin, Cait, Caitlan, Caitleen, Caitlen, Caitlene, Caitline, Caitlinn, Caitlyn, Catleen, Catlin, Catlyn, Catlynne, Catriona, Katelyn, Katlin.*

Camille (French) A religious helper. *Cam, Cama, Camala, Cami, Camila, Camile, Camill, Cammie, Cammille, Cammilyn, Cammy, Cammyl, Cammylle, Camyla, Chamille, Kamila, Kamilla, Kamille, Mila.*

Camryn (English) Female version of Cameron, meaning bent nose. *Camren, Camrin.*

Carmen (Hebrew, Latin) A garden; a song. *Carma, Carmaine, Carman, Carmel, Carmelina, Carmelinda, Carmelita, Carmelle, Carmencita, Carmene, Carmi, Carmia, Carmin, Carmina, Carmine, Carmita, Carmon, Carmynn, Carmynne, Charmaine, Chita, Karmel, Karmelita, Karmelle, Karmen, Mela, Melita.*

Caroline (Latin, French, German) Small and feminine. *Caralin, Caraline, Carileen, Carilene, Carly, Caro, Carolann, Carolanne, Carolenia, Carolin, Carolina, Carolyn, Carolynn, Carolynne, Carrie, Carroleen, Carrolene, Carrolin, Carroline, Cary, Charlene, Karolin, Karolina, Karoline, Karolyn, Karolyna, Karolyne, Karolynn, Karolynne.*

Cassandra (Greek) A prophet. *Casandera, Casandra, Casandrey, Casandri, Casandria, Casaundra, Casaundri, Casaundria, Casondra, Casondre, Casondri, Casondria, Cass, Cassandri, Cassandry, Cassaundra, Cassaundri, Cassie, Casson, Cassondra, Cassondri, Cassondria, Cassundra, Cassundri, Cassundria, Kasandera, Kasandra, Kass, Kassandra, Kassaundra, Kassie, Kasson, Kassondra, Sandra, Sandy.*

Cassidy (Gaelic) Clever; intelligent. *Casadee, Casdi, Casadie, Cass, Cassadi, Cassadie, Cassadina, Cassady, Cassiddy, Cassidee, Cassidey, Cassidi, Cassidie, Cassity, Kasady, Kassidey, Kassidi, Kassidie, Kassidy.*

Charlotte (French) Petite; womanly. *Carla, Carlotta, Carly, Char, Chara, Charla, Charle, Charil, Charl, Charla, Charle, Charlene, Charlet, Charletta, Charlette, Charlie, Charlisa, Charlita, Charlott, Charlotta, Charmaine, Charolette, Charolot, Charolotte.*

Chelsea (English) A port. *Chelcy, Chelese, Cheli, Chellsie, Chelse, Chelsea, Chelsee, Chelsey, Chelsi, Chelsie, Chelsy, Kelsey, Keslie, Kelsy.*

Chloe (Greek) In bloom. *Chlöe, Chloé, Chloee, Clo, Cloe, Cloey, Khloe, Kloe.*

Christina (Greek) A Christian. *Chris, Chrissa, Chrissy, Christa, Christeena, Christena, Christi, Christian, Christiana, Christie, Christin, Christine, Christinea, Christinna, Christy, Christyna, Chrys, Chrystena, Chrystina, Chrystyna, Christa, Cristeena, Christena, Cristina, Cristy, Crystal, Crystina, Kirsten, Kris, Krissy, Kristeena, Kristen, Kristin, Kristina, Kristine.*

Christine (Greek) A Christian; form of Christina. *Chris, Christeen, Christen, Christene, Christi, Christin, Cristine, Christy, Chrys, Chrystine, Cristeen, Cristine, Crystine, Kristine.*

Claire (Latin, Greek, French) Bright and clear. *Clair, Clairee, Claireen, Claireta, Clairette, Clairy, Clara, Clare, Clarette, Clarice, Claris, Clarisse, Clarrie, Clarry, Klair.*

Courtney (English, French) From the court. *Corey, Cort, Cortie, Cortney, Courtenay, Courtene, Courteney, Courtnay, Courtnee, Courtni, Courtnie, Courtny, Kort, Kortnee, Kortney.*

Dakota (Native American) Tribal name; friend. *Dacota, Dakohta, Dakotah, Dakotha, Dakotta, Dekoda, Dekota, Dekotah.*

Danielle (Hebrew, French) Judged by God; female form of Daniel. *Danae, Danee, Daneen, Daneille, Danela, Danele, Danella, Danette, Daney, Dani, Dania, Danial, Danialle, Danica, Danice, Danie, Daniela, Daniell, Daniella, Danika, Danila, Danita, Danniele, Danniell, Danniella, Dannielle, Danya, Danyel, Danyelle.*

Destiny (French) Fate. *Destanee, Destanie, Destannie, Destany, Desteney, Destinay, Destinee, Destinei, Destini, Destinie, Destinyi, Destnay, Destney, Destonie, Destony, Destyn, Destyni.*

Ella (English, Greek, German) Beautiful; all; a fairy. *Ellamae, Elle, Ellia, Ellie, Elly.*

Emilie (German) Form of Emily, meaning industrious. *Em, Emalee, Emalie, Emile, Emilee, Emiley, Emili, Emmilee, Emmile.*

Emily (German) Industrious. *Eimile, Em, Emaili, Emaily, Emalie, Emelene, Emelia, Emelina, Emeline, Emelyn, Emeylyne, Emi, Emie, Emila, Emile, Emilea, Emilee, Emili, Emilie, Emma, Emmalee, Emmali, Emmaline, Emmalynn, Emmeline, Emmi, Emmie, Emylynn, Emlyn.*

Emma (German) Complete; collective. *Emmie, Emmy, Ema, Em, Emmee, Emily, Emmalee.*

Erika (Scandinavian, English) All powerful. *Arika, Ayrika, Enricka, Enrika, Erica, Ericah, Ericca, Ericka, Erikka, Errika, Eryka, Eyrica.*

Erin (Irish, Gaelic) Peace; a name for Ireland; western island. *Eran, Eren, Erena, Erene, Ereni, Eri, Erian, Erina, Erine, Erinn, Erinna, Erinne, Errin, Eryn, Erynn, Erynna, Erynne.*

Evelyn (French, English, Hebrew) A hazelnut; positive; from Eve, meaning life. *Aveline, Eoelene, Ev, Evaleen, Evalene, Evalenne, Evaline, Evalyn, Evalynn, Evalynne, Eveline, Evelyne, Evelynn, Evelynne, Evlin, Evline, Evlun, Evlynn.*

Faith (English) Faithful; loyal. *Faithe, Fay, Faye, Fayth, Faythe.*

Fiona (Irish) Fair; white. *Fionna, Fionne, Fionnula.*

Gabriella (Hebrew) Form of Gabrielle, meaning devoted or faithful to God. *Gab, Gabbie, Gabby, Gabriala, Gabrialla, Gabriela, Gabriellia, Gabrilla.*

Gabrielle (Hebrew, French) Devoted or faithful to God. *Gabi, Gabielle, Gabrial, Gabriana, Gabriela, Gabriele, Gabriell, Gabriella, Gabrina, Gaby, Gabby, Galya, Gavra, Gavriella, Gavrila.*

Georgia (Latin, Greek) A farmer. *Georgeann, Georgeanne, Georgeina, Georgena, Georgene, Georgette, Georggann, Georgganne, Georgi, Georgiann, Georgianne, Georgie, Georgienne, Georgina, Georgy, Gina, Giorgi, Giorgia, Giorgie, Giorgyna, Jirina, Jirka, Jorga, Jorgia, Jorja.*

Grace (Latin) Graceful. *Engracie, Graca, Gracey, Graci, Gracia, Graciana, Gracie, Gracinha, Gracy, Grata, Gratia, Gray, Grayce, Grazia, Graziella, Grazielle, Graziosa, Grazyna.*

Gracie (Latin) From the name Grace, meaning graceful. *Graci, Gracy, Graecie, Gray.*

Hailey (English) A hay field. *Hailea, Hailee, Haili, Hailie, Hailley, Hailly, Halee, Haley, Hallie.*

Haley (Scandinavian) A hero. *Halee, Haleigh, Hali, Halie, Hailey, Hallie, Hayley.*

Holly (English) A holly tree. *Hollee, Holley, Holli, Hollie, Hollinda, Hollyann, Hollye.*

Isabella (Italian, Spanish) Consecrated to God; form of Isabel. *Isabela, Isabelle, Isabello, Izabela, Izabella.*

Jada (Hebrew) Wise. *Jadah.*

Jade (Spanish) A green gem. *Jada, Jadah, Jadea, Jadeann, Jadee, Jaden, Jadera, Jadi, Jadie, Jadielyn, Jadienne, Jadira, Jady, Jaeda, Jaida, Jaide, Jaiden, Jay, Jaycee, Jayde, Jadee, Jaydra.*

Jamie (Hebrew) Supplanter; female form of James. *Jama, Jamay, Jamea, Jamee, Jami, Jamia, Jamilynn, Jammie, Jamy, Jamye, Jayme, Jaymee, Jaymie.*

Jasleen (Sikh, Punjabi) Singing God's praises. *Jas, Jaslene, Jasline, Jaz.*

Jasmine (Persian) A jasmine flower. *Jas, Jasamine, Jasime, Jasimen, Jasmain, Jasmaine, Jasman, Jasme, Jasmeen, Jasmeet, Jasmene, Jasmin, Jasmina, Jasminen, Jasminne, Jasmira, Jasmit, Jasmon, Jasmond, Jasmyn, Jassma, Jassmain, Jassmaine, Jassmin, Jassmit, Jassmyn, Jazmin, Jazmine, Jaxxmun, Jazzy, Jess, Jessamine, Jessamy, Jessamyn, Mine, Mina, Yasiman, Yasman, Yasmina, Yasmine.*

Jayden (American) God heard; form of Jaden. *Jaden, Jay, Jaydeen, Jaydin, Jaydon, Jaydyn, Jaye.*

Jenna (Arabic, Scottish, English) Small bird; a white spirit; form of Jennifer. *Jena, Jenesi, Jenn, Jennabel, Jennah, Jennalee, Jennalyn, Jennasee, Jennat, Jennay, Jhenna, Jynna.*

Jennifer (Welsh) A white spirit. *Gen, Gennefur, Jen, Jenefer, Jenife, Jenifer, Jeniferr, Jeniffer, Jenipher, Jenn, Jenna, Jennae, Jennafer, Jenni, Jennie, Jeniffer, Jennifer, Jennipher, Jenniphur, Jenny, Jennyfer, Jennypher.*

Jessica (Hebrew) Wealthy; grace of God. *Jesi, Jesica, Jesika, Jess, Jessa, Jessaca, Jessalyn, Jessca, Jesscia, Jesse, Jesseca, Jessey, Jessi, Jessicca, Jessicka, Jessie, Jessika, Jessiya, Jessy, Jessyca, Jessyka, Jessykah, Jezeca, Jezica, Jezika.*

Jessie (Hebrew, Scottish) Form of Jessica and Jean, meaning God's grace. *Jescie, Jesey, Jess, Jessaca, Jessalynn, Jesse, Jessee, Jessi, Jessia, Jessika, Jessiya, Jessy, Jessye.*

Jillian (Latin, English) Youth; a girl. *Gilli, Gillian, Gillie, Jilana, Jilian, Jiliana, Jiliann, Jilianne, Jillienna, Jilienne, Jill, Jilliana, Jilliane, Jilliann, Jililanne, Jillie, Jillien, Jillienne, Jillion, Jilliyanne, Jilliyn, Jilyan, Jilyanna.*

Jocelyn (Latin) Happy. *Gosceline, Joce, Jocelie, Jocelin, Joceline, Jocelle, Jocelyne, Jocelynn, Jocelynne, Joci, Jocia, Jocie, Jocinta, Josaline, Joscelin, Josceline, Joscelyn, Joclyn, Joclynn, Jocylan, Jocylen, Joseline, Joselyn, Joselyne, Josiline, Josline, Jossalin, Joycelyn.*

Jordan (Hebrew) To decend or follow. *Johrdon, Jordain, Jordana, Jordane, Jordanna, Jorden, Jordenne, Jordeyn, Jordi, Jordine, Jordon, Jordonna, Jordyn, Jordyne, Jordynne, Joudane, Jourdan.*

Jordyn (Hebrew) Form of Jordan, meaning to decend or follow. *Jhordyn, Jordin, Jordine, Jordy, Jordyne, Jordynne.*

Julia (Latin) Young. *Iulia, Jula, Julcia, Julee, Juley, Juli, Juliana, Juliane, Julianna, Juliann, Julianne, Julica, Julie, Juliet, Julina, Juline, Julinka, Juliska, Julissa, July, Julya, Julyssa, Juka.*

Kaitlyn (Irish) Form of Caitlin, meaning pure. *Kaitlynn, Kaitlynne, Katelyn, Katelynn.*

Katelyn (Irish) Form of Caitlin, meaning pure. *Kaetlin, Kaetlyn, Kaitlin, Kaitlynne, Kat, Katalin, Katelan, Katelin, Katelynn, Kate-Lynn, Katline, Katy.*

Katherine (Greek) Pure; chaste. *Caitriona, Caren, Caron, Caryn, Caye, Cat, Cath, Catharine, Catherine, Ekaterina, Kaethe, Kai, Kaila, Kait, Kaitlin, Karen, Karena, Karin, Karina, Karine, Kat, Kata, Kataleen, Katalin, Katalina, Katarina, Kate, Katee, Katerina, Katey, Kath, Kathann, Kathanne, Katharine, Kathereen, Katheren, Katherene, Katherenne, Katherin, Katherina, Katheryn, Katheryne, Kathi, Kathleen, Kathryn, Kathy, Kathyrine, Katina, Katie, Katrina, Kattrina, Katy, Kay, Kit, Kitti, Kittie, Kitty.*

Katrina (German) Form of Katherine, meaning pure; chaste. *Catrina, Katja, Katreen, Katreena, Katrelle, Katrene, Katrice, Katrin,*

Katrine, Katrinia, Katriona, Katryn, Katryna, Kattrina, Kattryna, Katuska, Katya, Kay.

Kayla (Arabic, Hebrew) A crown of laurels. *Cala, Cayla, Kaela, Kaelee, Kaelene, Kaeli, Kaeleigh, Kaelie, Kaelin, Kaelyn, Kaila, Kailan, Kailee, Kaileen, Kailene, Kailey, Kailin, Kailynne, Kala, Kalan, Kalee, Kaleigh, Kalren, Kaley, Kalie, Kalin, Kalyn, Kayana, Kayanna, Kaye, Kaylah, Kaylan, Kaylea, Kaylee, Kayleen, Kayleigh, Kaylene, Kayley, Kayli, Kaylia, Kaylin, Kaylle, Keyla.*

Kaylee (American) Combination of Kay and Lee; form of Kayla, meaning crown of laurels. *Cayley, Kaelea, Kaeleah, Kaelee, Kaeli, Kaelie, Kailea, Kaileah, Kailee, Kayle, Kaylea, Kayleah, Kaylei, Kayleigh, Kaylie.*

Kelsey (English, Scottish) A port; an island. *Chelsey, Kelcey, Kelci, Kelcie, Kelcy, Kellsie, Kelda, Kellsee, Kellsey, Kellsie, Kellsy, Kelsa, Kelsea, Kelsee, Kelseigh, Kelsi, Kelsie, Kelsy, Keslie.*

Kendra (English) Knowledgeable. *Ken, Kena, Kenadrea, Kendrah, Kendre, Kendria, Kenna, Kenndra, Kennie, Kentrae, Kindra, Kinna, Kyndra.*

Kennedy (Irish) A helmeted chief. *Kenna, Kennady, Kennedie, Kenny.*

Kimberly (English) A ruler. *Kim, Kimba, Kimber, Kimber-Lea, Kimber-Lee, Kimbereley, Kimberely, Kimberlee, Kimberleigh, Kimberli, Kimberlie, Kimberlyn, Kimbria, Kimbrie, Kimbry, Kimmie, Kimmy, Kymberly.*

Kyla (Irish, English) Beautiful; a crown; narrow. *Kiela, Kila, Ky, Kylen, Kylene, Kylia, Kylynn.*

Kylie (Australian Aboriginal) Boomerang. *Kay, Kayle, Kayleigh, Keiley, Keilley, Keilly, Keily, Kiley, Kye, Kyla, Kylee, Kyleigh, Kylene, Leigh.*

Kyra (Greek) A lady. *Keera, Keira, Kira, Kyrah, Kyrene, Kyria, Kyriah, Kyrie, Kyry.*

Laura (Latin) A laurel. *Lara, Lauralee, Laureana, Larette, Laural, Laure, Laureana, Laurel, Laurelen, Lauren, Laurena, Lauret, Laureta, Lauretta, Laurette, Lauriana, Lauriane, Laurie, Laurin,*

Lauryn, Lolly, Lora, Loren, Lorena, Lorenza, Loret, Loreta, Loretta, Lorette, Lori, Lorin, Lorinda, Lorita, Lorna, Lorrie, Lorrin, Lorry, Loryn, Loura.

Laurence (French, Latin) A crown of laurels. *Laura, Laurance, Luarencia.*

Laurie (Latin) From Laura, meaning a laurel. *Laura, Laure, Lauri, Laury, Lor, Lore, Lori, Lorie, Lorry, Lory.*

Lea (Hebrew) Form of Leah, meaning weary; tired. *Lia, Liah.*

Leslie (English, Scottish) Small meadow; form of Lesley, meaning grey fortress. *Lee, Les, Leslea, Leslee, Lesleigh, Lesley, Lesli, Leslie, Lesly, Lesslie, Lezlee, Lezley, Lezli, Lezlie.*

Lily (Latin) A flower. *Lil, Lili, Lilie, Lilia, Lilian, Liliana, Lilianne, Lilias, Lilijana, Liliosa, LIlium, Lille, Lilli, Lillie, Lilly, Lillye, Lis, Lilye, Lilly Ann.*

Mackenzie (Irish) The daughter of a wise leader. *Mac, Macenzie, Mack, Mackensi, Mackensie, Mackenzee, Mackenzi, Mackenzia, Mackenzy, Mackenzie, Mackey, Mackie, McKinsey, McKinzie, Mekenzie, Mykenzie.*

Madeline (Hebrew) A woman from Magdala; a high tower. *Lena, Lene, Mada, Madalaina, Madaleine, Madalena, Madaline, Maddalena, Maddi, Maddie, Maddy, Madelaine, Madelayne, Madeleine, Madelena, Madelene, Madelia, Madelina, Madella, Madelle, Madelon, Madelyn, Madi, Madigan, Madge, Madlin, Madline, Madoline, Mady, Mae, Magda, Maida, Malena, Mattie, May.*

Madison (German, English) Warrior's son; son of Maud. *Maddie, Maddison, Maddy, Madisen, Madissen, Madisyn, Madysin, Madyson.*

Makayla (English, Hebrew) Female form of Michael, meaning who is like God. *Makaila, Makala, Michaela, Michaelya, Mikaela, Mikayla, Mikaylah.*

Makenna (Celtic, American) From McKenna, meaning able. *Mack, Mackena, Mackenna, Makena, Mckenna.*

Maria (Hebrew, Italian, Spanish) Form of Mary, meaning bitter. *Maja, Malia, Malita, Mar, Marea, Mareah, Maree, Mareea,*

Mariabella, Mariae, Mariah, Marica, Marie, Mariesa, Mariha, Marija, Marike, Mariya, Marja, Marucha, Marya, Mezi, Mitzi, Ri.

Marissa (Latin) Form of Maris, meaning from the sea. *Marce, Maressa, Mari, Marina, Marisa, Marisha, Marisse, Maritza, Marrissa, Marrissia, Marysa, Marysah, Merisa, Merissa, Morissa, Rissa.*

Maude (Hebrew, German) From Madeline, meaning woman of Magdala; strong in combat. *Maud, Maudie, Maudine, Maudlin, Maudline.*

Maya (Hindu, Latin) The creative power of God. *Maia, Maiya, Mayah, Mya, Myah, Mye.*

Mckenna (Celtic, American) Able. *Macenna, Mackenna, Makenna.*

Megan (Greek, Irish) Strong; a pearl. *Maegan, Magan, Margaret, Meagan, Meaghen, Meg, Megean, Megen, Meggan, Meggen, Meggi, Meggie, Meghan, Meghann, Megyn, Meygan.*

Melanie (Greek) Dark-skinned. *Malania, Malanie, Mel, Mela, Meila, Melainie, Melania, Melaine, Melana, Melane, Melani, Melania, Melaniya, Melanka, Melanney, Melannie, Melanny, Melany, Melanya, Melashka, Melasya, Melenia, Melina, Melka, Mellanie, Mellie, Melloney, Mellony, Melly, Meloni, Melonie, Melony, Melyne, Melynne, Milana, Milena, Milya.*

Melissa (Greek) Honey; a bee. *Malissa, Mallissa, Melesa, Melessa, Melicent, Melisa, Melisande, Melisandra, Melisandre, Melise, Melisha, Melisia, Melissande, Melissandre, Melisse, Mellissa, Mellissia, Meliza, Melizah, Mellie, Mellisa, Mellissa, Melly, Melysa, Melysah, Melyssuh, Milisa, Milissa, Millicent, Millie, Milly, Misha, Missy, Mylisa, Mylisia, Mylissa, Mylissia, Lis, Lisa, Lissa.*

Mia (Italian) Mine. *Me, Mea, Meah, Meya, Miah, Mya.*

Michelle (French) Who is like God. *Machele, Machelle, Mechele, Mechelle, Meschele, Meschelle, Meshele, Meshelle, Mia, Michele, Michell, Michella, Mish, Mishelle, Mitchele, Mitchelle, Nichelle.*

Miranda (Latin) Admirable; superb. *Maranda, Marenda, Meranda, Mira, Miran, Miranada, Mirandia, Mirinda, Mironda, Mirrie, Muranda, Myranda, Randa, Randee, Randey, Randi, Randie, Randy.*

Molly (Irish) Form of Mary, meaning bitter. *Moli, Moll, Mollee, Molley, Molli, Mollie, Mollissa.*

Morgan (Welsh) One who lives by the sea. *Mor, Morey, Morgana, Morganica, Morganne, Morganette, Morgen, Morgyn, Morrigan.*

Natalie (Latin) Born on Christmas. *Nat, Natala, Natalea, Natalee, Natalene, Natali, Natalia, Natalina, Nataline, Natalka, Natalle, Nataly, Natalya, Natalyn, Natasha, Natelie, Nathalia, Nathalie, Natalja, Nathaly, Nati, Natie, Natilie, Natlie, Nattalie, Nattie, Nattlee, Natty, Noel, Noelle, Talia, Tallie, Tally, Tasha, Tosh, Tosha.*

Natasha (Greek, Latin) Reborn; form of Natalie, meaning born on Christmas. *Nahtasha, Nastasia, Nastassia, Nastassja, Nastassya, Nastasya, Nat, Natacha, Natasa, Natashah, Natashia, Natashja, Natashka, Natasia, Natassija, Natassja, Natasza, Nathasha, Natisha, Netasha, Netosha, Nitasha, Notasha, Tashi, Tashia, Tasis, Tassa, Tassie.*

Nicole (Greek, French) People of victory. *Colette, Collette, Cosette, Nacole, Nakita, Necole, Nica, Nichol, Nichole, Nicholette, Nicholle, Nick, Nicki, Nickie, Nickol, Nickola, Nickole, Nickolia, Nicky, Nicol, Nicola, Nicolette, Nicolle, Nikki, Nikky, Nikol, Nikola, Nikole, Nikoletta, Nikolette, Nycki, Nyki, Nykki, Nykky, Nyky.*

Noemie (Hebrew) Form of Naomi, meaning pleasant one; beauty. *Noemi, Nohemi, Nomi.*

Olivia (Latin) An olive tree. *Lioa, Lioia, Llovie, Liv, Livie, Livvy, Olia, Oliva, Olive, Olivea, Oliveah, Olivetta, Olivette, Olivianne, Ollie, Olly, Olva, Olyvia.*

Paige (French) Form of Page, meaning a young child or attendant. *Payge.*

Paris (English, French) The capital city of France. *Pareece, Parie, Paries, Parice, Parisa, Pariss, Parissa, Parris, Parrish.*

Rebecca (Hebrew) Tied and bound. *Becca, Becki, Beckie, Becky, Rabecca, Rabecka, Reba, Rebbecca, Rebeca, Rebeccah, Rebeccea, Rebeckah, Rebeka, Rebekah, Rebekke, Rebeque, Rebi, Reby, Rheba, Riva, Rivca, Rivka.*

Riley (Irish) Brave; courageous. *Reilly, Rileigh, Rilie, Rylee, Ryleigh, Ryley, Rylie.*

Sabrina (Latin) One from a border land. *Breena, Brina, Brinna, Rena, Rina, Sabe, Sabre, Sabreena, Sabrena, Sabrinia, Sabrinna, Sebree, Sebrina, Zabrina.*

Sadie (English, Hebrew) A princess. *Sada, Sadah, Sade, Sadee, Sadi, Sady, Sadye, Saidee, Saydee, Saydie, Sydel, Sydell, Sydelle, Shaday.*

Sage (Latin, English) Wise; a spice. *Sagia, Saige, Sayge.*

Samantha (Aramaic, Hebrew) A good listener; one who listens to God. *Sam, Samanath, Samanatha, Samanitha, Samanta, Samanth, Samanthe, Samanthi, Samanthia, Samella, Samentha, Sami, Sammantha, Sammatha, Sammee, Sammey, Sammi, Sammie, Sammy, Semantha, Semmantha, Simantha, Symantha.*

Sara (Hebrew) Form of Sarah, meaning princess. *Saalee, Sae, Sarah, Saree, Sarra, Sarrie, Serra.*

Savannah (Spanish) A treeless plain; a place name. *Sahvannah, Sava, Savana, Savanah, Savanha, Savanna, Savannha, Savonna, Sevanna, Sevannah, Seven, Syvanna, Syvannah.*

Shayla (Irish) A fairy palace; form of Shea, meaning dignified. *Shay, Shaylagh, Shaylah, Shaylea, Shaylee, Shayley, Shayli, Shaylie, Shaylin, Shayly, Shaylyn, Shaylynn, Shea, Shey, Sheyla, Sheylyn.*

Shelby (English) A sheltered town; ledged estate. *Chelby, Schelby, Shel, Shelbe, Shelbee, Shelbey, Shelbi, Shelbie, Shellby.*

Sierra (Spanish) A saw-toothed mountain range; a place name. *Ciara, Ciera, Cierra, Seara, Searah, Searrah, Seera, Seiarra, Seira, Seirra, Siara, Siarah, Siarra, Siera, Sierrah, Sierre.*

Simran (Hindu) A gift from God. *Symran.*

Sophia (Greek) Intelligence; wise. *Sofeea, Sofi, Sofia, Soficita, Sofie, Sofya, Sophea, Sophey, Sophie, Sophy, Sophya, Zofia, Zosia.*

Sophie (Greek) Form of Sophia, meaning intelligence; wise. *Sofi, Sofia, Sofie, Sophey, Sophi, Sophy.*

Stephanie (Greek) A crown. *Stef, Stefania, Stefanie, Steffie, Stepania, Stepanie, Steph, Stephana, Stephania, Stephannie, Stephany, Stepheney, Stephenie, Stephie, Stephine, Stephney, Stephnie, Stesha, Steshka, Stevana, Stevanee, Stevi, Stevie.*

Sydney (French) From the French city Saint Denis. *Sy, Syd, Sydania, Sydel, Sydell, Sydelle, Sydna, Sydnie, Sydny, Sydnye.*

Talia (Hebrew, Greek) Heavenly dew; blooming. *Tahlia, Tai, Tali, Taliah, Talitha, Taliya, Talley, Tallia, Tallie, Tally, Tallya, Talora, Talya, Talyah, Thalie, Thalya.*

Taylor (English) A tailor. *Tailor, Taiylor, Talor, Talora, Tay, Taye, Tayia, Taylar, Tayler, Tayllor, Taylore.*

Teagan (Welsh, Irish) Beautiful; little poet. *Taegen, Teaghen, Teague, Teegan, Teeghan, Tegan, Teghan, Tegin, Teigan, Tiegan, Teige, Tigan.*

Tessa (Greek, Italian) A harvester; a countess. *Tesa, Tesha, Tesia, Tess, Tessia, Tessie, Teza, Tezia.*

Tianna (Greek) Form of Tiana, meaning princess. *Tana, Tea, Teana, Teanna, Teeana, Teeanna, Tia, Tiane, Tianne, Tiahna, Tianna, Tiona.*

Tiffany (Greek, French) The appearance of God. *Fannie, Fanny, Taffanay, Taffany, Tifaney, Tifanie, Tifany, Tiff, Tiffaney, Tiffani, Tiffanie, Tiffanny, Tiffeney, Tiffenie, Tiffi, Tiffie, Tiffiny, Tiffnay, Tiffney, Tiffnie, Tiffny, Tiffy, Tiphanie, Tiphany, Tyfannie.*

Trinity (Latin) A triad; three in one. *Trin, Trini, Trinie, Trinita, Trinitee, Triniti, Triny, Trynity.*

Vanessa (Greek) A butterfly. *Nes, Ness, Nessa, Van, Vanassa, Vanassah, Vanesah, Vanesha, Vanesia, Vanessah, Vanesse, Vanessia, Vanetta, Vaneza, Vania, Vaniece, Vaniessa, Vanija, Vanika, Vanisa, Vanissa, Vanita, Vanna, Vannessa, Vannesza, Vanni, Vannie, Vanny, Vanora, Venesa, Venessa, Vennessa.*

Victoria (Latin) Victor; winner. *Torey, Tori, Toria, Torie, Torrey, Torrie, Torrye, Tory, Vic, Vick, Vicki, Vicky, Victoire, Victoriah, Victoriana, Victorie, Victorina, Victorine, Victory, Vikky, Viktoria, Vitoria, Vittoria, Vyctoria.*

Zoe (Greek) Life. *Zoé, Zoë, Zoee, Zoelie, Zoeline, Zoey, Zoie, Zooey.*

KIDS' KORNER

Even though people often pronounce it wrong, Denique says she wouldn't ever want another name. The main reason she doesn't want a change? "My mom chose it," explains the 13-year-old, which is why she likes it so much.

Eight-year-old Madison wishes that her name wasn't so long. "I can't fit it on the page in bubble letters, even if it's the biggest page in the world," she complains. But she does like that it's pretty and raves about the fact that she was named after her parents' favourite place to eat.

Nine-year-old Taylor likes his name "because it means to cut and I like art." The one bad part about being called Taylor: "some kids make fun of it and this hurts my feelings," he says.

"My grandpa gave me this name and since everyone in my family respects him, they let him name me," explains 12-year-old Firieba. And she's quite pleased with his choice. "My name means unique and it really describes me," she says. But the one thing she doesn't like is the fact that it rhymes with her sister's name. "My mom has mixed up our names ever since my little sister was born," she complains.

When asked why he likes his name, four-year-old Jordan says, "Because I think it is silly." And he can't decide on anything bad to say about it. If forced to choose another name, he'd pick Alex "because that's my brother's name," he says.

Three-year-old Josh doesn't know why his parents gave him this name, but he likes it because it's spelled "J-O-S-H-U-A." If he had to pick another one, Josh says he'd choose "Peter. Yeah, Peter is a good name."

Ryan's parents chose his name because it sounds masculine and can suit both a kid and a grownup. "I like that it's short and that it stands for little king," says the 12-year-old. But as a kid, he used to get tripped up by the "y" and had a tough time spelling it.

Popularity Charts

Just because we share a nationality or a place of residence doesn't mean we agree on the names we like best. Take a look at the popular selections in Québec, for example. Only Sarah and Megan are common to top picks in other provinces while William is the sole match for boys. The most likely reason for this discrepancy is the abundance of creative names like Mathis and Olivier that French Canadians love.

But differences aren't limited to *la belle province*. Jasmine was a popular girl's pick for those living up north while Abigail is favoured in the Atlantic region. As for boys, there's even more of a variation. The favoured Ethan only made it onto the top lists in the Atlantic, Prairie and Western provinces. And while all of the top 10 popular boys' names in the Atlantic were shared with other regions, Daniel was only a favourite in Central Canada.

Below are charts of the top 20 names in each Canadian region. Since not every province keeps records of their most popular names, and there's no central Canadian source that houses this information, there are a few provinces and territories missing from the data.

Most Popular Baby Names in the Atlantic Provinces

Boys

Ethan	Benjamin	Joshua
Matthew	Connor	Alexander
Ryan	Nicholas	Logan
Jacob		

Girls

Emma	Sarah	Abigail
Madison	Olivia	Paige
Emily	Grace	Lauren
Hannah		

Most Popular Baby Names in Québec

Boys

William	Mathis	Thomas
Samuel	Olivier	Anthony
Jermey	Xavier	Alexis
Gabriel		

Girls

Noemie	Laurence	Jade
Gabrielle	Lea	Laurie
Megan	Sarah	Audrey
Ariane		

Most Popular Baby Names in Central Canada

Boys

Matthew	Michael	Andrew
Joshua	Ryan	Alexander
Nicholas	Daniel	Tyler
Jacob		

Girls

Emily	Hannah	Julia
Sarah	Madison	Samantha
Jessica	Victoria	Olivia
Emma		

 FUN FACTS

In Japan, the government approves characters that are allowed to be used in names. Japanese parents are currently asking that they ban symbols that represent negative images (cancer; prostitute; buttocks) from the approved list.

The name Trinity (after one of the main characters from the film *The Matrix*) gained huge popularity after the movie's release in 1999.

Elizabeth and Katherine (also spelled Catherine) have made the top 50 list in the U.S. for 100 years.

Can't find a name you know is popular? Many of today's common names have sprung from old-time favourites like Anthony and Isabel. And a large majority of them, like Hannah, Sarah, Jacob and Matthew, have strong religious connections. So your best bet is to check out Chapter 11: Traditional Names. You'll most likely find them there.

Most Popular Baby Names in the Prairies

Boys

Ethan	Ryan	Alexander
Joshua	Tyler	Logan
Matthew	Michael	Connor
Jacob		

Girls

Emily	Sarah	Sydney
Emma	Hailey	Megan
Madison	Olivia	Jessica
Hannah		

Most Popular Baby Names in Western Canada

Boys

Ethan	Ryan	Nicholas
Joshua	Alexander	Benjamin
Matthew	Liam	Nathan
Jacob		

Girls

Emma	Sarah	Jessica
Emily	Madison	Isabella
Olivia	Grace	Megan
Hannah		

CANUCK TRIVIA

In 2000, 1,410 baby boys were named Matthew in Ontario.
In 2000, 1,080 baby girls were named Emily in Ontario.

Most Popular Baby Names in Northern Canada

Boys

Cole	William	James
Matthew	Andrew	Logan
Joshua	Jacob	Liam
Michael		

Girls

Emily	Alyssa	Samantha
Hannah	Jasmine	Jessica
Emma	Olivia	Taylor
Sarah		

Web World

Still can't find a name to suit your unborn babe? Luckily, the Web is filled with pages that are chock full with helpful naming information. I'd be surprised if you can't find at least one name you like in the thousands listed on these sites:

www.babynames.com	*www.babyzone.com/babynames*
www.babycenter.com/babyname	*www.babynamesworld.com*
www.ssa.gov/OACT/babynames	*123-baby-names.com*
www.babychatter.com	*www.popularbabynames.com*

Chapter 11

-☆-

Traditional Names

Vivika Apple too out-there for your liking? Then a traditional name may be more your style. What I mean by "traditional" is a name that's been around for centuries (like since Jesus was born) or decades (since the days of Great Aunt Ethel). Whether they're based on religious beliefs or ancient history, these types of names have definite benefits: they're easy to spell, simple to pronounce and not so unusual that people ask "Huh?" when you first introduce yourself.

Traditional names are also easier for couples to agree on. Because many of the old-fashioned variety haven't been heard of for years, it's less likely that either you or your partner has poor associations with any of them—unless, of course, you had a particularly cruel grandparent or simply think the names sound ancient.

If you're worried that a traditional name will be too outdated for your little one, don't be. Popular names from the early twentieth century are coming back in style. Take Alexander, Matthew, Joshua, Emma, Emily and Hannah, for example. All of these graced a most-popular list in the 1900s, and each one has come back in full force over the past few years, jumping onto the nation's top 10 lists.

Religious Names

From saints to Bible bad guys, this list of spiritual names includes entries from religions around the world.

Religious Boys' Names

Abdul-Khaaliq (Muslim) The creator's servant.

Abel (Hebrew, Assyrian) Breath; child. The God-loving, obedient younger brother of Cain and son of Adam and Eve. *Abe, Abele, Abell, Abey, Abie, Able, Adal, Avel, Ibila.*

Adam (Hebrew) Earth; created by God. Eve's beau and the first man to inhabit the earth. *Adamson, Ad, Adahm, Adamek, Adamik, Adamo, Adao, Adas, Adamka, Adamko, Adem, Addamm, Addams, Addie, Addis, Addison, Addy, Adhamh, Adné, Adok, Adomas.*

Ajitesh (Hindu) Another name for Hindu Lord Vishnu. Preserver of the universe, Lord Vishnu has four hands. One holds a discus to remind us of the "wheel of time," a second holds a conch shell to represent the spread of the divine sound "Om," another holds a lotus, the symbol for magnificent existence and the final hand grasps a mace to represent Lord Vishnu's power to punish disobedience.

Akhuratha (Hindu) One with a mouse as his charioteer. Another name for the Hindu elephant god, Lord Ganesh.

Amarpreet (Sikh) God's immortal love. Sikhs worship only one god and do not use idols or images. They are free to pray anywhere and anytime. Their god is beyond mere description.

Anil (Hindu) Another name for Vayu, the god of wind. A somewhat ornery god with destructive tendencies, Vayu has trouble repressing his anger. He once attacked Mount Meru and broke its summit. He was also very unfaithful to his wife Vishwakarma and has many illegitimate children from numerous Hindu women.

Apollo (Greek) God of the arts. As lord of music and poetry, Apollo had close connections with many muses. With strong ties to law, philosophy, archery, prophecy and the care of flocks and herds, he was considered one of the most important gods in Greek mythology.

Balendra (Sikh) Another name for Lord Krishna. One of the most commonly worshipped lords in the Hindu faith, Lord

Krishna is thought to be the eighth incarnation of Lord Vishnu. He is famous for destroying evil powers and spreading love.

Benjamin (Hebrew) Son of my right hand. The Bible's youngest son of Jacob. *Behnjamin, Bejamin, Bemjiman, Ben, Benejamen, Benejaminas, Beniam, Beniamino, Benja, Benjaman, Benjamen, Benjamine, Benjamon, Benjemin, Benjermain, Benji, Benjie, Benjimen, Benjjmen, Benjy, Benni, Bennie, Benny, Benyamin, Benyamino, Binyamin, Minyamin, Minyomei, Minyomi.*

Bhupinderpal (Sikh) Preserved by God.

Cain (Hebrew) Spear; craftsman. The trouble-making eldest son of the Bible's Adam and Eve, brother to Abel. *Cainan, Caine, Caineth, Cane, Caino, Kain, Kaine, Kane.*

Caleb (Hebrew) Brave; faithful; dog. One of Moses' faithful traveling companions. *Caeleb, Calab, Cale, Caley, Calub, Kal, Kalb, Kaleb, Kalin.*

Chandresh (Hindu) Lord Shiva; moon. The third and most powerful god of the divine trinity, Lord Shiva is so complex that his shrine sits separately from others within the temple. Represented with hair piled high on his head, the river Ganges is said to flow from his tresses. With his important role in death and destruction, Lord Shiva is deemed the opposite of Lord Vishnu, the creator.

Daniel (Hebrew) The Lord is my judge. A Hebrew prophet and subject of the Old Testament's Book of Daniel. *Dacso, Dan, Danakas, Daneel, Daneil, Danek, Danel, Danforth, Dani, Danial, Dániel, Daniël, Daniele, Danieius, Daniell, Daniels, Danielson, Danielus, Danikar, Danil, Danilo, Daniyel, Danni, Dannie, Danniel, Dann, Danno, Dano, Danukas, Danyell, Danylets, Danylo, Dasco, Dayne, Deniel, Doneal, Doniel, Donois, Dusan, Nelo.*

David (Hebrew) Beloved. The Bible's King of ancient Israel, he beat the giant Goliath against all odds. *Dabi, Daevid, Dafydd, Dai, Daivid, Daoud, Dauid, Dav, Davad, Dave, Daved, Davee, Daveed, Daven, Davey, Davi, Davidde, Davide, Davido, Davidson, Davie, Davis, Davon, Davoud, Davy, Davyd, Dawes, Dawid, Dawit, Dawson, Dewey, Devlin.*

Dharamsheel (Sikh) Holy.

Dionysus (Greek) God of wine. Also known by his Roman name, Bacchus, Dionysus was the son of the famed god Zeus and a mortal woman named Semele. He was a kind god who brought much happiness. *Dionysos.*

Elijah (Hebrew) My God is the Lord. A Hebrew prophet of the Old Testament. *El, Elek, Eli, Elia, Eliakim, Elias, Eliasz, Elie, Eliha, Elija, Elijuo, Elisjsha, Eliya, Eliyahu, Ellis, Ellison, Ellsworth, Ellys, Elya, Elyas, Ilja, Ilya.*

Eryx (Greek) Son of Aphrodite. Eryx's father is said to be one of two men—the mortal Butes or the Greek god of the sea, Poseidon. Eryx was a Sicilian King ultimately killed in a wrestling match.

Ezekial (Hebrew) Strength of God. A prophet in the Bible. *Eze, Ezéchiel, Ezek, Ezekhal, Ezekial, Ezeeckel, Ezekeial, Ezekial, Ezikiel, Ezell, Ezequiel, Eziakah, Eziechiele, Eziequel, Ezkeil.*

Ezra (Hebrew) Happy; helper. A biblical prophet and leader of God's people. *Esdras, Esra, Ezrah, Zera, Ezera, Ezer, Ezri, Ezruh, Ezzret.*

Ganesha (Hindu) Lord of the hosts. Most often referred to as Shri Ganesha (Shri is a Hindu form of respect), Ganesha is son of Lord Shiva and Parvati. He is depicted as having an elephant head, four arms and a pot belly. *Ganesa, Ganesh.*

Gautam (Hindu) Lord Buddha. Formerly known as Siddhartha Gautama, Lord Buddha is the founder of Buddhism. He was born in Lumbini, Nepal in 623 B.C. He is thought to be the ninth reincarnation of the Hindu Lord Vishnu.

Haamid (Muslim) Praising and loving God.

Hermes (Greek) God of merchants and messenger of the gods. Cunning and shrewd, Hermes was the son of Zeus and a nymph named Maia.

Inderjeet (Sikh) The triumph of God.

Isaac (Hebrew, Dutch) One who laughs; laughter. The only son of the elderly couple Abraham and Sarah. He was named by God. *Ike, Ikey, Ikie, Isa, Isaak, Isak, Issac, Issak, Ishaq, Isia, Isiash,*

Issia, Issiah, Itzak, Itzhak, Ixaka, Izaac, Izaiah, Izaiha, Izzak, Izak, Sahak, Yitzhak, Zack, Zak.

Isaiah (Hebrew) Salvation of God (Yahweh). A Hebrew prophet in the Bible. *Isa, Isai, Isaia, Isaid, Isais, Isaish, Isay, Isayah, Isey, Isia, Isiah, Issiah, Izaiha, Izzie, Izzy.*

Ishmael (Hebrew) God will listen. Son of Abraham and surrogate mother Hagar. *Hish, Ish, Ishma, Ishmeal, Ismael, Ishmel, Ismail, Yishmael.*

Israel (Hebrew) Prince of God. *Iser, Isser, Israyel, Issy, Izrael, Izzy, Yisrael.*

Jacob (Hebrew) The supplanter; held by the heel. Married Rachel and Leah. The younger brother of Esau, Jacob was transformed by God into Israel, the Prince of God. *Iacob, Iacobe, Jaap, Jaccob, Jachob, Jack, Jackub, Jaco, Jacobb, Jacobe, Jacobee, Jacobi, Jacobis, Jacobo, Jacobs, Jacobus, Jacoby, Jacolby, Jacques, Jacquet, Jago, Jaime, Jakab, Jake, Jakes, Jakey, Jakiv, Jakob, Jakov, Jakubek, Jasha, Jecis, Jeb, Jeks, Jeska, Jim, Jocek, Jock, Jacoby, Jocolby, Jokubas, Kiva, Kivi.*

Jalaal (Muslim) Glory of faith.

Jesus (Hebrew) God will help; saved by God. The son of Mary and Joseph. Christians believe Jesus is the Son of God. *Hesus, Jecho, Jesu, Jesús, Jesuso, Jezus.*

Joachim (Hebrew) God will judge. *Akim, Jakim, Joacheim, Joakim, Joaquim, Joaquin; Jaquín, Joakin, Jov, Yachim, Yakim.*

Job (Hebrew) Patient; afflicted; oppressed. An innocent man who was greatly tested in the Bible. *Joab, Jobb, Jobe, Jobert, Jobi, Jobie, Joby.*

John (Hebrew) God is merciful. The author of the Bible's Gospel According to John. Also the name of John the Baptist and John the Evangelist. *Jack, Jacsi, Jaenda, Jahn, Jan, Janak, Janco, Janek, János, Jansen, Jantje, Jantzen, Jas, Jehan, Jenkin, Jenkyn, Jens, Jhan, Jhanick, Jhon, Jian, Joáo, João, Jock, Joen, Johan, Johann, Johnathan, Johne, Johnne, Johnni, Johnnie, Johnny, Johnson, Johnnye, Jon, Jonam, Jonas, Jonathan, Jone, Jones, Jonny, Jovan, Juan, Juana, Ian, Iain, Ivan, Iwan.*

Joseph (Hebrew) God adds. In the Bible, Joseph was the father of Jesus. *Guiseppe, Jo, Jobo, Jodie, Jody, Joe, Joeseph, Jose, Joey, Jooseppi, Josecito, Josef, Josep, Josephat, Josephus, Joselito, Josephe, Josephus, Josip, Joze, Jozef, Jozhe, Jozio, Sepp, Yusif.*

Joshua (Hebrew) The Lord is my saviour. Leader of the victorious Israelite armies against the Canaanites. *Johsua, Johusa, Josh, Joshau, Joshaua, Joshauh, Joshawa, Joshawah, Joshia, Joshu, Joshuah, Joshuam, Joshuea, Joshula, Joshus, Joshuwa, Joshwa, Josue, Jousha, Jozshua, Jozsua, Jozua, Jushua, Joshyam, Josue, Jozua.*

Judas (Latin) A form of Judah. Judas Iscariot was the disciple who betrayed Jesus. *Jude.*

Lazarus (Hebrew) God's assistance. *El'azar, Eleazer, Lasarus, Laszlo, Laza, Lázár, Lazar, Lazare, Lazaro, Lazaros, Lazarusie, Lazerus, Lazoros, Lazre, Lazzro.*

Luke (Latin) Light; another form of Lucius. Luke wrote the Gospel According to Luke and Acts of the Apostles in the New Testament. *Luc, Lucan, Lucas, Lucc, Luchock, Lucian, Luciano, Lucias, Lucius, Luck, Lucky, Luk, Luka, Lúkács, Lukas, Luken, Lukes, Luckus, Lukvan, Lukian, Lukyan, Lusio.*

Lokesh (Bengali) King of the world.

Mark (Latin) Warlike. Author of the Gospel According to Mark in the New Testament. *Marc, Marceau, Marcel, March, Marco, Marcus, Marek, Mariano, Marilo, Marius, Márk, Marke, Markee, Markel, Markell, Markey, Markie, Marks, Marko, Markó, Markos, Márkus, Markus, Markusha, Marky, Marque, Marquis, Marial, Marus, Marx.*

Marzouq (Muslim) Blessed; fortunate.

Matthew (Hebrew) Gift from God. Author of the New Testament's Gospel According to Matthew. *Mads, Makaio, Maitiú, Marty, Mat, Mata, Matai, Matek, Mateo, Mateusz, Matfei, Math, Mathe, Matheson, Matheu, Mathew, Mathian, Mathias, Mathieson, Mathieu, Matro, Mats, Matt, Matteo, Matteus, Matthaeus, Matthaios, Matthaus, Matthäus, Mattheus, Matthews, Matthia, Matthias, Mattie, Mattmias, Mattsy, Matty, Matvey, Matyas, Mayhew.*

HEY BABY!

Moses (Hebrew, Greek) Appointed for special things; taken by water. Set adrift in a basket on the river as a baby, Moses later brought God's Ten Commandments down from Mount Sinai. *Moe, Moey, Moise, Moïse, Moisey, Moisie, Moishe, Mosa, Mose, Mosese, Mosesh, Mosha, Moshe, Mosheh, Mosiah, Mosie, Moss, Mosya, Mousa, Moyse, Moyses, Moze, Mozes, Mozie.*

Nehemiah (Hebrew) Compassion of God. A priest, son of Hacaliah; one of the books in the Old Testament. *Nemia, Nemiah.*

Noah (Hebrew) Rest; wanderer. Patriarch and builder of the famous Ark, Noah was one of the only survivors of the Great Flood. *Noa, Noach, Noak, Noam, Noé, Noi, Noy.*

Orion (Latin, Greek) East; son of fire. A hunter in Greek mythology, Orion became a constellation in the heavens after his accidental death. *Orien, Oris.*

Paul (Latin) Little one; small. Born Saul, Paul's name was changed after he gave up his evil ways of persecuting Christians, repented and was baptized. He later became one of the persecuted. *Oalo, Paavo, Pablo, Pál, Pal, Pall, Paolo, Pasha, Pasko, Pauley, Pauli, Paulia, Paulie, Paulin, Paulino, Paulis, Paulo, Pauls, Paulus, Pauly, Powell, Pawl, Pawley, Pavel, Pavlo, Pavlos, Pawel, Pol.*

Peter (Latin, Greek) Rock. Jesus chose Peter as leader of the 12 apostles. *Panayiotos, Panos, Parkin, Parkinson, Parle, Parnell, Peadair, Pearce, Pears, Pearson, Pearsson, Peat, Peder, Pedro, Peer, Peers, Peet, Peeter, Peirce, Pekelo, Pelle, Per, Perico, Perion, Perkin, Perkins, Perren, Perrin, Perry, Pero, Petar, Pete, Petee, Péter, Peterson, Petey, Petie, Petö, Petr, Petri, Petrie, Petruno, Petrus, Petúr, Petur, Piaras, Pierce, Piero, Pierre, Piers, Pierson, Pieter, Pietor, Pietrek, Pietro, Piotr, Piter, Piti, Pjeter, Pyotr, Pytor .*

Pinak (Hindu) Lord Shiva's bow. In Hindu mythology, whoever was able to bend this bow would be granted permission to marry King Janak's daughter, Sita. Ram, the seventh incarnation of Vishnu (one of the most prominent Hindu gods), bent and broke the sword.

Poseidon (Greek) God of the sea and protector of water. One of the 12 gods of Olympus, Poseidon was worshipped most heavily by Greek fisherman. Brother to Zeus, Poseidon was also the god of horses, earth quakes and sea storms.

Rahim (Muslim) Another name for Allah, the Muslim god. Most commonly associated with the Islamic faith, the word Allah is used by Muslims throughout the world, regardless of their language. This word represents the presence of god. Allah is considered the only true reality to Islamic worshippers.

Romesh (Bengali) Another name for Vishnu; god of Rama. The second god in the Hindu Trinity, Lord Vishnu is known as a protector and creator. His famous incarnations include Lords Krishna and Rama.

Samuel (Hebrew) God listens. Son of Hannah and a Hebrew judge and prophet. *Sam, Samael, Samaru, Samauel, Samaul, Sambo, Samelle, Sameul, Samiel, Sammail, Sammell, Sammeul, Sammie, Sammo, Sammouel, Sammuel, Sammy, Samual, Samuele, Samuelis, Samuello, Samuelson, Samuka, Samuel, Samuru, Samvel, Sanko, Saumel, Schmuel, Shem, Shemuel, Simão, Simuel, Somhairie, Zamuel.*

Solomon (Hebrew) Man of peace; peaceful. A king of Israel in the Old Testament. *Salamen, Salamon, Salamun, Salaun, Salman, Salmon, Salom, Salomo, Salomon, Salomone, Selim, Shelomah, Shelomo, Shlomo, Sol, Solaman, Solamh, Sollie, Solly, Solmon, Soloman, Solomonas, Sulaiman.*

Zachariah (Hebrew) Remembered by God. A priest and the father of John the Baptist. *Zac, Zacaria, Zacarias, Zacarius, Zacaryah, Zaccary, Zach, Zacharia, Zacharias, Zacharie, Zachary, Zachery, Zachi, Zachie, Zachory, Zachury, Zack, Zackariah, Zacherias, Zackery, Zak, Zakarias, Zakarie, Zakary, Zako, Zaquero, Zechariah, Zeggery, Zeke, Zhachory, Zhack.*

Zeus (Greek) Living. Ruler of all gods in Greek mythology, Zeus was also ruler of the sky. *Zeno, Zenon, Zinon, Zues.*

REAL NAMES

Upon birth, Kathryn was given her mother's middle name. And she loves it so much that she has a no-nickname policy. "No one is usually allowed to call me anything else," explains the 28-year-old. So that means no Katie, Kath or Kathy for this classically-named woman.

For years, 40-year-old Suzanne has toyed with changing her "formal and prissy" name. In high school, she even went so far as to call herself Susée—anything to be different. "Somehow you feel that changing your name might change your image or how you feel about yourself," she explains. "The way that fantastic piece of clothing can make you feel."

Forty-two-year-old Deborah doesn't like her name at all, so she goes by either Deb or Debbie. "There are no young Deborahs," she says. "We're almost all over 40." If she had to choose another name, she says she'd choose Grace "because it embodies everything I'm not, like graceful, for example."

Julian has pretty much always liked having a unique name. "When I was younger, there weren't many kids named Julian. They were all named Mike, Paul or Tony," says the 32-year-old. And although he did go through a short phase of wanting a more common name to fit in, Julian now prefers being different.

As the last of eight children, Taryn's parents wanted to make sure she had a very distinct name to help her stand out. But as a child, she disliked being different. "Kids would always get my name wrong and I hated it," she says. "But now that I'm older, I've grown into my name and love that it's unique and that people talk to me about it."

"It defines me. It embodies my personality. It is everything about me," raves 34-year-old Gavin about his name. Other added bonuses: "It's unusual, unique and mostly unforgettable," he says. Now that's a guy who really likes his moniker.

Religious Girls' Names

Aaliyha (Arabic, Hebrew) Exhalted; to ascend. *Aalia, Aaliha, Alia, Aliya.*

Adalia (Hebrew) God's refuge. *Adahlia, Adailya, Adal, Adala, Adalee, Adali, Adalie, Adalin, Adallyuh, Adaly, Adalyn, Adaylia, Addal, Addala, Addaly.*

Aisha (Arabic) Life. A wife of the prophet Mohammed in the Arabic religion. Compassionate and loving, Mohammed preached the word of Allah. *Aesha, Aeshah, Aiesha, Aieshah, Aishah, Aishia, Aishia, Aisia, Aisiah, Asha, Ashah, Ashia, Ashiah, Ayasha, Ayeesah, Ayeisa, Ayesha, Ayeshah, Ayisha, Ayishah, Aysa, Ayse, Aysha, Ayshah, Aysha, Ayshe, Ayshea, Aytza, Azia.*

Amaris (Hebrew) God's promise. *Amares, Amaria, Amariah, Amarissa, Maris.*

Amatullah (Muslim) Allah's servant. Allah, which is Arabic for God, is the only reality for Islamic worshippers. He is considered all-powerful, all-pervading and omniscient by Muslim worshippers.

Amritaya (Hindu) Immortal.

Anya (Latvian, Russian) Grace of God; a form of Anna. *Anica, Anja, Anuschka, Anyuta.*

Ariadne (Greek) Holy one. The daughter of Crete's King Minos. *Ari, Ariana, Ariane, Arianie, Arianna, Arianne, Arianna, Ariyaunna, Aria, Ari, Rianna.*

Barakah (Muslim) Blessing. A servant who later served as nursemaid to the Prophet.

Bashemath (Hebrew) Sweet smell; fragrance. The name of two women in the Bible. Ishamel's daughter, wife of Esau. And Solomon's daughter, wife of Ahimaaz. *Basemath.*

Bathsheba (Hebrew) Daughter of the oath. The daughter of Eliam, Bathsheba was married to Uriah and had an affair with King David. *Bathseva, Batsheba, Bathshua, Batsheva, Batshua, Bersaba, Bethsabee, Bethsheba, Sheba.*

Bellona (Latin) To fight. The Roman goddess of war. Although Bellona didn't really do anything of great note, she was still honoured with a temple in Rome. *Bela, Bell, Bella, Belle, Belva, Belloma.*

Bilhah (Hebrew) Bashful. Rachel gave handmaiden Bilhah to Jacob as a concubine in the Bible.

Chanda (Hindu) Another name for Hindu goddess Devi. All-powerful and widely worshipped, Devi is considered the mother of all. She is goddess of health, fertility, rain, nature and death. She is also the Divine Mother of Hinduism. *Chana, Chandaa, Chandra, Chandrakanta, Shanda.*

Chandi (Hindu) Great goddess. Chandi is the name used to represent the malicious side of the omnipotent Hindu goddess Devi.

Chandramouli (Bengali) Shiva. In Hindu tradition, Lord Shiva is the third god of the powerful trinity. He represents death and destruction.

Deborah (Hebrew) A bee. One of the most powerful women in the Bible, Deborah helped lead God's army to free Israel from Jabin. She also acted as a prophet, judge and overall peacemaker. *Deb, Debbie, Debby, Debo, Deboreh, Deborrah, Debra, Debrah, Devora, Devorah.*

Delilah (Hebrew) Delicate and affectionate. In The Bible, Delilah is Samson's lover. *Dalia, Dalialah, Dalila, Daliliah, Delia, Delila, Delilia, Lila, Lilah.*

Demira (Hindu) Devoted to Lord Krishna. One of the most commonly worshipped lords in the Hindu faith, Lord Krishna is thought to be the eighth incarnation of Lord Vishnu. He is famous for destroying evil powers and spreading love.

Devahuti (Hindu) God. Another name for Devi, Hindu goddess of health, fertility, rain, nature and death. She is the Divine Mother of Hinduism. *Deva.*

Devna (Hindu) Godly. Another name for the supreme Hindu goddess, Devi who is considered the mother of all. *Deva, Devi.*

Dinah (Hebrew) Vindicated; judged. Daughter of Leah and Jacob in The Bible. *Deanna, Deena, Denora, Dina, Dinna, Dinorah, Diondra, Dyna, Dynah.*

Eden (Hebrew) Pleasure; delight. The Garden of Eden was Adam and Eve's paradisiacal first home. It also housed the tree of knowledge. *Eaden, Eadin, Ede, Edena, Edene, Edenia, Edana, Edin, Edyn.*

Ereshva (Muslim) Righteous.

Esther (English, Hebrew, Persian) Star. In The Bible, Esther rose from being an exiled prisoner to the Queen of Persia. *Es, Essie, Essy, Esta, Estee, Ester, Esthur, Eszter, Eszti, Etti, Ettie, Etty.*

Eve (Hebrew) Life. The first woman created by God, tempted by Satan and tossed from the Garden of Eden. *Eva, Evathia, Evelina, Eveline, Evelyn, Evey, Evie, Evita, Evuska, Evvy, Evyn, Ewa.*

Gaia (Greek) Goddess of the earth. Known as Mother Earth, Gaia was second to be created. She emerged from Chaos, a great void and gave birth to Ouranos, the Heaven. She and Ouranos created the Titan gods. *Gaea, Gaioa, Gaja, Gaya.*

Gianna (Italian) God is gracious. *Geonna, Gi, Gian, Giana, Giann, Gianne, Giannni, Giannetta, Giannina, Ginny.*

Gurinder (Sikh) Lord. Another name for God, Sikh worshippers believe in only one God, to whom they can pray anywhere and at anytime.

Hannah (Hebrew) God's grace. In the Bible, Hannah is the mother of Samuel the prophet. *Hana, Hanae, Hanah, Hanan, Hanna, Hannaa, Hannalore, Hanne, Hanneke, Hannele, Hanni, Hannie, Hannon, Honna.*

Helah (Hebrew) Rust. One of Ashur's wives in the Bible. Ashur was the son of Hezron and Abiah. He founded the town Tekoa. *Hela.*

Hera (Greek) Queen of gods, wife of Zeus. The goddess of marriage, Hera gained her ultimate status: Queen of the Olympians, when she married Zeus. She was a strong enemy of Heracles.

Jael (Hebrew) To climb; mountain goat. In the Bible, she killed Sisera, the captain of an enemy army. *Jaela, Jaelee, Jaeleen, Jaeli, Jaelie, Jaelle, Jaelynn, Jahia, Jahiea.*

Jasminder (Sikh) God's Glory.

Judith (Hebrew) Praised. A widow who uses her beauty as power to behead Holofernes and save Judas in the Bible. *Giuditta, Ioudith, Jitka, Jodi, Jodie, Jody, Jucika, Judana, Jude, Judey, Judi, Judie, Judine, Judit, Judita, Judite, Juditha, Judithe, Judy, Judye, Judyta, Judyth, Judythe, Jutka.*

Leah (Hebrew) Tired; weary. In the Bible, Leah is Jacob's wife and the mother of Reuben, Simeon, Levi, Judah, Issachar, Zebulun and Dinah. *Lea, Léa, Leatrice, Lee, Leea, Leeah, Leia, Leigh, Leigha, Lia, Liah.*

Kezia (Hebrew) Cassia tree; cinnamon. The name of Job's second daughter in The Bible. *Lakeisha, Kazia, Kaziah, Keesha, Keisha, Keshia, Kesiah, Keishia, Ketzi, Ketzia, Keziah, Kezzy, Kissie, Kizzie, Kizzy.*

Kulthoom (Muslim) Daughter of the Prophet Mohammed. Meaning highly praised, Mohammed is considered the Prophet of Islam. Compassionate and loving, Mohammed preached the word of Allah.

Magdalen (Greek) A high tower. Saint Mary Magdalen was a close friend and disciple of Jesus. *Mada, Mag, Magda, Magdala, Magdalena, Magdalene, Magdalina, Magdaline, Magdalyn, Magdaelana, Magdelane, Magdelene, Magdelin, Magdelina, Magdeline, Magdelyn, Magdlen, Magdolna, Maggie, Magola, Mahda, Makda, Mala, Maudlin.*

Maimoona (Muslim) Blessed.

Malak (Muslim) Angel. Muslims believe that god created angels from light to carry out his commandments.

Mara (Hebrew) Bitter; sadness. Naomi adopted this name to represent her troubles in the Bible. *Amara, Mahra, Marah, Maralina, Maraline, Marra.*

Mary (Hebrew) Bitter. In the Bible, Mary was the virgin mother of Jesus. *Maire, Manette, Manya, Mara, Marabel, Mare, Maree, Marella, Marelle, Mari, Maria, Marial, Mariam, Marian, Maricara, Marice, Marie, Mariel, Marieke, Marika, Marilee, Marilyn, Marion, Marisha, Marita, Marité, Marja, Marye, Maryk, Maryla, Marynia, Maryse, Marysia, Maura, Meree, Meridel, Merrili, Merry, Mhairie, Mitzie, Moira, Morag, Moya, Muire.*

Naamah (Hebrew) Pleasant; sweet. Daughter of King Ammon and wife of Solomon in the Bible. *Naama, Naamana, Nammi, Naamia, Naamiah, Naamit, Naamiya.*

Naomi (Hebrew) Pleasant one: beauty. Mother-in-law of Ruth, Naomi suffered many trials but maintained her strong faith in God. *Mimi, Mims, Mimsy, Naoma, Naomia, Naomie, Naomy, Navit, Naynay, Nene, Neoma, Noami, Noemi, Noemie, Noma, Nomah, Nomi, Nyome, Nyomi, Omie.*

Puah (Hebrew) Splendid. A midwife who objected to killing Hebrew boys upon their birth in the Bible. *Pua.*

Rachel (Hebrew) Lamb. Jacob's wife. *Rach, Racha, Rachael, Rachaele, Rachal, Racheal, Rachelann, Rachele, Rachell, Rachelle, Rachie, Rae, Raechal, Raelene, Rakel, Rakhil, Rasch, Raquel, Raquela, Raquella, Raquelle, Raycene, Rey.*

Rebekah (Hebrew) Bound; joined. Another form of Rebecca. Married to Isaac, Rebekah bore twin sons Esau and Jacob and daughter Bethuel. *Becca, Becha, Becka, Becki, Beckie, Becky, Bekki, Rebecca, Rebeccah, Reba, Rebakah, Rebbecca, Rebbie, Rebeca, Rebeccah, Rebecha, Rebecka, Rebeckah, Rebeka, Rebekha, Rebekka, Rebekkah, Rebekke, Rebeque, Rebi, Reby, Ree, Reeba, Revecca, Reveka, Reveeka, Reyba, Rheba, Riba, Rifka, Rivca, Rivka, Rivy.*

Rhoda (Greek) Rose; from the island of Rhodes. In the Bible, Rhoda was the mother of John Mark; she lived with Mary. *Rhodante, Rhodanthe, Rhode, Rhodeia, Rhodia, Rhodie, Rhody, Roda, Rodi, Rodie, Rodina, Rody, Roe.*

Ruth (Hebrew) Compassionate; a friend. In the Bible, Ruth is the daughter-in-law of Naomi. She later married Boaz and had a son named Obed. *Rue, Ruthanne, Rutha, Ruthalma, Ruthe, Ruthella, Ruthetta, Ruthi, Ruthie, Ruthina, Ruthine, Ruthven, Ruthy.*

Salome (Hebrew) Peace. Along with Mary Magdalene, Salome was a disciple of Jesus. According to Mark, she was present at the crucifixion. *Sal, Salohme, Saloma, Salomé, Salomey, Salomi, Salomia.*

Sarah (Hebrew) Princess. The beautiful wife of Abraham and mother of Isaac in The Bible. She was also known as Sarai. *Sadee, Sadey, Sadie, Sadye, Sae, Sahra, Saidee, Sairne, Saleena, Salena, Salina, Sallee, salley, Sallianne, Sallie, Sally, Sallyann, Sara, Saraha, Sarahann, Sarai, Sarann, Saree, Sarene, Sarett, Saretta, Sarette, Sari, Sarina, Sarine, Sarita, Saritia, Sarra, Sarri, Sarrie, Sary, Sasa, Sayre, Sorcha, Zara, Zarah, Zaria.*

Sherah (Hebrew) Kinswoman. Light-hearted. Daughter of Ephraim in the Old Testament. She built three towns. *Sheera, Sheerah, Shenay, Shenda, Shene, Shenea, Sheneda, Shenee, Sheneena, Shenica, Shenika, Shenina, Sheniqua, Shenita, Sheena, Shera.*

Tabitha (Greek, Arabic) Gazelle. In the Bible, Peter helped her rise from the dead. *Tabatha, Tabbatha, Tabbee, Tabbetha, Tabbey, Tabbi, Tabbie, Tabbitha, Tabbi, Tabbie, Tabby, Tabetha, Tabithia, Tabotha, Tabtha, Tabytha.*

Tamar (Hebrew; Sanskrit) Palm tree; spice. Short for Tamara. In the Bible, Tamar married two of Judas's sons. She then bore Judas's twin sons Pharez and Zerah. *Tama, Tamara, Tamarah, Tamarind, Tamarr, Tami, Tamika, Tamary, Tamer, Tammie, Tammy, Tamor, Tamour.*

Vashti (Persian) Lovely; beautiful. Queen of Ahasuerus and wife of the Bible's Ahasuerus, the King of Persia. *Vashtee, Vashtie.*

Zillah (Hebrew) Shadow. Wife of Lamech and an ancestor of Cain in the Bible. *Zila, Zilla, Zilah, Zylia, Zylla.*

Zipporah (Hebrew) Bird. Daughter of Ruele and wife of Moses in the Bible. *Cipora, Tzipeh, Tzipora, Tzippe, Zipeh, Zipora, Ziporah, Zippi, Zippie, Zippora, Zipporia, Zippy, Ziproh.*

KIDS' KORNER

Daniel's parents gave him this name because "they wanted to call me Danny," says the 13-year-old. And even though he doesn't particularly like when people call him Dan, he says, "I really wouldn't want to change my name because I can't imagine it not being Daniel. I can't imagine it being different."

Although it's short and only has two syllables, 12-year-old Lisa doesn't always like her name. "I don't like that it rhymes with my sister's name," she complains. "And it sounds like there is an 'e' in it."

Sometimes Kevin, who's named after an ancestor as well as a basketball star, wishes his name wasn't so common. The reason? "I get confused when someone calls a different Kevin's name," says the 12-year-old. If he got to choose another moniker for himself, Kevin would pick Jamick "because it has the first initial of my parents' home land—Jamaica—and I won't get confused [with other people]."

Julie doesn't mind being named after her mother's dog. "It's very pretty and elegant and the name just rolls off your tongue," explains the 17-year-old. But occasionally she wishes she had a name that no one else has so she could be more unique. "My mother nearly called me Persephone," she says. "I think that would be an amazing name to have because...everyone would know who you were."

Keeley says her parents gave her this name because they liked it. And she's definitely glad they did. "I like everything [about it]," beams the five-year-old.

Nine-year-old Domenico sometimes wishes that his name wasn't so long and hard to pronounce. And he always hated when kids shortened it to Dum to make fun of him. But overall Domenico likes his name (which came from his Nonno) because "hardly no one has it" and "it means that I'm different, I'm strong and fast."

Old-Fashioned Names

To me, a name popular in the 50s doesn't deserve old-fashioned status. In order to be considered traditional, names should sound old and distinguished. That's why all of the following entries were common from 1900 to 1920.

Old-Fashioned Boys' Names

Albert (German) Bright and noble. *Adelbert, Ailbert, Al, Albertik, Alberto, Alberts, Albertus, Albie, Albin, Albrecht, Alby, Ally, Alvertos, Aubert, Bertel, Berty, Bertie, Elbert.*

Alvin (English) Noble, loyal friend. *Al, Aliwyn, Aliaon, Aloin, Aluin, Aluino, Alva, Alvan, Alven, Alvie, Alvino, Alvy, Alvyn, Alwin, Alwyn, Alwynn, Aylwin, Elwin.*

Anthony (Latin, Greek) Praiseworthy; priceless; flourishing. *Anathony, Andonios, Andonis, Andor, András, Anfernee, Anferny, Anntonin, Anothony, Antal, Antawas, Anth, Anthawn, Anthey, Anthinan, Anthino, Anthoney, Anthonu, Anthonysha, Anthoy, Anthyoine, Anthyonny, Antin, Antjuan, Antoine, Anton, Antone, Antonello, Antoni, Antonin, Antonino, Antonio, Antonius, Antons, Antony, Antos, Antwan, Antwon, Antwone, Nee, Tee, Tone, Toney, Toni, Tonie, Tonio, Tony.*

Arthur (Celtic) Bear; noble; follower of Thor. *Art, Artair, Arte, Artek, Arther, Arthie, Arthor, Artie, Artis, Arto, Artu, Artur, Artus, Atur, Arturo, Arty, Aurthar, Aurther, Aurthur.*

Bernard (German) Brave; bold. *Barnard, Barnardo, Barney, Barnhard, Barnhardo, Barnie, Barny, Bearnard, Benek, Ber, Berardyn, Berend, Bern, Bernabé, Bernardas, Bernardel, Bernardin, Beranrdino, Bernardo, Bern, Bernel, Bernerd, Berngards, Bernhard, Bernhardo, Bernhards, Bernhardt, Bernie, Berny, Bjorn, Burnard.*

Brian (Celtic) Strong; virtuous. *Bri, Briand, Briann, Briano, Briant, Briante, Brien, Brience, Brienn, Brient, Brin, Briny, Brion, Bry, Bryan, Bryant, Bryon.*

Bruno (German) Dark skin, brown hair. *Bruin, Bruins, Brune, Brunne, Brunon, Brunoh, Bruns, Broun.*

Carl (English, German) Manly; strong one. *Caril, Cario, Carle, Carles, Carless, Carlie, Carlis, Carlisle, Carlson, Carlston, Carlton, Carlo, Carlos, Carlus, Carly, Carlyle, Carolos, Karla, Karel, Karoly, Karl, Karlo.*

Cecil (Latin) Unseeing; blind. *Cece, Cecel, Cecile, Cecilio, Cecillo, Cecillus, Celio, Siseal.*

Chester (Latin) Camp. *Ches, Cheslav, Chesley, Chess, Chessie, Chessy, Cheston, Chet.*

Clarence (Latin) Bright; clear. *Clair, Clarance, Clare, Calren, Clarendon, Clarens, Clarense, Clarey, Clarons, Claronz, Clarrance, Calrrence, Clearence, Klarence, Klarens.*

Clifford (English) Cliff near a slope or river crossing. *Cleford, Clif, Clifton, Cliff, Cliffy, Cliford, Clyff, Clyfford.*

Clyde (Scottish, Welsh) A Scottish river; heard from a distance. *Clide, Cly, Clydey, Clydie, Clydy, Clye, Clywd, Klyde, Kyle.*

Dennis (Greek) Follower of the Greek god of wine, Dionysus. *Den, Denes, Deni, Denies, Denis, Deniss, Denit, Deniz, Dennes, Dennet, Denni, Dennies, Dennison, Denniston, Dennit, Denniz, Denny, Dennys, Deno, Denzel, Denzell, Denzil, Dino, Dion.*

Donald (Scottish, Old English) A world leader. *Don, Donal, Dónal, Donaldo, Donaldson, Donall, Donalt, Donát, Donaugh, Doneld, Donghal, Donild, Donn, Donne, Donnie, Donny.*

Douglas (Scottish) Of dark water. *Doug, Dougal, Dougie, Douglass, Dougles, Dugald, Dugan, Dughlas.*

Earl (English) Nobleman; leader. *Airle, Earid, Earland, Earle, Earleen, Earley, Earlie, Earlson, Early, Eori, Eri, Erie, Erl, Erle, Erleen, Erlene, Errol, Erryl.*

Edgar (English) Fortunate; success; spear. *Ed, Eddie, Edek, Edgard, Edgardo, Edgars, Edghur, Edgur.*

Edward (English) A guardian of property. *Ed, Eddey, Eddi, Eddie, Eddy, Edik, Edko, Edo, Edoardo, Edorta, Édouard, Eduard, Eduardo, Edus, Edvard, Edvardo, Edwar, Edwardo, Edwards, Edwerd, Edwy, Edzio, Ekewaka, Etzio, Ewart.*

Edwin (English) A wealthy friend. *Eadwinn, Edik, Edlin, Eduino, Edwinn, Edwyn, Edwynn.*

Elmer (English) Noble; famous. *Aylmar, Aylmer, Aymer, Elemér, Ell, Ellmer, Elm, Elmar, Elmir, Elmo, Elmoh.*

Eugene (Greek) Noble; well-born. *Eoghan, Eugean, Eugen, Eugéne, Eugeni, Eugenie, Eugenio, Eugenius, Evgeney, Gene, Ugene.*

233

Everett (German, English) Wild boar; strong. *Eberardo, Eberhard, Eberhart, Ev, Everard, Evered, Everet, Everette, Everitt, Evert, Evrett, Evrit.*

Floyd (English) The hollow. Another form of Lloyd. *Floid, Flood, Floode, Floyde.*

Francis (Latin, French) Free; from France. *Ferenc, Fran, Franc, France, Francessco, Franchot, Franci, Francisco, Francise, Franciskus, Franco, François, Frang, Frank, Frankie, Franky, Frans, Franscis, Fransis, Franta, Frants, Franus, Franz, Frencis.*

Frank (English) Owner of land. A short form for Franklin. *Franc, Franck, Franco, Franek, Frang, Franio, Franke, Frankee, Frankey, Frankie, Franko, Franky.*

Frederick (German) A peaceful, merciful ruler. *Fred, Freddie, Freddy, Fredek, Frederic, Frederich, Frederico, Frederik, Fredric, Fredrick, Fredrich, Friedel, Friedrick, Fridrich, Fridrick, Friedrike, Fritz, Fritzi, Fritzie, Fryderyk.*

Gary (English) A spear carrier. Short form of Gareth. *Gare, Gareth, Garey, Garrey, Garri, Garrick, Garrie, Garry, Garvie, Garvie, Gervais, Gervase, Gervis.*

George (Greek) Farmer of the earth. *Geordie, Georg, Georgas, Georges, Georget, Georgi, Georgil, Georgio, Georgios, Georgiy, Georgy, Gevork, Gheorghe, Giorgio, Giorgos, Goerge, Goran, Gordios, Gorge, Gorje, Gorya, Grzegorz, Gyorgy, Jorg, Jorge, Jorgen, Jurek, Jorges, Jürgen, Jurgen, Jurgi, Jorrin, Yegor, Yura, Yurchik, Yuri, Yurik, Yurko, Yusha.*

Gerald (German) Ruler with the spear. *Garald, Garrard, Garrod, Garold, Garolds, Gary, Gearalt, Gellert, Gérald, Geralde, Geraldo, Gerale, Gerardo, Geraud, Gerbert, Gerek, Geri, Gerick, Gerik, Gerold, Gerrald, Gerre, Gerrell, Gérrick, Gerrild, Gerrin, Gerrit, Gerrold, Gerry, Geryld, Giraldo, Giraud, Girauld, Girault, Giraut, Jarard, Jarett, Jarrett, Jerald, Jeralde, Jeraud, Jerold, Jerrald, Jerri, Jerrold, Jerry.*

Glenn (Irish) Valley. *Gleann, Glen, Glendon, Glennie, Glennis, Glennon, Glenny, Glynn.*

Gregory (Greek) Watchman; vigilant. *Gergely, Gergo, Greagoir, Greagory, Greer, Greg, Gregary, Greger, Gregery, Gregry, Gregg, Greggory, Grégoire, Gregor, Gregori, Gregorie, Gregorio, Gregorios, Gregos, Greig, Gries, Grigor, Grisha, Grzegorz.*

Harold (Scandinavian) Ruler of the army. *Araldo, Aralt, Aroldo, Arry, Garald, Garold, Hal, Harailt, Harald, Haraldas, Haraldo, Haralds, Hareld, Haroldas, Haroldo, Harry, Heraldo, Herold, Heronim, Herrick, Herryck.*

Henry (German) Household ruler. *Hagan, Hank, Harro, Harry, Heike, Heinrich, Heinz, Hendrick, Henery, Heniek, Henning, Henraoi, Henree, Henri, Henrick, Henrik, Henrim, Henrique, Henrry, Henryk, Hersz.*

Herbert (German) Skilled army or ruler. *Bert, Erbert, Harbert, Hebert, Hébert, Heberto, Hiebert, Herb, Herbart, Herberto, Herbie, Herbirt, Herby, Heriberto, Hurb, Hurbert.*

Herman (German, Latin) Army man; high-ranking. *Harman, Harmon, Herm, Hermahn, Hermann, Hermie, Herminio, Hermino, Hermon, Hermy, Heromin.*

Howard (English) Guardian; watchman. *How, Howe, Howerd, Howie, Howurd, Howy, Ward.*

James (Hebrew) Someone who replaces. A form of Jacob. *Jacques, Jago, Jaime, Jaimes, Jaimito, Jakome, Jamesie, Jamesy, Jamey, Jamie, Jamsey, Jamze, Jas, Jasha, Ja, Jayme, Jaymes, Jaymie, Jem, Jemes, Jim, Jimi, Jimmey, Jimmie, Jimmy, Seamus.*

Kenneth (Irish, Scottish, Old English) Good-looking; born of fire; a royal oath. *Ken, Kendall, Keneth, Kenn, Kennath, Kennet, Kennethen, Kennett, Kenney, Kennie, Kennieth, Kennith, Kennth, Kenny, Kennyth, Kenyon, Kevin.*

Lawrence (Latin) A crown of laurel. *Labhras, Larance, Laren, Larian, Larien, Laris, Larrance, Larrence, Larry, Lars, Larson, Laughton, Laurance, Laurence, Laurencio, Laurens, Laurent, Laurenz, Laurie, Lauris, Lauritz, Laurus, Law, Lawerance, Lawford, Lawrance, Lawren, Lawrey, Lawrie, Lawron, Lawrunce, Lawry, Lencho, Lon, Loreca, Loren, Lorence, Lorencz, Lorens, Lorenz, Lorenzo, Loretto, Lorne, Lorin, Lorry, Lourenco, Lowrance.*

Leo (Latin) Lion. *Leão, Lee, Leib, Leibel, Léo, Leon, Leonas, Leone, Leonek, Leons, Leosko, Leontios, Leopold, Lev, Lio, Lion, Liutas, Lyon.*

Leon (Greek) Lion. Short for Leonard. *Leo, Léon, Leonas, Léonce, Leoncio, Leondris, Leone, Leonek, Leoni, Leonid, Leonidas, Leonirez, Leonizio, Leonn, Leonon, Leons, Leontes, Leosko, Liutas.*

Leroy (French) The king. *Le Roy, Lee, Leeroy, LeeRoy, Leigh, Lerai, Leroi, LeRoi, LeRoy, Roy, Roye.*

Lester (Latin, English) From the chosen camp; from Leicester. *Leicester, Les, Lestor.*

Lewis (English, German) Renowned; a famous warrior. Another version of Luis. *Lew, Lewes, Lewie, Lewus, Lewy.*

Lloyd (Welsh) Of gray hair. *Loy, Loyd, Loyde, Loydde, Loydie, Loye.*

Melvin (Celtic) A chief. *Mal, Malvin, Malvinn, Malvon, Malvonn, Mel, Melvern, Melvine, Melvino, Melvon, Melvyn, Melwin, Melwinn, Melwyn, Melwynn, Milvin.*

Milton (English) A mill town. *Melton, Milt, Milten, Miltey, Milti, Miltie, Milty, Mylt, Mylton.*

Norman (English, French) From the north; a northerner. *Norm, Normand, Normando, Normen, Normie, Normon, Normun, Normy.*

Oscar (Scandinavian, Gaelic) A divine spear; deer lover. *Okko, Osgar, Osgood, Oskar, Oskari, Osker, Ossie, Oszkar, Oskar, Oz, Ozkár, Ozzie.*

Philip (Greek) Horse lover. *Felipe, Filbert, Filip, Filippo, Phelps, Pehlipe, Phil, Philip, Philipe, Philipp, Philips, Philippe, Philippo, Philipson, Phillip, Phillipos, Phillp, Philly, Philo, Philp, Phipps, Piers, Pilib, Pilipo, Pippo.*

Ralph (English) Wolf; wise counselor. *Radolphus, Rafe, Raif, Raff, Raffi, Ralf, Ralph, Ralpheal, Ralphel, Ralphie, Ralphy, Ralston, Raoul, Raul, Raulas, Raulf, Raulo, Rolf, Rolph.*

Raymond (German, English) A protector; strong. *Radmond, Raemond, Raemondo, Raimondo, Raimund, Raimunde, Raimundo, Rajmund, Ramon, Ramón, Ramond, Ramonde, Ramone, Ray, Rayman,*

Raymand, Rayment, Raymon, Raymonde, Raymondo, Raymond, Raymont, Raymun, Raymund, Raymunde, Raymundo, Raymy, Reamonn, Redmond, Reimond.

Richard (German, English) Strong ruler; brave. *Dic, Dick, Dickie, Dicky, Ricard, Ricardo, Riccardo, Ricciardo, Rich, Richar, Richardo, Richards, Richardson, Richart, Richer, Richerd, Richey, Richi, Richie, Richshard, Rick, Rickard, Rickert, Rickey, Rickie, Rickward, Ricky, Rico, Rihardos, Rihards, Rikard, Riki, Rikkert, Riks, Riocard, Riqui, Risa, Rishard, Ritch, Ritchard, Ritcherd, Ritchie, Ritchy, Rocco, Rostitslav, Rostya, Rye, Ryszard.*

Robert (English) Brilliance; fame. *Bert, Berty, Bob, Bobbey, Bobbie, Bobby, Dob, Dobbs, Rab, Rabbie, Raby, Riobard, Riobart, Rob, Robars, Robart, Robb, Róbert, Robben, Robbie, Robbin, Robbins, Robby, Robbyn, Rober, Roberd, Robers, Roberto, Robertos, Roberts, Robey, Robi, Robin, Robinet, Robinson, Roburt, Robyn, Rosertas, Rubert, Ruberto, Rudbert, Rupert, Ruperto, Ruprecht, Tito.*

Ronald (English) Mighty; powerful. *Naldo, Ranald, Renaldo, Ron, Ronal, Ronaldo, Ronan, Ronel, Ronn, Ronney, Roni, Ronnie, Ronnold, Ronny, Ronoldo, Ronuld.*

Roy (French, Gaelic) King; red. *Rey, Roi, Royal, Royale, Royall, Ruy.*

Russell (French) With red hair. *Roussell, Rus, Rusel, Rush, Russ, Russel, Russelle, Russy, Rusty.*

Stanley (English) Rocky meadow. *Stan, Stanberry, Stanbury, Standish, Stanfield, Stanford, Stanhope, Stanlea, Stanlee, Stanleigh, Stanli, Stanly, Stanmore, Stanton, Stanway, Stanwick, Stanwyck.*

Stephen (Greek) Crown. *Esteban, Estevan, Etienne, Stamos, Stavros, Stefan, Stefano, Stefanos, Stefans, Stefen, Steffan, Steffel, Stefos, Stepa, Stepan, Stepanek, Stepanos, Stepek, Stephan, Stephanas, Stéphane, Stepháne, Stephano, Stephanos, Stephanus, Stephens, Stephenson, Stephfan, Stephin, Stephon, Stephone, Stepka, Stepven, Steve, Stevee, Steven, Stevenson, Stevi, Stevie, Stevy.*

Theodore (Greek) A gift from God. *Fedor, Feodor, Fyodor, Téadóir, Teador, Ted, Tedd, Teddey, Teddi, Teddie, Teddy, Tedor, Telly, Teodor, Tedorek, Teodomiro, Teodoro, Teodus, Teos, Tewdor, Theo, Theo, Theodor, Theodors, Theodorus, Theodosios, Theos, Tivadar, Todor, Tolek, Tudor.*

Thomas (Greek) Twin. *Massey, Tam, Tamas, Tameas, Tammy, Tavish, Tevis, Thom, Thoma, Thomason, Thomé, Thomes, Thomeson, Thomison, Thommy, Thompson, Thomson, Thomus, Thos, Thumas, Thumo, Tom, Toma, Tomaisin, Tomas, Tomaso, Tomasso, Tomasz, Tomaz, Tomcio, Tomcy, Tomek, Tomelis, Tomey, Tomi, Tomie, Tomey, Tomislaw, Tomm, Tommy, Tomsen, Tomson, Tomus, Toomas, Tuomas, Tuomo.*

Timothy (Greek) Worshipping God. *Tim, Timithy, Timka, Timkin, Timmathy, Timmothy, Timmoty, Timmthy, Timmie, Timmy, Timo, Timofeo, Timofey, Timok, Timon, Timontheo, Timoteo, Timotheus, Timonthy, Timót, Timote, Timotei, Timoteo, Timoteus, Timothé, Timothe, Timothée, Timotheo, Timotheos, Timotheus, Timothey, Timthie, Timuthy, Tomothy, Tymon, Tymmothy, Tymothy.*

Vernon (French, Latin) Alder tree; like spring. *Vern, Verda, Verna, Vernal, Verne, Vernen, Verney, Vernin, Vernis.*

Victor (Latin) Conqueror; victor. *Vic, Vick, Vickter, Victa, Victer, Victoir, Victoriano, Victorien, Victorin, Victorino, Victorio, Vikki, Viktor, Vince, Vitenka, Vitin, Vitor, Vitorio, Vittore, Vittorio, Vittorios, Wiktor.*

Walter (German) Leader of the army; strong warrior. *Gauthier, Gautier, Ualtar, Valter, Vova, Walder, Wallie, Wally, Walt, Waltli, Walher, Waltr, Waltur, Walty, Wat, Waterio, Watkin, Watkins, Watson.*

Wayne (English) A wagon maker. *Waggoner, Wain, Wainwright, Wanye, Way, Wayn, Waynell, Waynne, Waynwright, Wene.*

Willard (German) Brave; bold. *Wilard, Willerd.*

William (English) Fearless protector. *Bill, Billie, Billy, Guillaume, Guillaums, Guillermo, Uilleam, Uilliam, Vas, Vasili, Vasilak, Vasilious, Vasily, Vaska, Vassos, Vasyl, Vila, Vildo, Vilek, Vilem, Vilhelm, Vili, Viliam, Viljo, Vilkl, Ville, Villiam, Vilmos, Vilous, Welfel, Wilek, Wiliama, Wiliam, Wilkes, Wilkie, Will, Willem, Wilford, Wilhelm, Will, Willaim, Willaime, Willam, Willard, Willeam, Willem, Williame, Williams, Williamson, Willi, Willie, Willil, Willkie, Willis, Wills, Willy, Willyam, Wiley, Wilmar, Wilmer, Wilmos, Wilmot, Wilson, Wilton, Wilyam, Wilyum, Wim, Winton, Wyley, Wylkes.*

Woodrow (English) A forester; row by the woods. *Wood, Woodie, Woodman, Woodrowe, Woodruff, Woody.*

FUN FACTS

In Japan, popular girls' names have a large foreign influence, like Anna, Maria and Rina. Boys, on the other hand, are most commonly given names ending in ta, ya, ki, hei and suke.

According to an Ohio University study, girls' names go out of fashion much quicker than boys' names, some of which can remain popular for 30 years or more.

Did you know that there'll only ever be one Hurricane Andrew? Once the name's been used for a particularly devastating storm, it's officially retired.

Old-Fashioned Girls' Names

Agnes (Latin, Greek) Lamb; pure; virginal. *Aganetha, Agenta, Aggie, Aggy, Agna, Agne, Agneis, Agnelia, Agnella, Agnés, Agnesa, Agnesca, Agnese, Agnesina, Agneska, Agness, Agnessa, Agneta, Agneti, Agnetta, Agnies, Agnieszka, Agniya, Agnola, Agnolah, Agnolla, Agnolle, Agnus, Aneska, Anka, Annice, Annis Ines, Inez, Nesa, Nessa, Nessi, Nessia, Nessie, Nessy, Nesta, Neza, Senga, Ynes, Ynesita, Ynez.*

Alice (Greek, German) Honest; noble. *Adelice, Ailis, Al, Alece, Alecia, Aleece, Alexis, Ali, Alica, Alican, Alicea, Alicie, Alicyn, Aliece, Alies, Aliese, Alika, Alis, Alisa, Alisha, Alise, Alison, Alix, Alize, Alla, Alles, Allesse, Allice, Allie, Allis, Allisa, Allise, Allison, Alliss, Allisse, Allix, Ally, Allyce, Allys, Alseia, Alyce, Alyse, Alysse, Alysha, Alyshea, Alyshia, Alyson, Lisie, Lisy, Lyssa, Lysse.*

Anna (English, Italian, German, Czech, Swedish, Russian, Polish) Gracious. Another form of Hannah. *Ana, Anae, Anah, Ania, Anica, Anita, Anja, Anka, Annah, Anne, Annina, Annora, Anona, Anuh, Anya, Anyu, Aska.*

Barbara (Greek, Latin) Foreigner; stranger. *Babara, Babb, Babbie, Babe, Babett, Babette, Babina, Babs, Barb, Barbara-Ann, Barbarella, Barbarit, Barbarita, Barbary, Barbe, Barbeeleen, Bärbel, Barbey, Barbie, Babina, Barbora, Barborka, Barbra, Barbrann, Barbro, Barby, Basha, Basia, Bebe, Bobbi, Bobbie, Bobi, Vaoka, Varenka, Varvara, Varya, Vava.*

Beatrice (Latin) Happy; bringing joy. *Bea, Beat, Beata, Béatrice, Beatricia, Beatriks, Beatris, Beatrisa, Beatrise, Beatriss, Beatrissa, Beatrix, Beatriz, Beattie, Beatty, Bebe, Bee, Beitris, Beitriss, Bibi, Treece, Trice, Trixie, Trixy.*

Bernice (Greek) One who brings victory. *Bema, Beranice, Berenice, Berenike, Bernelle, Berneta, Bernessa, Bernetta, Bernette, Benicia, Berni, Bernie, Berise, Bernyce, Brona, Bunny, Nixie.*

Betty (Hebrew) Sacred to God. *Bett, Bette, Betti, Bettina, Bettye, Bettyjean, Betty-Jean, Bettyjo, Bettylou, Betuska, Bety, Biddy, Boski.*

Blanche (French) White. *Blanca, Blanch, Blancha, Blanchette, Blanka, Blanshe, Blenda, Blinney.*

Brenda (English, Scandinavian) A fiery hill; sword. *Bren, Brendalynn, Brendell, Brendelle, Brendette, Brendie, Brendyl, Brenna, Brennda, Brenndah, Brenunda, Brinda, Brindah, Brinna, Brynn, Brynna.*

Catherine (Greek) Pure. *Cadie, Caddie, Cat, Catalina, Catarina, Catarine, Cate, Cateline, Caterina, Catha, Cathann, Cathanne, Catharin, Catharina, Catharine, Catharyn, Catharyna, Catharyne, Cathe, Cathee, Cathenne, Catheren, Catherene, Catherin, Catherina, Catheryn, Cathi, Cathleen, Cathrine, Cathryn, Cathy, Catlaina, Catrice, Catrika, Catrin, Catrina, Catrine, Catryn, Catryna, Cattiah, Caty, Ekaterina, Kat, Kate, Katherine, Kathie, Kathy, Katie, Katrina, Katryn, Kitty.*

Cheryl (French) Beloved. *Charel, Charil, Charyl, Cher, Cherel, Cherelle, Cheri, Cherie, Cherilyn, Cherish, Cherrelle, Cherryl, Cheryle, Cherylee, Cherylene, Cheryll, Cherylle, Cheryline, Cheryn, Sheri, Sherrill, Sherry, Sherryl, Sherryll, Sheryl, Sheryll.*

Clara (Latin) Bright; clear. *Clair, Claire, Clairette, Clairine, Clarabelle, Clare, Claresta, Clareta, Clarette, Clarice, Clarie, Clarinda, Clarine, Claris, Clarisa, Clarissa, Clarisse, Clarita, Clary, Claryce, Clerissa, Clerisse, Cleryce, Clerysse, Klara, Klarice, Klarissa, Klaryce, Klaryssa.*

Donna (Italian) Lady; woman of the house. *Dahna, Danielle, Dom, Domina, Don, Dona, Dondi, Donisha, Donetta, Donnaica, Donnalee, Donnalyn, Donnay, Donnell, Donnella, Donni, Donnica, Donnie, Donnika, Donnise, Donnita, Donny, Dontia, Donya, Madonna.*

Doris (Greek) A place name; of the sea. *Dor, Dore, Dori, Dorice, Dorisa, Dorise, Doriss, Dorlisa, Dorolis, Dorosia, Dorrie, Dorris, Dorrise, Dorrys, Dory, Dorys, Doryse.*

Dorothy (Greek) Gift from God. *Dodo, Dodi, Dolley, Dollie, Dolly, Dorathy, Dorethea, Dorika, Doritha, Dorlisa, Doro, Dorolice, Dorota, Dorotea, Dorotha, Dorothea, Dorothee, Dorothia, Dorrit, Dortha, Dorthea, Dosi, Dossie, Dosya, Dot, Dotson, Dottie, Dotty.*

Edna (Hebrew) Delight. *Eddie, Ednah, Edneisha, Ednita, Eydie.*

Elizabeth (Hebrew) God's oath; devoted to God. *Alzbeta, Babette, Bess, Bessey, Bessi, Bessie, Bessy, Bet, Beta, Beth, Betina, Betine, Betka, Betsey, Betsi, Betsy, Bett, Betta, Bette, Betti, Bettina, Bettine, Betty, Betuska, Eliabeth, Elis, Elisa, Elisabet, Elisabeta, Elisabeth, Elisabethe, Elisabetta, Elisabette, Elisaka, Elisauet, Elisaveta, Elise, Elisebet, Eliska, Elissa, Elisueta, Eliza, Elizabet, Elizabete, Elizabetta, Elizabette, Elizebeth, Ellice, Elliza, Elsa, Elsabeth, Elsbet, Elsbeth, Elsbietka, Elschen, Else, Elsi, Elsie, Elspet, Elspeth, Elspie, Elsy, Elysabeth, Elyse, Elyssa, Elzbieta, Elzunia, Helsa, Illizzabet, Isabel, Isabelita, Lib, Libbee, Libbey, Libbi, Libbie, Libby, Libbye, Lieschen, Liese, Liesel, Lis, Lisa, Lisbet, Lisbete, Lisbeth, Lise, Lisenka, Lisettina, Lisveta, Liz, Liza, Lizabeth, Lizanka, Lizbeth, Lizka, LIzzi, Lizzie, Lizzy, Ysabel, Zizi.*

Ella (English, German) Beautiful; a fairy; all. *Ellamae, Elle, Ellia, Ellie, Elly.*

Elsie (German) God's servant. *Elsee, Elsi, Elsy.*

Ethel (English) Noble. *Adele, Ethelda, Ethelin, Etheline, Ethelle, Ethelred, Ethelbert, Ethelyn, Ethelynn, Ethelynne, Ethille, Ethlin, Ethyl.*

Evelyn (Celtic, French, Hebrew) Pleasant; hazelnut; life. *Avalina, Avaline, Avelina, Aveline, Eileen, Eilen, Eoelene, Ev, Evaleen, Evalene, Evalenne, Evalina, Evaline, Evalyn, Evalynn, Evalynne, Evel, Eveleen, Evelina, Eveline, Evelyne, Evelynn, Evelynne, Evette, Evlin, Evline, Evlun, Evlynn, Ewalina.*

Florence (Latin, Italian) Blooming; Italian place name. *Fleur, Florenza, Flo, Flora, Florance, Florencia, Florency, Florendra, Florense, Florentia, Florentina, Florentyna, Florenza, Florenze, Floretta, Florette, Floria, Florie, Florina, Florine, Floris, Flory, Floryn, Flossie.*

Frances (Latin, French) From France; free. *Fanny, Fran, Franca, France, Francee, Francena, Francesca, Francess, Francesta, Franceta, Francetta, Francette, Francey, Franci, Francine, Franchesca, Francie, Francise, Franchon, Francois, Francyne, Fran, Frank, Frankie, Franni, Frannie, Franny, Franse, Franzetta, Franziska.*

Gertrude (German) Spear maiden. *Gerda, Gerdi, Gert, Gerta, Gertey, Gerti, Gertie, Gertina, Gertraud, Gertrud, Gertruda, Gerty, Jera, Jerica, Truda, Trude, Trudey, True, Trudi, Trudie, Trudy.*

Gladys (Welsh) Lame. *Glad, Gladdie, Gladdy, Gladi, Gladice, Gladis, Gladiz, Gladness, Gladwys, Gwladus, Gwladys.*

Hazel (English) A hazelnut tree; commander. *Hazal, Hazaline, Haze, Hazeline, Hazell, Hazelle, Hazen, Hazie, Hazle, Hazyl, Hazy.*

Heather (English) A flowering shrub; heather. *Heath, Heathe, Heatherlee, Heatherly.*

Helen (Greek) Bright one; light. *Elana, Elin, Halina, Hela, Helaine, Hele, Helena, Helene, Helle, Hellen, Helli, Hellin, Hellon, Helon, Heluska, Helyn, Lena, Lenore.*

Ida (English, German) Prosperous; work. *Idaia, Idaleena, Idalena, Idalene, Idalia, Idalina, Idaline, Idalya, Idalyne, Idarina, Idarine, Idaya, Ide, Idell, Idella, Idelle, Idetta, Idette, Idia, Iduska, Idys.*

Irene (Greek) Peace. *Arina, Arinka, Eirena, Eirene, Eirini, Erena, Erene, Ereni, Errena, Ira, Irana, Iranda, Iranna, Irayna, Ireen, Irén, Irena, Irenea, Irenee, Irenka, Iraiana, Irien, Irina, Irine, Irini, Irisha, Irka, Iryna, Orina, Orya, Oryna, Reena, Reenie, Rene, Rina, Yarina, Yaryna.*

Isabel (Spanish) Holy; God loving. A Spanish form of Elizabeth. *Isabella, Isabela, Isabelle, Isobel, Izabelle, Izabela, Ysabel, Sabel, Issie, Izzy, Iza.*

Janet (English) God's gift; a form of Jane. *Jan, Janeta, Janete, Janett, Janetta, Janette, Janita, Janith, Janitza, Jannet, Janneta, Janneth, Jannetta, Jannette, Janot, Jante, Janyte, Jenet, Jenett, Jenetta, Jenette, Jennetta, Jennette, Jessie, Jinett, Joanet, Johnette, Jonetta, Jonette, Sinéad, Siobhán.*

Janice (Hebrew, English) God is gracious; another form of Jane. *Genese, Jan; Janece, Janecia, Janeece, Janeice, Janese, Janiece, Janika, Janitza, Jannice, Janniece, Jannika, Janyce, Jynice.*

Jean (French) The Lord is gracious. *Jeana, Jeanann, Jeancie, Jeane, Jeanette, Jeanie, Jeanine, Jeanmarie, Jeanna, Jeanne, Jeanney, Jeannie, Jeannot, Jeanny, Jeantelle Jeanny, Jena, Jenay, Jenna, Jenette.*

Joanna (Hebrew) God's gift. *Giovanna, Janka, Jo, Jo-Ana, Joan, Joana, Joandra, Joanka, Joananna, Joananne, Jo-Anie, Jo-Anna, Joann, Joanna, Joannah, Joas, Joeanna, Joetta, Johana, Johanna, Johannah, Johanne, Juaniqua, Juanita, Jurnel, Shawna, Ohanna, Yoanna.*

Josephine (Hebrew) God will increase. *Fena, Fina, Giuseppina, Jo, Jody, Joes, Joey, Jojo, Josee, Josée, Josefa, Josefena, Josefina, Josefine, Josepha, Josephe, Josephene, Josephin, Josephina, Josephyna, Josephyne, Josetta, Josette, Josey, Josi, Josie, Jozaphine.*

Kathleen (Irish, Greek) Little darling; pure. *Caitlin, Cathleen, Katheleen, Kathelene, Kathileen, Kathlyn, Kathlyne, Kathlynn, Kathie, Kathy, Katleen, Kaatlin.*

Lillian (Latin) A lily. *Lian, Lil, Lila, Lilas, Lileana, Lileane, Lilia, Lilian, Liliana, Liliane, Lilika, Lill, Lillas, Lilla, Lilli, Lillia, Lillie, Lillianne, Lilyan, Lillyanna, Lillyann, Lilyanne, Liyan.*

Lois (German) Renowned soldier. *Lo, Loes.*

Louise (German) Famous maiden warrior; female form of Louis. *Aloisa, Aloise, Aloysia, Eloisa, Eloise, Lisette, Lois, Loise, Lolah, Lou, Louie, Louisa, Louisetta, Louisette, Louisiane, Louisine, Louiza, Loulou, Lova, Lovisa, Lowise, Loyce, Loyise, Lu, Luana, Luane, Luisa, Luise, Lulu, Luwana, Ouise, Ouisa.*

Lydia (Greek) Woman from Lydia. *Lida, Liddi, Liddie, Lidi, Lidia, Lidija, Lidiya, Lidka, Likoxhk, Lyda, Lydiah, Lydie.*

Mable (Latin) Lovable. *Amabel, Mab, Mabbel, Mabella, Mabelle, Mabie, Mable, Mabyen, Maibelle, Maibie, Maybel, Maybell, Maybelle, Maybie.*

Mae (Celtic) A form of Mary. *Maelle, Maeona, May.*

Margaret (Greek, Latin, Persian) Pearl; child of the light. *Greeta, Greetje, Grere, Gret, Greta, Gretal, Gretchen, Gretel, Gretle, Madge, Mag, Maggi, Maggie, Maggy, Maire, Mairi, Maisie, Margalith, Margalo, Margara, Margareta, Margarethe, Margarett, Margaretta, Margarette, Margarida, Margarita, Margarite, Marge, Margeret, Margerey, Margery, Margie, Margo, Margot, Margret, Margrett, Marguerette, Marguerite, Marj, Marjoe, Marjorie, Marmie, Marta, Maymie, Meaghan, Meaghen, Meg, Megan, Megen, Meggi, Meggie, Meggy, Meghan, Midge, Peg, Pegg, Peggey, Peggi, Peggie, Peggy, Reet, Reeta, Reita, Rheeta, Rita, Ritta.*

Marion (French) An alternate form of Mary. *Mare, Mariana, Mariano, Marrian, Marrion, Mary, Maryian, Maryon, Maryonn.*

Marjorie (Greek, English) Pearl; a form of Margaret. *Madge, Majorie, Marcail, Marg, Marge, Margeree, Margerey, Margerie, Margery, Margey, Margorie, Margory, Marjarie, Marjary, Marje, Marjerie, Marjery, Marjie, Marjorey, Marjori, Marjory, Marjy.*

Martha (Arabic) Lady. *Macia, Maita, Marella, Marit, Marite, Marlet, Mart, Marta, Martaha, Martell, Marth, Marthan, Marthe, Marthena, Marthina, Marthine, Marthy, Marti, Marticka, Martina, Martita, Marty, Martyne, Masia, Matti, Mattie, Matty.*

Mildred (English) Gentle. *Hildred, Mil, Mila, Mildraed, Mildread, Mildrene, Mildrid, Mildryd, Milli, Millie, Milly.*

Miriam (Hebrew) Bitter; older version of Mary. *Maijii, Maikki, Mair, Maire, Mairi, Mairona, Mame, Mamie, Mamy, Mariam, Mariame, Masha, Mashenka, Mashka, Meryem, Miliana, Mima, Mimi, Mimma, Mimmie, Mimsie, Miri, Miriama, Miriame, Mirian, Mirjam, Mirriam, Mirrian, Miryam, Mitzi, Myriam.*

Nancy (Hebrew) Gracious. *Nainsey, Nainsi, Nan, Nana, Nance, Nancee, Nancey, Nanci, Nancie, Nancine, Nancsi, Nancye, Nanette, Nanice, Nanine, Nanna, Nanncey, Nanncy, Nanni, Nannie, Nanny, Nanouk, Nanscey, Nansee, Nansey, Noni, Nonie.*

Opal (Sanskrit) A precious jewel. *Opale, Opalina, Opaline.*

Patricia (Latin) A noble woman. *Pat, Patia, Patreece, Patreice, Patria, Patrica, Patrice, Patriceia, Patricka, Patrisha, Patrishia, Patrizia, Patrizzia, Patsie, Patsy, Patti, Pattie, Patty, Ricky, Tish, Tricia, Trish, Trisha.*

Pauline (Latin) A form of Paula. *Pauleen, Paulene, Paulina, Paulyne, Pawlina.*

Phoebe (Greek) Bright one. *Febe, Fee, Feebe, Feebs, Phaeve, Pheabe, Pheba, Phebe, Pheby, Pheebee, Phoeb, Phoebey, Phoebie, Phoebs, Phoebus.*

Phyllis (Greek) A leaf. *Filida, Filise, Fillys, Fyllis, Philicia, Philida, Philis, Phillis, Philliss, Phillisse, Phillys, Phyl, Phylis, Phyliss, Phylisse, Phyllida, Phyllis, Phyllys.*

Priscilla (Latin) Of ancient times. *Cilla, Piri, Precila, Precilla, Prescilla, Pricila, Pricilla, Pris, Prisca, Priscella, Priscila, Priscille, Prisella, Prisila, Prisilla, Priss, Prissie, Prissilla, Prissy, Prysilla.*

Rita (Greek) Pearl; short for Margarita. *Reatha, Reda, Reeta, Reida, Reitha, Reta, Rheta, Rhetta, Rida, Riet, Ritaamae, Ritamarie.*

Rose (Latin) Rose; a flower. *Rasia, Roanna, Rois, Roise, Rosa, Rosabel, Rosabell, Rosabella, Rosabelle, Rosalee, Rosaleen, Rosaley, Rosalia, Rosalie, Rosalin, Rosamund, Rosebud, Rosella, Roselle, Rosellen, Rosemarie, Rosemary, Rosemonde, Rosemund, Rosena, Roseta, Rosetta, Rosette, Rosey, Rosi, Rosie, Rosina, Rosita, Rosly, Rosmund, Rosse, Rosy, Roz, Roze, Rozee, Rozsi.*

Ruby (French) A precious red gem. *Rube, Rubetta, Rubette, Rubey, Rubi, Rubia, Rubiann, Rubie, Rubyann, Rubye, Rue.*

Sandra (English, Greek) Helper; protector. *Sahndra, Sandee, Sandi, Sandie, Sandira, Sandrea, Sandria, Sandrica, Sandrine, Sandy, Saundra, Shandra, Sondra, Zandra.*

Shelley (English) A meadow on the ledge. *Shelee, Shell, Shella, Shellee, Shellene, Shelli, Shellian, Shellie, Shellina, Shelly.*

Shirley (English) A bright meadow. *Sherlee, Sherleen, Sherley, Sherli, Sherlie, Sherey, Sherly, Sheryl, Shir, Shirelle, Shirl, Shirlean,*

Shirlee, Shirleen, Shirleigh, Shirlene, Shirlie, Shirlly, Shirly, Shirlyn, Shirlynn, Shurl, Shurlee, Shurley, Shurlie, Shurly.

Stella (Greek, Latin) A star. *Estella, Estelle, Starla, Starling, Stela, Stele, Stelie, Stellar, Stelle, Stellina.*

Thelma (Greek) Will. *Telma, Thel, Thelmalina.*

Vera (Latin, Russian) True; faith. *Vara, Veera, Veira, Veradis, Verah, Verasha, Vere, Verenia, Veria, Verie, Verin, Verina, Verine, Verla, Verouska, Viera, Vira.*

Viola (Latin, Italian) A violet; a stringed instrument. *Vi, Violah, Violaine, Violanta, Violante, Viole, Violeine, Violet.*

Violet (Latin, French) A violet; purple flower. *Vi, Viola, Viole, Violetta, Violette, Vylolet, Vyolet, Vyoletta, Vyolette*

Virginia (Latin) Chaste; virginal. *Gina, Ginger, Ginia, Giniah, Ginny, Jinny, Verginia, Verinya, Virge, Virgen, Virgenia, Virgenya, Virgie, Virgine, Virginie, Virginnia, Virginya, Virgy, Virjeana.*

Willie (English, German) Short for Wilhelmina. *Willi, Willina, Willisha, Willy.*

Wilma (German) Unwavering protector; short form of Wilhelmina. *Williemae, Wilmah, Wilmayra, Wilmetta, Wilmette, Wilmina, Wilmyne, Wylm, Wylma.*

Last Names as First Names

Think traditional names sound too old for a newbie? Try honouring an ancestor by using his or her last name instead. The last-name-as-first-name trend hit the map in the late 90s with popular names like Madison, Mackenzie, Taylor and Morgan. Although the trend is more popular for girls, there are quite a few Averys, Masons and Landons around.

Last Names for Boys

Ackland	Anderson	Barton
Acton	Ash	Becker
Addison	Bailey	Beckett

Bennett	Irving	Parker
Brennin	Jackson	Payne
Boyd	Jansen	Peyton
Burton	Jenkins	Porter
Calder	Johnson	Quinn
Campbell	Kelsey	Remington
Carter	Kendall	Sawyer
Charlton	Langdon	Scott
Dante	Lennox	Smith
Deacon	Mackay	Sweeney
Decker	Mackenzie	Reilly
Denton	Mackinnon	Tamir
Dover	Manley	Taylor
Emerson	Madden	Traynor
Findley	Marsh	Tucker
Gulliver	Mason	Turner
Hamilton	McConnell	Vermond
Hanson	Montgomery	Watson
Heaton	Morgan	Walker
Hogan	Morley	Weston
Holden	Nasir	Wolf
Holt	Newman	Wylie
Houston	Newton	Wynston

 CANUCK TRIVIA

The most popular girls' names in British Columbia in 1920 were Margaret, Mary, Dorothy, Elizabeth and Kathleen.

The most popular boys' names in British Columbia in 1920 were John, William, Robert, James and George.

Nicknames

Fiercely opposed to hearing your son Richard called Dick, Dickie or Rich? Unfortunately, there's not much you can do about it. Nicknames have been around for as long as names have existed and they often last a lifetime. Whether it's because people are too lazy to pronounce a full name or because they feel creative enough to invent their own, there's really no stopping the short form. So, here are a few things to keep in mind when choosing a name for your little tyke.

Be formal

As soon as someone tries to shorten little Matthew's name, whether it's Grandma or your best friend, firmly tell that person that you'd prefer if they used his full name instead.

Go short

The shorter the name, the more likely it is to be nickname-proof. Good examples include Glenn, Brett, Sam, Gail, Paige, and Bria.

Go long

The longer the name, the more nickname possibilities. Take Elizabeth for example. Liz, Lizzie, Beth and Betsy are just a few of the numerous names she could be called. This means you'll have more options to choose from, so if you hate one of the names, you can ask people to use another one instead. Longer names also give your child a more decisive role to play in the naming process. Later on, she can choose to be known by the one she likes best.

Accept the inevitable

No matter how hard you try, there's always going to be someone who'll try to shorten your child's name. And if kids can't find a way to create a nickname out of a name, they'll invent a new one based on a physical or character trait (like Tiny for the biggest guy in the class). Those often stick just as long as the shortened versions.

Last Names for Girls

Astrella	Dixie	Morgan
Aubrey	Doucette	Orchard
Averill	Gilly	Page
Bailey	Halley	Parke
Beckley	Hannah	Parker
Bellamy	Innes	Paxton
Berkeley	Ireland	Raina
Breese	Ivey	Ramsey
Bromley	Keane	Reese
Burr	Kelly	Reis
Cade	Kendall	Ryder
Cady	Logan	Saberi
Cassidy	Malaka	Saterlee
Chatsey	Mallery	Sedore
Chilton	Mallory	Severn
Coventry	Mason	Sinclair
Darley	Matalin	Temple
Darling	McKenna	Witney
Devane		

Chapter 12

-☆-

Trendy Names

"How do popular names differ from trendy ones?" you ask. Popular types grace the top baby name lists across the provinces, territories and rest of the globe. And they stay at the top year after year. Trendy names, on the other hand, scream "live-in-the-moment" and "fly-by-the-seat-of-your-proverbial-pants." These names are hip, cool and definitely with it—for now. But beware: they have a tendency to fall out of favour fast, lasting little longer than the Spice Girls' popularity. So, in just a year, your little Dallas could be begging you to rename him John or Matthew.

Like your choice of movies, the baby name you pick says a lot about your personality. Lovers of Mary tend to be more traditional and many have strong religious connections, for instance, while those who prefer California are more likely to watch indie flicks and listen to a wide variety of music. Those who opt for trendy names often want to be viewed as having a finger on the pulse of what's happening. By naming a daughter Kennedy, for example, parents are showing that they, too, can fit in with the cool crowd who eat raw food, drink low-fat lattés and carry purse-size dogs.

But just as we now consider sushi to be totally yesterday, so might we turn our noses up at trendy names like Brock and Chase. If you're still willing to take the risk, or merely want to take a peek at what's considered way cool at the moment, here are a few trendy names that are currently still in. And hey, some of these could be like 80s fashion, which seems to keep coming back into style whether we like it or not.

REAL NAMES

When Caitlin was born 28 years ago, she was the only person she knew with her name. She liked being unique and thought her name sounded beautiful. Then, about five years ago, everything changed. "Every little girl started to be named Caitlin or Kaitlyn or Katelyn," she says. Now it's totally common. If she had to pick another name for herself, Caitlin would choose her mother's name, Claire. "It's unique and pretty and I would be honoured to share a name with my mother because she's an amazing individual," she says.

Aileen was always proud of having her grandmother's name. "She was beautiful and eccentric [and I adored her]," the 48-year-old reminisces. But sometimes she wished her name was a bit easier to understand, like Amy. "There are so many similar names which sound like Aileen," she says. As a child, she hated having to correct people who thought her name was Elaine, Arlene or Eileen.

Trendy Boys' Names

Armani	Dublin	Phoenix
Axel	Fabio	Prince
Banjo	Frost	Reece
Blaze	Huck	Rider
Boston	Jet	Rio
Braxton	Kenzo	River
Brock	Kyler	Shadow
Chase	Lark	Sinbad
Colby	Lash	Slade
Colten	Leaf	Stone
Cuba	London	Storm
Dakota	Maverick	Tanner
Dallas	Melbourne	Templar
Dante	Memphis	Tiger
Denim	Milan	Thor
Devin	Orlando	
Dubai	Oslo	

KIDS' KORNER

Shannal's parents chose her name to reflect how special she is. "I am named after a perfume," says the 12-year-old. "And it is cool and it suits me, too." She just wishes that she didn't have to share it with other people.

"I've only met two people that have the same name as me," says 10-year-old Craig. And it's cool because it's just one word. "People can't have a short form for my name," he points out. But sometimes, he complains, kids think his name is short for something like Craigory, so they'll call him that instead.

Trendy Girls' Names

Aspen	Harmony	Plum
Autumn	Hope	Porsche
Bella	Ice	Rain
Brooklyn	India	Raven
Cairo	Ireland	Savannah
California	Kennedy	Scarlett
Chelsea	Kenya	Siena
Cheyenne	Kiwi	Sierra
China	Lake	Skye
Clementine	Lettice	Skylar
Clover	London	Starbright
Daisy	Maia	Strawberry
Dakota	Maya	Sunshine
Destiny	Meadow	Trinity
Diamond	Montana	Violet
Genesis	Paris	Willow

> ## ☺ FUN FACTS
> The name Morpheus (after a character from *The Matrix*) flew onto the baby naming map after the film's release in 1999.
> Over 5,000 babies named Mohammed were born in Britain in 2004.
> Recently a pregnant Palestinian woman was stuck for five days at the border between Israel and Egypt. She finally gave birth to "Maabar," meaning "Terminal," in an Egyptian ambulance.

Designer Names

Not a fan of traditional, trendy or popular names? Why not express your unique qualities by inventing a moniker of your own? Here are a few tips to help you get started.

Drop a letter

One of the easiest ways to invent a name is by using a common one like Olivia and dropping a letter to make it into something else, like Livia. Or, you could take a popular name like Malcolm and drop an entire syllable, changing it to Colm.

Rhyme it

Another quick way to create something new involves taking a name you like and changing its first initial or spelling. So Jason, for example, could turn into Mason or Rayson. As long as it still rhymes, you're on the right track.

Add something

Take a name you like and add another letter or syllable to make it unique. For example, change Ash to Ask or Ashloya and Kent to Klent or Kenton.

Change the spelling

If you really like a name but hate its commonality, try altering the spelling. Change Lucy to Luci or Devon to Devin, for instance. Just don't make it so different that your child will have trouble spelling it herself.

Put it together

Honour parents, grandparents or yourselves by combining your names to create a new one. Andrew + Leah could yield Andrelea or Colin and Ashley could name a little one Ashlin.

Get creative

Find a name you like and fiddle around with it until you've created something you're proud of. Take mine for example—Shandley. After naming six kids, my parents decided to get more creative. They started with Chantel, then added our family's Irish roots and changed it to start with an "S" so I'd have the same initials as my dad.

Don't go too weird

Remember, a name is something that your child is stuck with for life. Out of the ordinary, hard to pronounce and difficult to spell is a really bad combination. If you're opting for something different, try to make sure it looks good phonetically and is easy for a child and others to spell.

Remember the last name

Made up names are best suited to plain, short last names like Brown, Smith and Jones, especially if the name is long and complicated. Those with more interesting last names may want to stick with a short and easy name or one that's more common. My sister Dawn, for instance, named her daughter Megan because she loved it and thought that anything more distinctive would clash with her husband's last name, Torisawa.

Chapter 13

- ☆ -

Unisex Names

These days, you can't judge a person's sex based on the first name alone, especially if you've only met over e-mail. With androgynous monikers like Montana, Dakota, and Taylor taking centre stage, you'd better be sure that the Sydney you're writing to is a guy before you refer to him as Mr.

Unisex names came onto the naming scene in the early 60s, with nicknames like Toby and Jody being used frequently to refer to people of both sexes. It wasn't until the 80s, however, that boys' names like Kelsey and Jamie hit the popular female name charts. And in the early 90s, Taylor, Madison, MacKenzie, Morgan and Sydney swept those former stars under the rug.

Although society deems it acceptable and even desirable to give children unisex names, it's still more common to find a girl sporting a boy's name than it is the other way around. Many people are still set in old stereotypes. They view giving a girl a boy's name as an easy way to instill her with masculine qualities like strength and determination. Naming a boy Kimberly, on the other hand, is seen as feminizing the male, making him weak and over sensitive.

Weird Names

Ever met or heard of someone whose name was just too strange to believe? Like a kid named Leonardo Da Vinci or a man named Gay? While I'm sure you have many that you could add to this list, here are a few of my favourite weird but true names.

Christopher Columbus
(not the explorer)

David Davidson

Deborah Martinez Martinez

Ferda Derdler

Gaye Males

Harley Davidson

Harold Dick (Shortened to
Harry, of course)

Honey Huckaluck

John Johnson

Michael Bolton (not the singer)

Phil Ng

Rich Hardigan (nickname Dick)

Richard Shitten (shortened to
Dick)

Sandi Beach

Tu Morrow

Tudor Sherrard

Wayne McShane

 REAL NAMES

When 28-year-old Mandi was growing up, the spelling of her name was unique, which she liked. Since Mandi felt that her name was "a little plain," anything that made it stand out a bit was appreciated. "My mom wanted to name me Randy, but my dad thought that was only a boy name, so they came up with Mandi," she says. "I wish [they] would have stuck with naming me a boy's name."

Deirdre loves the fact that her name is versatile. "I can choose when to be formal (Deirdre) or not (Dee)," explains the 30-year-old. But the fact that barely anyone can pronounce it correctly gets under her skin. From Deadtree to Deedra, she's gotten just about every variation possible. "The real way to say it," she explains, "is Deardree."

Who's Choosing These Names?

Parents who bestow a masculine name on their daughter often want to bust through gender stereotypes to give their child a leg up in the world. Naming her something like Devon or Tyler, they think, will encourage confidence and ability, while producing yet another Sarah may cause their daughter to fall into old ways of pink dresses, soft voices and a fear of getting dirty.

Those who give feminine names like Courtney or Kelly to their sons may also be striving to break this gender barrier. Giving a softer name to their son, some believe, could encourage him to be more compassionate, creative and sensitive.

Those who don't have feminist ideals are probably opting for a unisex moniker as a way to set their child apart from the millions of Emilys, Emmas, Ethans and Joshuas in the world. Naming a girl Daryl or a boy Alexis will help distinguish them from others in their day care, school or soccer league. And an androgynous name can make a child unique and trendy at the same time.

Other parents opt for unisex names as a way to honour an area they like or a family member they're fond of. Place names like Dakota and Montana are commonly used for both boys and girls while surnames like Mason and MacKenzie have also hit the naming scene. Plus, for those who've always wanted to name a child after their father but keep having girls, there may be no alternative to calling her Sydney or Noah.

But before you rush out to present your little prince or princess Harry, it's important to consider the pros and cons of giving kids an androgynous name. Here's what you need to know:

The Pros
Power
Girls with masculine names are often assumed to be cool, tough and level-headed, even if none of these adjectives describe them. Their name alone could help them gain self-confidence and success later in life.

KIDS' KORNER

Christopher really wishes that people would call him by Chris instead of using the "topher" part of his name. And if they just can't do that, says the 12-year-old, he'd like to be renamed Nathaniel "because that's what my parents were gonna name me if they hadn't have heard Christopher."

"My parents named me using both their initials," says eight-year-old Jordyn Taylor, daughter of Joe and Teresa. "It makes it special." She does wish, however, that people would stop saying, "That's a boy's name," when they meet her.

Half the Work

Don't want to find out the sex before your baby's born? No problem. Choosing an androgynous name cuts out half the work of naming your child. No matter which unisex option you choose, it'll be perfect for either a boy or a girl.

Job Equality

When applying for jobs, employers will look at the resume of an androgynously named applicant to judge his or her qualifications instead of basing their opinions solely on gender. It's hard to know who you're getting when Hunter and Tory apply.

 FUN FACTS

It is more popular for girls to have a unisex name than it is for boys. And once an androgynous name has become popular for girls (e.g., Morgan), it rarely jumps back to being masculine.

In 2000, there were 298 girls and 273 boys in the U.S. named Armani, after the clothing line.

Chief Rastas of a Ghaliatu Village in the Solomon Islands named his son Ramsi to honour the intervention force working hard to maintain peace in the islands. The child's name is an acronym for the Regional Assistance Mission to Solomon Islands.

The Cons
Loss of Masculinity

As mentioned before, boys have a much tougher time with unisex names than girls do. Beyond schoolyard teasing are the stereotypes given to them by peers and adults in university and the workforce. Your Courtney may be the best football player in the province, but many may see him as better suited to designing clothes than scoring touchdowns.

Loss of Femininity

Just because a girl's named Corey doesn't mean she has to wear baggy jeans and a cropped hair cut. Similar to boys who have a feminine name, girls with androgynous names are often presumed to favour playing with trucks and dirt over dolls and colouring kits. Their names could create visions of butchiness instead of femininity.

Humiliation

The last thing anyone wants is for their child to be the target of teasing. And unfortunately, this is a more common occurrence for boys with unisex names than it is for girls. Take my brother Lindsay, for example. He was teased incessantly through childhood for having the same name as girls in his class. It wasn't until he reached high school and established a strong personality that the teasing stopped and he grew comfortable with his name. The moral of the story: it's important to think of the consequences before giving your child a name he or she might be embarrassed by.

Confusion

Another key problem for those with androgynous names is gender confusion. When dealing with people who've never met them, kids often have to explain whether they're a boy or a girl. And throughout their lives, they're pretty much guaranteed to be called he rather than she or *Ms.* instead of *Mr.*

CANUCK TRIVIA

There were 239 boys and 164 girls named Baby in B.C. in 1985, making it the thirteenth most popular name in the province for both sexes. Of course, most of these were probably kids who simply didn't have a name at the time of registration, so parents just labeled them as baby.

Jessie was the eleventh most popular girls' name in British Columbia between 1872 and 1898.

Unisex Names

Now that you've weighed the pros and cons of choosing an androgynous name for your child, it's time to do the fun part—pick a few that you like best.

Aaron	Cassidy	Gene
Addison	Chase	Gerry
Adrian	Chris	Glenn
Alex	Connor	Hadley
Alexis	Corey	Harley
Andy	Courtney	Hudson
Ashley	Dakota	Hunter
Aubrey	Dale	Ira
August	Dallas	Israel
Bailey	Dana	Jade
Billy	Daryl	Jaden
Brett	Devon	Jamie
Brice	Dilot	Jesse
Brooklyn	Drew	Jo
Caden	Dylan	Jordan
Cameron	Eliot	Jules
Carmen	Emerson	Kai
Carmine	Erin	Kelly
Carson	Evan	Kelsey
Casey	Frances	Kerry

Kendall	Orion	Sawyer
Kennedy	Paris	Scout
Kyle	Parker	Sean
Lane	Pat	Shane
Lee	Payton	Skylar
Leslie	Perry	Spencer
Lindsay	Quinn	Stacy
Logan	Rae	Sydney
London	Reagan	Taylor
Mackenzie	Reed	Terry
Madison	Reese	Tony
Mallory	Regan	Tory
Marley	Rene	Tracy
Mason	Ricky	Tyler
Montana	Riley	Tyne
Morgan	Robin	Tyson
Nevada	Rory	Wallace
Nicky	Ryan	Wesley
Noah	Ryder	Whitney
Noel	Sam	Zane

Hard-to-spell Names

One of the most challenging parts about being a kid is learning how to read and write. And one of the first things you ever learn to spell is your name. Imagine if you were called Vyacheslav Deborskerov? That's hard enough to pronounce, let alone spell. The only upside to a name like this (spelling-wise, that is) is you'll learn the alphabet quickly.

Why not make it easy on your child and give him an easy-to-spell first name, or use a short nickname to start off with until he gets the hang of it?

Chapter 14

-☆-

Place Names

Naming children after a city, lake, country or region is hardly a new concept. After all, names like Dakota, Georgia and Montana have graced elementary school rosters for over fifteen years. Even Victoria and David Beckham have followed suit, naming their son Brooklyn after the New York suburb.

Choosing a place name can be a good way to remember an area of special significance. Whether it was a spot visited on your honeymoon or your favourite weekend retreat, some places hold deep meaning and wonderful memories—perfect for honouring your new addition. My husband and I considered naming a daughter Seville, after the Spanish city in which we were engaged. In the end, we chose Vail (as in Colorado) for our daughter's middle name to honour the last trip she took with us in utero.

Unfortunately, some places don't lend themselves well to baby names. Take one of my favourite spots, Kings Canyon in the Australian Outback. Not only is it too wordy and pretentious, but it also doesn't fit with our daughter's name of Brown. So even though you might love the area, it's important to stick to a name that will work for a child. The last thing you want is to ruin your memories by having your kid teased for being the only Las Vegas or Northwest Territories in the class.

In addition to making sure the name would suit a child, it's important to think about the stereotypes surrounding the place you choose. It's hard enough to be a kid, let alone one who's saddled with a name like Baghdad or Congo, which has been surrounded by controversy.

Don't have a place in mind? From the Yukon to Hong Kong, I've scoured the globe to come up with a few for you to choose from.

Canadian Place Names

Considering we live in the second largest country in the world, with almost 10,000,000 square kilometers of land, there's bound to be at least one Canadian place name you like.

Canadian Place Names for Boys

Aklavik Land in this Northwest Territories' region is shared by both the Gwic'in and Inuvialuit peoples.

Alberni Life in British Columbia's Port Alberni revolves around fishing and forestry.

Amherst The remains of Fort Amherst can be found in St. John's, Newfoundland.

Amos A haven for clean water, the spring variety from this small Québec town is bottled and sold under the name Périgny.

Arviat Once known as Eskimo Point, the settlement of Arviat is the most southern of all communities in Nunavut.

Atlin A small town located near Whitehorse, British Columbia.

Avalon The name of a peninsula housing almost half the population of Newfoundland.

Boyd A cave in central Newfoundland where tourists can see archeological ruins of a Beothuk village.

Brackley Brackley Beach is a national park in the central region of Prince Edward Island.

Brandon Also known as "wheat city," Brandon is the second largest city in Manitoba, behind Winnipeg.

Breton Cape Breton Island is Nova Scotia's large, rugged island known for beautiful mountain and sea views.

Burin A photogenic old town on Newfoundland's Burin Peninsula.

Campbell Known as the salmon capital of the world, Campbell River is found on the east coast of Vancouver Island in British Columbia.

Canso A small town on Nova Scotia's Eastern Shore, Canso is surrounded by history.

Charlevoix Situated in what is known as rural Québec, this beautiful region boasts lush mountains, rolling hills, crevices and cliffs, all along the St. Lawrence River.

Comox Like fishing, swimming and hanging out on the beach? Then Comox Valley in British Columbia is the vacation spot for you.

Cortes Just east of Quadra Island in British Columbia, Cortes Island is just as impressive with tons of wildlife to spy on.

Cypress Nature lovers should make Cypress Hills Interprovincial Park a must-stop on their next Saskatchewan visit. With spectacular lakes, hills, hiking trails and camp sites, what more could you want?

Dawson Known as the official starting point ("Mile 0") of the Alaska Highway, Dawson Creek, British Columbia, is a good place to watch the Northern Lights. This is also the name of a small town by the Yukon and Klondike rivers.

Dempster A highway running between the Yukon and Northwest Territories.

Denman A small Gulf Island in British Columbia, Denman is worth visiting for its beautiful nature views and the community's handmade arts and crafts.

Digby Anyone who loves seafood should definitely visit the Nova Scotian town of Digby, famed for its fresh scallops and smoked herring.

Dover Port Dover is a popular Ontario summer spot complete with boat tours, interesting shops, a beach and a lighthouse.

Dryden If you like fishing or hunting, Dryden is the place to be. If not, you might want to find another Ontario town to explore.

Dufferin A two-hour drive from Halifax, Port Dufferin is situated on Nova Scotia's Eastern Shore.

Dugald Just east of Winnipeg, this town's main feature is the Costume Museum of Canada.

Estevan While visiting Saskatchewan's town of Estevan, make sure to look for the way-larger-than-life statue of coal miner, Lignite Louie.

Fogo A mere 25 km in length, Fogo Island is a good spot for Iceberg hunting in Newfoundland.

Frederic Fredericton is one of the most major cities in the Maritimes and the capital of New Brunswick.

Galiano Virtually untouched, most of this British Columbian island is undeveloped forest land.

Gander An unexciting town in central Newfoundland, Gander is often used as a fuel stop for planes, trucks and cars.

Gimli Home of the Icelandic Festival of Manitoba, Gimli is mainly a fishing and faming village located about an hour north of Winnipeg.

Haines Craving an outdoor adventure? The Yukon's Haines Junction is the perfect starting place for everything from serious hiking to mountain climbing.

Hamilton A highly industrial city in southwestern Ontario, Hamilton is considered the centre of the country's iron and steel industries.

Hardy With a population of just under 5,000, Port Hardy is a small town based at the northern tip of Vancouver Island.

Herschel Lying in the Beaufort Sea, Herschel Island is also known as Qikiqtaruk, which means "it is an island" in Inuktitut.

Hillman The name of a marsh along the shore just north of Point Pelee in Ontario. It offers good bird-watching opportunities and a pleasant walking trail.

Ingraham A 70 km trail in the Northwest Territories, the Ingraham Trail is located east of Yellowknife.

Irving A nature park in Saint John, New Brunswick.

James James Bay takes up 350,000 square kms of land in Québec. On it are eight Cree Indian reserves.

Jourimain The Cape Jourimain Nature Centre in New Brunswick covers 1,667 acres of land, all protected by the Canadian Wildlife Service.

Kamloop Kamloops, British Columbia, is situated in the Thompson Nicola region. Known as the Tournament Capital of Canada, this city is as rich in history as it is in recreational activities.

Kent Kentville is a small town located at the east end of the Annapolis valley in Nova Scotia.

Kluane Kluane National Park houses the largest collection of wildlife on the continent. Visit this huge Yukon nature region to catch a glimpse of everything from grizzly bears to moose. While you're there, hop on a mountain bike or head out fishing.

Labrador Essentially a part of Newfoundland, Labrador is three times larger than its host province.

Lennox Prince Edward Island's Lennox Island is home to many Mi'kmaq families. It's a great place to enjoy fresh blueberries and lobster.

Liard Sitting just 37 km north of the Northwest Territories and British Columbia border, Fort Liard is a small hamlet with a population of about 500.

Mahone A popular spot for Halifax weekenders, Mahone Bay is a quaint area full of gorgeous views and antique shops.

Manan Grand Manan Island is located just south of Campobello Island in New Brunswick. It's also the largest island in the Bay of Fundy.

Maurice With lush campgrounds, winding walking trails and numerous fishing areas, Québec's La Maurice National Park is a favourite spot for nature lovers.

Morin Val Morin is a quiet village hidden in the mountains near Montreal. It's famous for fantastic cross country ski trails.

Nelson The buildings of Nelson are nestled in beautiful hills by Kootenay Lake and the Selkirk Mountains.

Odanak A small village housing an Abénaki Native Indian reservation in Québec.

Orford A 58 square km park, Parc du Mont Orford lies in the Eastern Townships of Québec.

Owen If you're interested in the arts, head to Ontario's Owen Sound, named one of the country's five "Cultural Capitals" in 2004; you're sure to find some form of entertainment that suits you.

Parry A popular summer spot for Ontarians, Parry Sound is situated on Georgian Bay.

Penticton What a beautiful spot to visit in British Columbia's Okanagan Valley. Ski, swim or attend a wine tasting—just don't miss this quaint town.

Prescott An historic Ontario town near Ottawa, Montreal and Syracuse, New York.

Quidi Home of the oldest cottage in North America, Quidi Vidi is a tiny yet pretty village just outside St. John's, Newfoundland.

Rupert The second largest city on main land British Columbia, Prince Rupert is mainly a fishing town.

Selkirk Mmm, catfish. You should try some when you visit this Manitoban town.

Shelburne Found along Nova Scotia's South Shore, Shelburne is both beautiful and historical. This is also the name of a small town near Toronto.

Siméon A somewhat uninteresting town in Québec. Its most famous attraction: Les Palissades Centre Éco-forestier.

Simpson With a population near 1,200, Fort Simpson is the largest community in its region in the Northwest Territories.

Stanley A waterfront town in southern Ontario, Port Stanley is a summertime favourite. In Vancouver, this name was given to the city's huge and well-frequented Stanley Park.

Tillsonburg A small town in southern Ontario famous for its tobacco-growing district.

Tobermory An attractive village in the Bruce Peninsula of Ontario, Tobermory is popular for both tourism and fishing.

Tofino One of British Columbia's gems, Tofino lies on the west coast of Vancouver Island in Clayoquot Sound. If you love spending time outside and eco-tourism is your thing, Tofino can't be missed.

Trinity A bay that runs along Newfoundland's Avalon peninsula.

Truro Smack dab in the middle of Nova Scotia, Truro is a small town unpopular with tourists.

Ucluelet A fantastic place to fish for Salmon, this British Columbian town also offers good places to camp.

Valcourt The Québec birthplace of Joseph Armand Bombardier, creator of the snowmobile.

Vernon Although not as beautiful as neighbouring Okanagan towns Kelowna and Penticton, Vernon is surrounded by three lakes and a picturesque valley.

Watson Known as the Gateway to the Yukon, the town of Watson Lake can be found in the territory's southeast region.

Wendake Located only 15 km or so northwest of Québec City, this small town is often visited for its Huron-Wendat village.

Wetaskwin Home of the Reynolds-Alberta Museum, just south of Edmonton.

Weyburn This Saskatchewan town was the birthplace of author W.O. Mitchell.

Wheatley A happening spot for migrating birds, this small Ontario town boasts a provincial park and popular beach area.

Windsor A largely industrial town in southwestern Ontario, Windsor is located directly across from Detroit.

Yukon One of Canada's three territories, the Yukon covers more than 483,000 square km.

Famous people with place names

From Chevy Chase to Dakota Fanning, even the rich and famous are named after places. Here are a few you might recognize.

Famous men with place names:

Chevy Chase (actor, comedian)

Christopher Khayman Lee (actor)

Clint Eastwood (actor, director)

Denholm Elliott (actor)

Etienne De Crecy (singer)

Harrison Ford (actor)

Horton Foote (actor)

Orlando Bloom (actor)

Montgomery Clift (actor)

Montserrat Caballé (singer)

Robert Englund (actor)

Shelton Dane (child actor)

Sterling Hayden (actor)

Stone Cold Steve Austin (wrestler)

Famous women with place names:

Alberta Watson (actress)

Ann Hampton Callaway (singer)

Asia Argento (actress)

Dakota Fanning (child actress)

Delta Burke (actress)

India.Arie (singer)

Irán Castillo (singer)

Kathy Ireland (model)

Olympia Dukakis (actress)

Paris Hilton (actress and socialite)

Rosario Dawson (actress)

Sienna Guillory (actress)

Victoria Beckham (former singer)

Virginia Hay (actress)

Winona Ryder (actress)

REAL NAMES

"I never really liked it that much, but others say they do," 40-year-old Shane says about his name. "So I guess it's nice that others like it." The main reasons for his discord: as a child, other kids thought it was a girls' name and for some reason, people constantly call him Shawn.

Bonnie describes her name as "different without being bizarre." While the 31-year-old admits that most people have heard her name before, she says she was the only Bonnie in her elementary and high schools. "Now, however, I'm in a small town of 1,500 people and there are five of us," she says. What are the chances?

Cedrick considers his name, which is the same as his grandfather's, to be unique. And he's proud of the fact that it runs in the family. If he absolutely had to choose another name for himself, the 37-year-old says he'd stick to tradition and pick "Charlton, because it is my father's name."

Caroline pretends that she doesn't mind when people call her Carolyn, but underneath, it drives her crazy. "I always liked that [my name] was not Carolyn," she explains. "To me, the two names are totally different." This 46-year-old, however, always did love the nickname she received from a school friend's father: Good Queen Caroline.

Canadian Place Names for Girls

Adèle Ste Adèle is a quaint and beautiful village near Montreal.

Agathe The village of Ste Agathe des Montes sits along Québec's Lac des Sables near Montreal.

Anicinabe A northern Ontario campground complete with showers and a beach.

Annapolis Nova Scotia's Annapolis Valley harvests some of the country's tastiest apples.

Argentia Located in the southwestern region of Newfoundland's Avalon Peninsula, Argentia is home to a ferry terminal with service to Nova Scotia.

Atikokan The place to stay when visiting Quetico Park, Atikokan has comfy motels, lodges and restaurants.

Aurora The name of a small suburb about 20 minutes north of Toronto.

Awenda A wonderful place for hiking and camping, Awenda Provincial Park lies near Penetanguishene, along Georgian Bay in Ontario.

Brier Whale-watching aficionados love Nova Scotia's Brier Island. The beautiful scenery and numerous hiking trails are an added bonus.

Calgary City meets Rockies in this picturesque Alberta town.

Cavendish Birthplace of novelist Lucy Maud Montgomery, author of *Anne of Green Gables*, this large city has everything from a wax museum to a nearby amusement park.

Elmira Perhaps the most interesting thing about Elmira, Nova Scotia is its railway museum.

Glace Glace Bay is located within Sydney's industrial area in Nova Scotia.

Hecla A provincial park along Lake Winnipeg in Manitoba, Hecla contains numerous islands and wildlife.

Inuvik Known as the land of the midnight sun, Inuvik is the second largest town in the Northwest Territories.

Iqaluit The capital city of Nunavut, Iqaluit means "place of many fish" in Inuktitut.

Ivvavik The name of this Yukon national park means "a place for giving birth" in the language of the Inuvialuit peoples.

Jasper Jasper National Park is Canada's largest Rocky Mountain National Park. With unbeatable mountain scenery, it's no wonder Jasper is a hot spot for tourists.

Kawartha A beautiful lake region in southwestern Ontario, the Kawartha Lakes are home to quaint towns like Bobcaygeon and Fenelon Falls.

Kelowna Sip on a homemade merlot while enjoying the stunning views of Kelowna in British Columbia's Okanagan Valley.

Kenora A small town near Winnipeg, Kenora is known for its pulp-and-paper industry. It's also a popular spot for summer cottaging and fishing.

Liscomb A great place for a hike, Liscomb Mills is an attractive part of Nova Scotia's Eastern Shore.

Louise One of the most beautiful places you'll ever visit, Lake Louise is one of Alberta's favoured attractions.

Lunen A short drive from Halifax, Lunenburg is a picturesque, vibrantly coloured town, especially along the waterfront.

Madeleine Québec's Îles de la Madeleine are found in the Gulf of St. Lawrence. Known for their breathtaking landscapes and laid-back lifestyle, these islands are referred to as the Magdalen Islands in English.

Manitoba A Canadian province settled between Saskatchewan and Ontario.

Maple Maple Creek is a small Saskatchewan town just on the outskirts of Cypress Hills.

Miquelon The name of an area in Newfoundland consisting of two islands marginally separated by a narrow area of sand.

Moraine Only about 15 km from Lake Louise, Lake Moraine may not be as famous, but it's certainly as impressive.

Nahanni Strap on your hiking boots and be prepared for an adventure trip through the Northwest Territory's Nahanni National Park Reserve. With hot springs, tundra views, mountain ranges and forests, what's not to love?

Neepawa Known as the World Lily Capital, this Manitoban town is a must-see for avid gardeners.

Nicolet Also known as the "town of bells," this quaint Québec religious spot was founded in 1672.

Paulatuk A small community of Kangamalit peoples on the Arctic coast in the Northwest Territories.

Peggy Just over 40 km west of Halifax, the lighthouse of Peggy's Cove is one of the most photographed spots in Nova Scotia.

Providence Fort Providence, Northwest Territories, is situated on the Mackenzie River. It's a good place for fishing and scenic views of the river.

Quadra At the north end of the Georgia Strait in British Columbia, Quadra Island is a wonderful place for bird-watchers. And if you sit quietly for long enough, you're sure to see a seal or two.

Regina Saskatchewan's capital city, Regina houses the country's only training centre for the Royal Canadian Mounted Police. Another interesting tidbit: almost all of the 350,000 trees in this city were hand-planted.

Saguenay A natural beauty in Québec's countryside, this region runs along the Rivière Saguenay. Contained within it are a 100 km-long fjord, 500-metre cliffs and distinct marine life.

Saturna One of British Columbia's Gulf Islands, Saturna's overall beauty is worth the trouble it takes to get there.

Shepody Shepody Bay Shorebird Reserve is located on Mary's Point on New Brunswick's Bay of Fundy.

Summer A cooler retreat during hot summer months, Summerside is located in the western region of Prince Edward Island.

Sydney The main city on Cape Breton Island, Sydney contains the largest toxic waste site in North America—the Sydney Tar Ponds.

Terra With over 100 km of trails, Newfoundland's Terra Nova National Park is a must-see for nature enthusiasts and hikers alike.

Tintina May and September are great months to visit the Tintina Trench in the Yukon. That's when various birds, including tundra swans and peregrine falcons, migrate and nest in the wetlands, marshes and cliffs.

Wascana The largest park in Regina, Wascana Centre features a large manmade lake.

Winnipeg The capital of Manitoba, Winnipeg houses 60 per cent of the province's population.

Victoria British Columbia's capital city, Victoria houses some of the country's most beautiful gardens.

Vuntut Meaning "among the lakes" in the Gwich'in language, this Yukon-based national park spans over 4,300 square km of pure, beautiful wilderness.

 KIDS' KORNER

Seven-year-old Cambria loves her name. "It has a C in it instead of a K," she boasts. "My favourite letter is C." The one thing she isn't fond of is the "b" in the middle. "Sometimes I mix up my "b"s and "d"s," she says, which makes it hard to spell.

Brittany is six years old and she is very fond of her name. "It sounds pretty and I like how it's spelled," she says. If she had to choose another name, she'd pick Angel. "I just like that name," she explains.

"I like my name because it is unique and I like the meaning of it," says 12-year-old Avery, who was given the last name of one of his mother's favourite co-workers. "Because it means 'ruler of the fairies,' it makes me feel capable of being a leader," he says.

 FUN FACTS

Not sure what to name your new business? Enlist the help of a professional naming company. They'll come up with names and conduct market research to find out which one's best. If only they did it for kids as well.

Tiger Woods' real name is Eldrick. His father began calling him Tiger to honour the nickname of a fellow soldier and family friend.

Japanese names most often appear as last name first followed by first name. In the Western world, where this process is reversed, it is often hard to determine which name to use.

CANUCK TRIVIA

John and Mary were the most popular names in Nova Scotia in 1950.

The city of Ottawa was named Bytown until 1855.

International Place Names

In terms of finding a baby name, the world really is your oyster. With almost 200 countries and thousands of cities, villages and hamlets, there's a bevy of places to choose from. Here are a few to get you started.

International Place Names for Boys

Agadir	Delhi	Nepal
Alger	Delos	Orlando
Beaumont	Dryden	Osaka
Belfast	Dublin	Prague
Berlin	Farnham	Renfrew
Birmingham	Houston	Rome
Bombay	Israel	Santiago
Borneo	Jordan	Sudan
Boston	Logan	Tehran
Brooklyn	Madras	Tibet
Cambridge	Madrid	Toledo
Carson	Melbourne	Wellington
Crete	Melville	Zurich
Cyprus		

International Place Names for Girls

Aberdeen	Athens	Calais
Alabama	Athinai	Calcutta
Albany	Bali	Cannes
Ankara	Cairns	Capri
Asia	Cairo	China

275

Dakota	Killarney	Sarajevo
Dallas	London	Savannah
Dayton	Manila	Seoul
Easter	Milan	Seville
Egypt	Monaco	Skye
Flanders	Nagoya	Sydney
Florence	Nassau	T'aipei
Georgia	Nice	Tokyo
India	Odessa	Tulsa
Indiana	Paris	Umbria
Ireland	Persia	Vail
Jakarta	Provence	Vienna
Kansas	Rhodes	Virginia
Kenya	Santorini	Zaria

Chapter 15

-☆-

Surnames

Historically, surnames were used as a way to distinguish the hundreds of Williams and Marys from one another. Whether they were derived from a first name (Johnson), an occupation (Smith) or a location (Woods), a last name followed the paternal side of the family through the generations. And up until two decades ago, pretty much everyone assumed that a child had to be named after her father's family. Those who didn't follow this tradition were frowned upon.

Today, in a society of increasingly equal opportunity and stay-at-home dads, more and more women are choosing to keep or hyphenate their names upon marriage. And they're giving their kids a whole new generation of last names. From mom's maiden name to a hyphenated combination of both parents' surnames, grade school rosters are full of different choices. Oh, and just because two kids have the same mom and dad doesn't mean they share a last name.

Confused yet? Don't worry. This chapter is designed to help you decide which surname is best for your child. Peppered with anecdotes from real moms who've chosen different surnames for their kids, you'll get first-hand input on their last-name experiences. Plus, I've included a few of the pros (and sometimes cons) associated with each surname choice.

REAL NAMES

"Names are funny because you actually become them," says 28-year-old Karen. At six, she wished she could have been called Wonder Woman, Jem or Strawberry Shortcake, but now, she says, "I can't picture myself as anyone but Karen...I think a new name would change me somehow."

Whether she was born a girl or a boy, Kelly's parents were going to name her Kelly. And she's glad they did. "I am so comfortable with my name," says the 27-year-old, and "it's always interesting when you meet someone with the same name as you. You feel an immediate connection."

Legally Yours

As with most things, naming your child and even registering the birth is surrounded by legalities. Here are a few of the basics to help you maneuver around the red tape.

Choosing a surname

Thinking of giving your child the last name Picasso in hopes of bringing out her inner artist? Not so fast. The only legally acceptable surnames for a baby are the mother's married, maiden or legally changed name; the father's surname; or a combination of the two. So, unless you live in P.E.I., Nova Scotia, Manitoba, Saskatchewan or B.C., where rules are more slack, you can't pick any name you like. But even in those provinces, the powers that be can reject your choice if they deem it to be confusing, derogatory or embarrassing.

Changing names

Whether it's due to a divorce, marriage or personal preference, changing your child's surname isn't an easy or cheap task. In Ontario, for instance, the waiting time for a name change can be up to 55 weeks. And in all provinces and territories, both parents have to agree to the change. If one parent lacks custody, written notice of the impending name change must be delivered to him. If this can't be obtained, you may have to go through the court system. The cost varies by province, prices ranging from $10 to $185 for the change and up to $37 to amend the birth certificate. If you want to change your own surname at the same time as your child's, you're looking at up to $185 for yourself and up to $25 for each kid. For more information, check with your Vital Statistics office or visit their Web site.

Name change fees

Wondering how much you'll be charged for changing a name in your region? Check out the prices below:

New Brunswick $125 plus $50 for each child

Newfoundland $36.50 plus $25 for each child

P.E.I. $185 plus $110 for each child

Nova Scotia $157.15 plus $20 for each child

Québec $216.50 plus $25 for each child

Ontario $137

Manitoba $119

Saskatchewan $35.70

Alberta $120

British Columbia $174 plus $22 for each child

North West Territories $10

Nunavut $10

Yukon $50 plus $17.50 for each additional person and $10 for a certificate

What about traveling?

According to the Canadian Passport Office, having different surnames within a family isn't as much of a problem for traveling as it used to be. The reason? Parents aren't allowed to include their kids' names on their own passports. So all children, regardless of age, must apply for and travel on their own passport. Therefore, having a different last name from their parent or siblings won't make a difference for kids who are leaving or entering the country.

KIDS' KORNER

Eight-year-old Laura hates when babies call her "Lawa" and sometimes wishes she was called Lisa, which would be easier for them to pronounce. But she likes the fact that she was named in honour of her father's mother and grandmother because "they were special people," she says.

Nathaniel really likes his first name, which he says his parents chose for religious reasons. It's his last name that he'd really like to change. "It's a Zodiac sign and it's annoying when people ask me about it," complains the 12-year-old. "I want to change my last name to my grandma's last name."

Choosing the Mother's Maiden Name: Why Do It?

Bust Patriarchy

What better way to counter ancient ways than by naming your child after his mother's family? Not only will you defy patriarchal beliefs that a child (and wife) must have the man's surname, but you'll also enable the woman's family to ensure its history for at least another generation.

Forget the Past

There's no rule stating that you have to honour a deadbeat dad with your child's surname. Many women, especially single mothers, are choosing to give children their own last names instead.

Who's Doing It?

Although it may seem like more and more women are giving children their maiden names, statistics say that it's still dad who's got the influence. But there are still many women, from single moms to feminists, who've bestowed their own last names on their kids.

Take Mary-Ann Lefley-Hean, for example. She has six children from two different men. Robert and John have her maiden name, Grace, while the younger four, Silas, Rainey, Famke and Ulysses are named Lefley-Hean, after their father. "I was single when I had my first two, so they have my maiden name," she explains. "And I'm married now, so the others have my husband's last name. Call me old-fashioned, but I think when you marry, you take your husband's name, therefore your children get it also." Other than some confusion at school—she often has to explain that even though her last name is Lefley-Hean, she actually is Robert and John Grace's mom—the 36-year-old mom says they haven't noticed any difficulties with the kids' last names.

Choosing the Father's Surname: Why Do It?
Tradition

Sometimes it's easier to go with the proverbial flow than it is to break tradition, especially when it comes to a child's last name. Not only will sticking with the father's surname be easier for grandparents to accept, but it will also help to maintain the father's lineage.

Reduce Confusion

The majority of the time, having a father's surname is just plain easier. First of all, pretty much everyone assumes that a child's last name is the same as his father's anyway, so it may be simpler to just comply with their beliefs. And secondly, keeping the same last name in the family (for mom, dad and kids) will help prevent school mix-ups and hassles at the border.

Who's Doing It?

With the exception of Nunavut, where only 35 percent of children are given their father's surname, a whopping majority of Canadian kids are still named after their dads.

Karen Boms is among this majority. Although she didn't take her husband's last name of Meddings when she got married, Karen doesn't have a problem passing on his surname to her expected son. "I think it's better for the child to have a surname that isn't hyphenated," she says. "And since we know we're having a boy, I think it's nice for my husband to pass on his lineage." If her next child is a girl, Karen's determined to give her the last name Meddings as well. The reason? As a teacher, she has first-hand experience of the confusion that two siblings with different surnames can cause to other teachers and kids. "Once you give your first child one of the parent's surnames, it seems only appropriate and beneficial to give your other children the same," she says.

Alicia Martin-Boyle had a more difficult time making her decision. Although she hasn't picked out a first name for her daughter-to-be, pregnant Alicia has already decided on the surname—her husband's last name, Boyle. After much deliberation, Alicia and her husband Jamie decided against adding her maiden name of Martin to the baby's last name. "I realized I wanted to hyphenate it for selfish reasons," she explains. "I felt that she wouldn't be mine as much as Jamie's if she didn't have my last name, too." Now that the decision's made, the parents-to-be are happy with their choice. "It creates a sense of unity and cohesion in the family and sounds better," Alicia says.

Pam Forgrave named her kids Smith, after her husband's family, because she doesn't like the look of hyphenated names. "I didn't want to burden my children with really long names, so we decided to give them just one last name," she explains. "We also live in a small town and most people assume I use my husband's last name." In order to preserve her own family's history, she gave her maiden name, Forgrave, as a second middle name to son Lowell, three, and daughter Makeda, two.

Michela Barnhart chose to take her husband's last name when they got married so she would have a special connection to both her husband and his son Brandon Savage-Barnhart (Savage is from his mother). When her daughter Crea was born three years ago, Michela named her Barnhart. "There have been numerous difficulties encountered because Brandon's name is so long," she explains. "We decided that Crea would just have my husband's name [because] that is simpler and yet Brandon is still a part."

Who's Doing What?

Curious to see what people are choosing as a last name for their kids? Here's a quick list of the percent of children given various surnames across the country. Since many of the Vital Statistics offices were unable to provide me with this data, these are estimates only, based on the information I was able to collect.

Estimated percentage of children given their father's surname:

Western Canada	–	86.1%
Central Canada	–	87.4%
Northern Canada	–	46.95%
Eastern Canada	–	82.5%

Estimated percentage of children given their mother's surname:

Western Canada	–	7%
Central Canada	–	9%
Northern Canada	–	45.25%
Eastern Canada	–	13%

Estimated percentage of children given a hyphenated surname:

Western Canada	–	3.2%
Central Canada	–	3.7%
Northern Canada	–	7.85%
Eastern Canada	–	4%

> ‑ **FUN FACTS**
> In Chinese tradition, all members of a family have the same last name.
> The city of Dubai currently holds the record for the largest gathering of people sharing the same name—between 1,500 and 2,000 males named Mohammed gathered at one of the city's parks.
> 375 Marias gathered in Spain in 2003, creating the former world-record for the largest gathering of people with the same name.

Choosing a Hyphenated Surname: Why Do It?

Fair play

Although they may be long and cumbersome to spell, hyphenated surnames are a wonderful way to recognize the family heritage of both parents. And in an increasingly equal society, why shouldn't each parent get a chance at sharing a surname with their kids?

Who's Doing It?

While many women are hyphenating their own names upon marriage, that doesn't mean they're all choosing to pass these names on to their kids. In Canada, for instance, there are still fewer than eight percent of kids with hyphenated last names.

Diana Fairbairn (née Wiebe) is a member of this minority. She and her husband Scott gave daughters Maia, six, and Chloe, two, the hyphenated surname Fairbairn-Wiebe. "The girls are a product of love between my husband and me," she explains. "It was really important to me that their last names reflect that joining of our lives, our families and our love." Although the 32-year-old mom is happy about the surname choice, she says it hasn't always been easy. Both grandmothers have trouble understanding that the kids have both last names and criticize the length of Fairbairn-Wiebe. And a customs agent recently quizzed her at the U.S. border about the kids' last names. "He wanted to know where the Wiebe came from since my last name is Fairbairn," she explains. Other problems have included confusion at school (staff members aren't sure what to call Diana) and difficulty fitting the kids' full names on official forms. As for the kids, Chloe's too young to notice, while "Maia says the best thing about her surname is that it sounds good," says Diana. "And she says it doesn't matter that it's really long or hyphenated."

Georgie Binks, mother of 17-year-old Julie and 13-year-old Ian Stewart-Binks, says her kids love having a hyphenated surname. "It is a [combination] of their father's and my last name," says Georgie. "They like it because they know they are the only ones who have it." Another added bonus of the combined names: it helps outsiders to know that Georgie, who's now divorced, is related to her kids. Although the kids have never experienced grave problems with having hyphenated last names, Georgie says they're sometimes called Stewart instead of Julie or Ian. Once, Georgie was so infuriated when a doctor called her daughter Stewart that she found a new physician.

Giving Siblings Different Surnames: Why Do It?

To Recognize Different Fathers

Kids from different marriages usually have separate last names. Take my family, for example. My mom had two daughters when she married my dad. Their last name was Bailey after their father. My dad's four kids from previous marriages were McMurray. And when my little sister and I came along, we were given McMurray, too.

Can't Decide

If you simply can't decide (or agree on) whose last name to use, you could always try a compromise. Give one child his father's surname and name the next after her mother's family.

 CANUCK TRIVIA

Tremblay, Gagnon, Roy, Côté and Bouchard are among the most common surnames in Québec.

Every child born to the same parents in New Brunswick must have the same last name.

285

Who's Doing It?

Divorce is the most common reason for siblings to have different last names. That said, some families choose to give their children a dissimilar surname for a variety of reasons—from wanting to recognize each parent to craving a more unique approach to naming traditions. Take the Thorson/Boron family, for example:

Eight-year-old Abby was given her mother's maiden name, Thorson, while her seven-year-old sister Annika got their dad's surname, Boron. "We both wanted our names carried on and in both cases our children are the only ones in their generation to have those names," explains mom Stephanie. "I feel very fortunate to be with a man who is willing to buck the trends—or set them." And surprisingly enough, there's rarely confusion over the kids' names.

The only glitch they've noticed has been at dance class where administrators can't remember which last name the kids are registered under in their computer. Other than that, it's been smooth sailing so far. And the kids generally like their different last names. Abby thinks it's cool to have a distinct surname, something that sets her apart from her sister and from other kids. And although Annika sometimes says her last name makes her feel as if she isn't in the same family as her mom and sister, she still thinks it's kind of neat to be different, says her mom.

How Do I Get a Birth Certificate?

There are so many things to think about when your child is born. Which name will you choose, will you breastfeed, did your partner remember to bring the car seat? The last thing you need to worry about is how to apply for your child's birth certificate. So I've done the investigating for you. This quick and easy guide will tell you how to register a birth and apply for a birth certificate in each region in Canada.

New Brunswick

Complete and sign the Registration of Birth, Form C-1, available from a hospital staff member or midwife shortly after the birth of your child. If the hospital or midwife cannot send the form in for you, you'll have to drop it off or mail it to the Registrar General's office at the Vital Statistics office near you. You'll then receive a birth certificate in the mail.

Nova Scotia

Complete and sign a Live Birth Registration form, available from the hospital or midwife at the time of birth. You must sign this before you leave the hospital and give it to the Local Division Registrar or your midwife who will forward it to the Vital Statistics office. Then, download the birth certificate application form online (see "Online resources" below) and mail or fax it to the Vital Statistics office.

Newfoundland

While in the hospital, staff will collect information from you to complete a Live Birth Notification form. They will then forward this to the Vital Statistics office. Within 30 days of returning home, you should complete a Return of Birth form, available from any Vital Statistics office, government service centre or member of the clergy. Return this to a Vital Statistics office or have the clergy member do this on your behalf. It's then best to wait for two or three weeks to give time for the Vital Statistics office to register the birth. After this time, you can apply for the birth certificate. Either pick up a form from a Vital Statistics office or download it from the Web (see "Online resources" below) and mail it in.

P.E.I.

You must register your child's birth within 30 days with the Vital Statistics Office. Forms, which can be obtained at the hospital or from your midwife, must be filled out, signed and sent to the Vital Statistics Office. Once they receive your registration, they'll send you a Confirmation of Birth, which you must fill out and return within 30 days. This form allows you to request a birth certificate.

Québec

You'll receive an Attestation of birth from whoever assists with your delivery. You'll then need to fill out a Declaration of Birth form, which you can obtain at the hospital (or from Le Directeur de l'état civil) and send it in to Le Directeur de l'état civil within 30 days. Often, the hospital will do this for you. The office of Le Directeur de l'état civil will then send you a Notice of Registration of Birth form and Request for Certificate or Copy of Act form. The latter form allows you to apply for the birth certificate.

Ontario

You must first complete and sign a Statement of Live Birth, which should be given to you by the hospital or midwife. You'll then send the form into the appropriate Division Registrar's office in your municipality. They'll forward it on to the Office of the Registrar general who will register the birth and send you a Notice of Birth Registration by mail. Only once you receive this can you apply for the birth certificate. You can get the form online (see "Online resources" below) or from an Office of the Registrar General, Land Registry Office or Government Information Centre.

Manitoba

Within five days of your child's birth, you must fill out a Registration of Live Birth form at the hospital or through your midwife. Your caretaker will then forward this form to the Vital Statistics office. You can obtain a birth certificate application form from the hospital staff, midwife or online (see "Online resources" below). Once you've completed and signed this form, send it in by fax or mail to the Vital Statistics office.

Saskatchewan

Before leaving the hospital, you must complete and sign the Registration of Live Birth Form, which is available from hospital staff.

They will mail it to the division registrar. If you give birth outside of a hospital, you must contact the Vital Statistics office in order to obtain a form to complete. Once your child's birth is registered, you can then complete an Application for Certificate Form, which is available online (see "Online resources" below) or from the Vital Statistics office. You can then drop it off in person, or mail it or fax it (if you pay by credit card) to the Vital Statistics office.

Alberta

First, you have to complete a Registration of Birth form, which is available from the hospital or midwife. Once you have signed it, return it to a member of the hospital's staff. They will mail it to the Vital Statistics Office. This must be done within 10 days of your child's birth. To apply for a birth certificate, you have to visit a private registry agent (look under "licensing" in the Yellow Pages) to complete the form. They will then forward your request to the Vital Statistics agency. Because this process is conducted through a private representative, charges can vary from $20 up to $100 or more. So you might want to shop around.

British Columbia

Within 30 days of your child's birth, you must complete the Registration of Live Birth form, available from hospital staff or your midwife. They will then forward this form to the Vital Statistics office. You may then fill out an application for a birth certificate, available in the package you'll receive from the hospital or your midwife. If you didn't receive the form, contact a Vital Statistics Office near you or download the application online (see "Online resources" below) and mail or fax it to the appropriate office.

Northwest Territories

Complete the Registration of Live Birth form in the hospital or with your midwife. They will be responsible for mailing this form to the Vital Statistics office. Then, download an application form online (see

"Online resources" below) or call the Vital Statistics office to have a form mailed or faxed to you. Once you've completed the form, send it in to the Vital Statistics office.

Nunavut

Once you've filled in the Registration of Live Birth form in the hospital or with your midwife, they'll send it off to the Vital Statistics Office. You can then contact the Office to obtain an application form for the birth certificate.

Yukon

Fill in the Registration of Live Birth form at your hospital or with your midwife. They will send this in to the Vital Statistics office. Then, download a birth certificate application form online (see "Online resources" below) or pick one up from the Vital Statistics office or hospital. Once you've completed the form, mail it back to the Vital Statistics office.

Online resources:

Want to download an application form or find out more about applying for a birth certificate? Try one of these sites.

New Brunswick • *gnb.ca*
Click "Vital Statistics" (under "Individuals and Families") and then choose "Birth Registration Guide."

Newfoundland • *gs.gov.nl.ca*
Under "Top Ten Pages" click "Birth Certificate."

P.E.I. • *gov.pe.ca*
Click on "InfoPEI," then "Government," then do a search for "Birth Certificates."

Nova Scotia • *gov.ns.ca*
Click "Agencies," then click "Vital Statistics," then choose "Birth certificate request."

Québec • *etatcivil.gouv.qc.ca*
Click "Birth."

Ontario • *cbs.gov.on.ca*
Click "Births, Deaths and Marriages."

Saskatchewan • *health.gov.sk.ca*
Click "Birth Certificates."

Manitoba • *gov.mb.ca/cca/vital*
Click "Download forms,"
then click "Application form."

Alberta • *gov.ab.ca*
Do a search for "Birth
Certificates."

British Columbia • *vs.gov.bc.ca*
Choose "Birth Registration &
Certificates."

Northwest Territories
hlthss.gov.nt.ca
Click "Application Forms,"
then click "Application for Birth/
Marriage/Death certificate."

Nunavut
There's no pertinent Web
information available. Call
(867) 645-8001 to obtain an
application.

Yukon • *hss.gov.yk.ca*
Choose "Vital Statistics Agency"
(under "Branches") then click
"How to order a Yukon birth
certificate."

How Much do They Cost?

Unfortunately, most birth certificates aren't free. Here's what you can expect to pay for a certificate in your area:

New Brunswick Free for the first, wallet-sized certificate

Newfoundland $25

P.E.I. $25

Nova Scotia $26.50 for a short form, $32.00 for a long form

Québec $15

Ontario $25 for a birth certificate, $35 for the certified copy of birth

Manitoba $25

Saskatchewan $25, $50 for a certified photocopy

Alberta $25.35, depending on the private registry agent's fees

British Columbia $27

Northwest Territories $10 for a wallet or paper-size

Nunavut $10

Yukon $10 for a long or short form

-☆-

Chapter 16

The Great Canadian Name Quiz

Can't bear to look at another baby name? Sounds like it's time for a break. Why not try your luck with the Great Canadian name quiz? Filled with pertinent naming trivia that's unique to our nation, you definitely won't find these questions elsewhere.

From Prime Minister's nicknames to the popularity of certain monikers during 1920 and beyond, here's your chance to learn everything you never knew you wanted to know about Canadian names.

1. Which province doesn't allow a woman to take her husband's last name?
    a) Québec
    b) Ontario
    c) Nunavut
    d) none of the above

2. Which girl's name appears on every province and territory's top 10 list for 2002?
    a) Madison
    b) Jessica
    c) Sarah
    d) Morgan

3. Which provinces allow you to give your child any surname you'd like?
   a) B.C. and the Northwest Territories
   b) Yukon, New Brunswick and Québec
   c) Alberta, B.C., Nova Scotia and Nunavut
   d) Nova Scotia, B.C., P.E.I, Saskatchewan and Manitoba

4. Which popular Prime Minister was also known by the nickname, Mike?
   a) Pierre Trudeau
   b) Lester B. Pearson
   c) Sir John A. Macdonald
   d) Mackenzie King

5. What do singer KD Lang's initials stand for?
   a) Karen Day
   b) Kelly Deborah
   c) Kristen Diane
   d) Kathryn Dawn

6. What were the three most popular boys' names in Nova Scotia in 1975?
   a) Scott, Kevin and Matthew
   b) Jason, Michael and Christopher
   c) John, David and Jason
   d) Daniel, Steven and Paul

7. What is Wayne Gretzky's middle name?
   a) Michael
   b) Douglas
   c) Steven
   d) David

8. Which of the following girls' names mean beauty?
   a) Ashley, Christine and Sade
   b) Elizabeth, Katrina and Vanessa
   c) Jessica, Sarah and Rachel
   d) Belinda, Ella and Shayna

9. Which singer's name is French for April?
   a) Céline Dion
   b) Jann Arden
   c) Avril Lavigne
   d) Chantel Kreviazuk

10. How many of Canada's Prime Ministers have shared the name John?
    a) five
    b) three
    c) two
    d) seven

11. Which author named his children's book characters after his own kids?
    a) AA Milne
    b) Michael Ondaatje
    c) Farley Mowat
    d) Mordecai Richler

12. Which of the following boys' names mean strength?
    a) Brian, Ethan and Mather
    b) Matthew, Jeremy and Kevin
    c) Jason, Ryan and Trevor
    d) Geoffrey, Mark and Shane

13. Which boy's name was the most popular in Manitoba from 1994 to 2000?
    a) Joshua
    b) Tyler
    c) Matthew
    d) Ethan

14. What does the name Nunavut mean?
    a) place of peace
    b) our land
    c) man's home
    d) great river

15. What was "Pocket Rocket" Richard's first name?
a) Marcel
b) Guy
c) Henri
d) Gilbert

16. Which of the following names were considered when naming Canada?
a) Acadia
b) Cabotia
c) Ursalia
d) all of the above

17. Which author's real name was Jean Margaret Wemyss?
a) Margaret Laurence
b) Jane Urquhart
c) Margaret Atwood
d) Carol Shields

18. Which hockey player was nicknamed "Jake the Snake?"
a) Justin Papineau
b) Jaromir Jagr
c) Jacques Plante
d) Joel Bouchard

19. What is rap musician K-os's real name?
a) Kheaven Brereton
b) Marshall Scobie
c) Devon Francis
d) Keenan Williams

20. Which former Canadian Prime Minister's real first name is Martin?
a) Brian Mulroney
b) Jean Chrétien
c) John Turner
d) Joe Clark

21. Which of the provinces' names means New Scotland?
a) New Brunswick
b) Nova Scotia
c) Newfoundland
d) Ontario

22. In which province or territory are the majority of children given their mother's surname?
a) Nunavut
b) Manitoba
c) British Columbia
d) Nova Scotia

23. What is Shania Twain's real name?
a) Janine Edwards
b) Stephanie Edwards
c) Eileen Edwards
d) Mary Edwards

24. What is the meaning of the name Canada?
a) many trees
b) big land
c) decisive
d) village

25. Which boy's name was popular in every decade from 1920 through to 1980?
a) Matthew
b) Michael
c) John
d) James

26. Which two girls' names have remained among Canada's top 10 since 1980?
a) Sarah and Jessica
b) Jennifer and Hannah
c) Madison and Montana
d) Megan and Olivia

27. Which three names are most commonly given to boys born in Canada?
a) William, Benjamin, Nicholas
b) David, Ryan, Alexander
c) Matthew, Joshua, Jacob
d) Ethan, Michael, Logan

28. Which three names are most commonly given to girls born in Canada?
a) Emma, Emily, Madison
b) Megan, Jessica, Samantha
c) Sarah, Olivia, Hannah
d) Grace, Jennifer, Anna

29. Which group of Canadians keep their spiritual names a secret in order to guard their sacredness?
a) Acadians
b) First Nations groups
c) Inuit
d) Métis

30. In which province or territory are over 86 per cent of kids given their father's surname?
a) Nova Scotia
b) Northwest Territories
c) British Columbia
d) Alberta

ANSWERS

1. a) Québec. Women who were married and are living in Québec are not legally allowed to take their husband's surname, even after they have kids.

2. c) Sarah. This is the only name common to every province's and territory's 2002 list of popular names. The next most popular, appearing on all but three of the lists, are Emily and Emma.

3. d) Nova Scotia, B.C., P.E.I, Saskatchewan and Manitoba. All other provinces and territories mandate that a child be given the surname of the mother, father or a combination of the two.

4. b) Lester B. Pearson. Many years prior to taking office, Lester Bowles Pearson was given the nickname Mike by his flying instructor in World War I.

5. d) Kathryn Dawn. One of Canada's most unique and well-recognized voices, KD Lang uses her initials as a stage name.

6. b) Jason, Michael and Christopher. These popular names were closely followed by John, David and James.

7. b) Douglas. Undisputedly the world's greatest hockey player, Wayne has a very traditional middle name.

8. d) Belinda, Ella and Shayna. Other names that represent beauty include Alana, Calista, Harmony, Jacinda and Vashti.

9. c) Avril Lavigne. This famous punk rockin' youngster's name reflects her father's French Canadian roots.

10. a) Five. Macdonald, Abbott, Tompson, Diefenbaker and Turner all shared the first name John.

11. d) Mordecai Richler. The award-winning fiction writer named characters in his popular *Jacob Two-Two* books after his five kids—Daniel, Noah, Emma, Martha and, of course, Jacob.

12. a) Brian, Ethan and Mather. Other strong names: Arsen, Bogart, Charles, Kale and Hardy.

13. c) Matthew. In addition to being the number one name for six years in a row, Matthew has graced Manitoba's top three list from 2001 to 2003. The second most popular boy's name is Joshua.

14. b) Our land. Canada's largest and youngest territory, Nunavut was given an Inuktitut name to represent its Inuit heritage.

15. c) Henri. Brother of the famed Maurice "Rocket" Richard, Henri played in the NHL for 20 seasons and won 11 Stanley Cup rings.

16. d) All of the above. When considering names for Canada, a few of the most popular included Cabotia, Acadia and Ursalia. Other runners-up included New Britain, Laurentia, Columbia and Britania.

17. a) Margaret Laurence. Born in Neepawa, Manitoba, she changed her surname to Laurence upon marriage and preferred the name Margaret to Jean.

18. c) Jacques Plantes. Joseph Jacques Omer Plantes was born in Mont Carmel, Québec. Known as "Jake the Snake," Plantes was the first goalie to regularly wear a mask in the NHL.

19. a) Kheaven Brereton. A talented Toronto native, Kheaven Brereton, better known as rap artist K-os, is a multiple Juno award winner.

20. a) Brian Mulroney. Born Martin Brian Mulroney in Baie-Comeau, Québec, this ex-Prime Minister was in power from 1984-1993.

21. b) Nova Scotia. Once known as Acadia, Nova Scotia got its name from the British in the early 1600s.

22. a) Nunavut. Just over 60 per cent of children born in Nunavut receive their mother's last name. In B.C., on the other hand, only about seven per cent of kids are named after their mom.

23. c) Eileen Edwards. Somehow Eileen Edwards seemed a bit too boring for Canada's most celebrated country pop star.

24. d) Village. Thought to have derived from the name kanata of Huron-Iroquois origin, Canada means village or settlement.

25. d) James. A member of the top 10 list from 1920 to 1980, this name proves that boys' names really do have staying power.

26. a) Sarah and Jessica. Popular since the 80s, these two names may not stay in the top 10 for more than a few more years. The reason? Girls' names seem to fall out of fashion much faster than boys'.

27. c) Matthew, Joshua, Jacob. The three most popular boys' names in Canada, these are closely followed by Ryan, Alexander and Nicholas.

28. c) Sarah, Olivia, Hannah. These three names top the charts throughout Canada. They're followed by Emma, Emily, and Madison.

29. b) and c) First Nations groups and Inuit. Although many First Nations and Inuit peoples have an English- or French-sounding first name, their real, spiritual name holds great significance to them. As a result, they're kept as a well-guarded secret in hopes of preserving their sacred meanings.

30. d) Alberta. Over 87 per cent of babies born in Alberta are given their father's last name. In B.C., close to 86 per cent are named after their dad, while a mere 35 per cent are given their father's surname in Nunavut.

Index

A

Abbott, John Joseph Caldwell, 133
Abdul-Jabbar, Kareem, 28
Acadian names, 40–45
Adams, Bryan, 142
Affleck, Ben, 142
Affleck, Casey, 155
African names, 87–92
Alberta
  birth certificate application, 289
  place names, 268, 271, 272
Allen, Woody, 155
alliteration in names, 9
Anderson, Pamela, 151
Andretti, Michael, 29
Angelil, Rene, 155
Angus, Colin, 67
Aniston, Jennifer, 138, 149
Arden, Jann, 149
Argento, Asia, 269
Armstrong, Jeannette, 73
Armstrong, Lance, 28
Arquette, David, 157
associations with names, 8, 10–11, 13, 14, 26, 85, 179–181, 182, 276–285
Atlantic Provinces, popular names, 212
Atwood, Margaret, 66, 74, 78, 81, 83, 84
Austen, Jane, 64
Austin, Stone Cold Steve, 269
Australia, popular names, 162
Austria, popular names, 163
authors' names, 66-76
Ayer, Debbon, 159
Aykroyd, Dan, 142

B

backup names, 12
Backus, Chris, 158
Badu, Erykah, 156, 158
Bailey, Donovan, 27

Baldwin, Billy, 156, 157, 158
Banderas, Antonio, 140
Banks, Tyra, 152
Barnhart, Michela, 282
Barrymore, Drew, 147
Beatty, Warren, 147
Beck, Leslie, 74
Beckham, David, 153, 155, 269
Beckham, Victoria, 153, 155, 269
Bedouin traditions, 15
Bell, Marilyn, 32
Bellow, Saul, 70
Bellucci, Monica, 157
Bening, Annette, 147
Benjamin, Andre, 156
Bennett, Richard Bedford, 133
Berry, Halle, 149
Berton, Pierre, 69
Biblical names, 7, 39, 126, 166. *See also* Religious names
Binks, Georgie, 285
Birdsell, Sandra, 76
Birney, Earle, 67
birth, registering, 278
birth certificates, applying for, 286–291
bissett, bill, 66
Blanchard, Rachel, 151
Blanchett, Cate, 147, 154, 155
Blaser, Robin, 70
Blodgett, E.D., 67
Bloom, Orlando, 145, 269
Bluger, Marianne, 75
Bolster, Stephanie, 76
Boms, Karen, 281
Bon Jovi, Jon, 154, 155, 159
Bono (Paul Hewson), 142, 157
Borden, Robert Laird, 133
Bowell, Mackenzie, 133
Bowering, Marilyn, 75
Boyens, Ingeborg, 73
boys' names. *See also* Authors' names
  Acadian, 41–42

African, 87–91
athletic, 26–30
cars, 34
celebrities, 142–147, 153–156
characters, literary, 76–81
Chinese, 92–93
designers, 174-175
English, 94–95
French-Canadian, 49–51
German, 97–98
Greek, 102–103
Irish, 105–106
Italian, 108–110
Japanese, 112–113, 239
last names used as first,
 246–247
Métis, 59–61
movie characters, 137
old-fashioned, 232–238
place names, 263–269, 275
Polish, 114–116
popular, 186–197
popular, by decade, 127–128,
129, 131, 134, 135
popular, by country, 162–174,
 212, 213, 214, 215, 255
religious, 217–223
royal, 160
Russian, 117–119
Spanish, 120–122
trendy, 251
Brady, Tom, 29
Brand, Dionne, 72, 82, 83
Brando, Marlon, 139
Brandt, Di, 72
Brenner, Veronica, 34
Briatore, Flavio, 158
Brinkley, Christie, 159
British Columbia
birth certificate application, 289
place names, 264, 265,
 266, 267, 268, 272, 273, 274
popular names, 165, 247, 260
Broderick, Matthew, 154
Bronte, Charlotte, 64
Brooks, Martha, 75, 80
Brossard, Nicole, 75, 84
Browning, Kurt, 28
Bublé, Michael, 145

Burke, Delta, 269
Bush, George, 156, 158
Bush, Laura, 157, 158
Bussieres, Pascale, 152

C

Caballé, Montserrat, 269
Callaway, Ann Hampton, 269
Callwood, June, 73
Cameron, Rod, 146
Campbell, Kim, 133
Campbell, Neve, 152
Canada
place names, 264–269, 270-274
popular names, 164, 212, 213,
 214, 215, 255
Candy, John, 144
Capshaw, Kate, 156
Carnahan, Matthew, 158
car names, 34–35
Carpenter, David, 67
Carrey, Jim, 143, 158
Carrier, Roch, 70
Carter, Vince, 29
Cartier, Jacques, 49
Cassel, Vincent, 157
Castillo, Irán, 269
celebrities, 45, 138–160, 180
children of, 153–159
Central Canada, popular names, 213
Chalke, Sarah, 152
Chang, Michael, 29
characters' names, 76–84
Charest, Isabelle, 31
Chase, Chevy, 269
Chase, Jessica, 32
Chaucer, Geoffrey, 64
Cheadle, Don, 142
Cher, 139
Child, John, 28
China, 88
Chinese names, 92–94, 282
Chouinard, Josée, 32
Chrétien, Jean, 133
Church, Jarvis, 143
Clark, Charles Joseph (Joe), 133
Clark, Susan, 152
Clarke, Austin, 66, 80, 81, 83

Clarke, George Elliott, 68
classical names, 127–139
Clemens, Roger, 29
Clift, Montgomery, 269
Clinton, Bill, 157
Clinton, Hilary, 157
Clooney, George, 142
clothing names, 181
Cohen, Leonard, 144
Collins, Wilkie, 154
Colwill, Nina Lee, 75
Comaneci, Nadia, 33
Combs, Holly Marie, 154
Connor, Ralph, 69
Cook, Peter, 159
Correl, Mady, 150
Coupland, Douglas, 67
Cox, Courteney, 148, 157
Cox, Deborah, 148
Craven, Matt, 145
created names, 13, 260–261
Cronkite, Walter, 140
Cronyn, Hume, 143
Cross, Kendall, 149
Crozier, Lorna, 74
Crudup, Billy, 156
Cruise, Tom, 146, 152
Cruz, Penélope, 151
Cullen, Seán, 146
Cumming, Peter, 69
Cuthbert, Elisha, 148
Czerny, Henry, 143

D

Damon, Matt, 145
Dane, Shelton, 269
Davies, Robertson, 70, 78
Davis, Geena, 154, 155
Dawson, Rosario, 269
de Assis Moreira, Ronaldo, 29
De Crecy, Etienne, 269
De Lint, Charles, 67, 83, 84
De Matteo, Drea, 148
Denmark, popular names, 164–165
designers, 174-175
DiCaprio, Leonardo, 144
Dickens, Charles, 64
Diefenbaker, John George, 55, 133

Dion, Celine, 147, 155
disagreements, solving, 36–37
divorce, 286
Domi, Tie, 29
Donoho, David, 154
Douglas, Michael, 157
Downie, Gord, 143
Dukakis, Olympia, 269
Duncan, Sandy Frances, 76

E

Eastern European names, 63
Eastwood, Clint, 143, 269
Egoyan, Atom, 142, 147
Einstein, Albert, 179
Elliott, Denholm, 269
English names, 94–97, 165
Englund, Robert, 269
ethnic names, 10, 126. See also Names
  by origin
Evangelista, Linda, 150
Evert, Chris, 31
expectations associated with names,
  179–181

F

Fairbairn, Diana, 282
family, honouring, 12, 17-18, 23-24, 32, 39,
  77, 88–89, 102, 129, 134, 153, 211, 231,
  251, 270
Fanning, Dakota, 269
Farrow, Mia, 155
Feldman, Corey, 156
Feore, Colm, 141
Ferrell, Will, 155
Ferri, Claudia, 148
Findley, Timothy, 65, 70, 80
Finland, 166, 178
First Nations names, 46–49
Fogwill Porter, Helen, 73
Foley, Dave, 142
Follows, Megan, 150
food names, 181
Foote, Horton, 269
Ford, Harrison, 143, 269
Forgrave, Pam, 282
Fox, Michael J., 145

Foxx, Jamie, 143
France, popular names, 167
Fraser, Afton, 154
Fraser, Brendan, 154
Freeman, Morgan, 145
French-Canadian names, 49–52
Frost, Sadie, 155
Furtado, Nellie, 152

G

Gagnon, Marc, 28
Galbraith, John Kenneth, 68
Gallant, Mavis, 75
geographic names, 179
German names, 88, 97–100, 167
Gibson, Thomas, 156
Gibson, William, 71
Gilpin, Peri, 156, 159
girls' names. *See also* Authors' names
  Acadian, 43–45
  African, 91–92
  athletic, 32–35
  cars, 35
  celebrities, 147–152
  characters, literary, 81–84
  Chinese, 93–94
  designers, 175
  English, 95–97
  French-Canadian, 51–52
  German, 99–100
  Greek, 103–105
  Irish, 106–107
  Italian, 110–111
  Japanese, 113–114, 239
  last names used as first, 249
  Métis, 61–63
  movie characters, 137–139
  old-fashioned, 239–246
  place names, 270–274, 275–276
  Polish, 116–117
  popular, 15, 16, 197–210
  popular, by decade, 128, 129, 131,
    134, 135, 136
  popular, by country, 162–174, 212,
    213, 214, 215, 255
  religious, 225–230
  royal, 160
  Russian, 119–120
  Spanish, 122–124

trendy, 252
Goldman, Michael, 155
Gosling, Ryan, 146
Gosselaar, Mark-Paul, 144, 155
Govier, Katherine, 74, 78, 79
Gray, Charlotte, 72
Greek names, 87, 100–105. *See also*
  Names by origin
Green, Tom, 147
Gretzky, Wayne, 29
Gross, Paul, 145
Guillory, Sienna, 269

H

Hamm, Mia, 33
Hanks, Tom, 136, 147
Hanlon, Ned, 29
Hannah, Daryl, 136
Hardaway, Anfernee, 26
Harden, Marcia Gay, 157, 158
Hawke, Ethan, 138
Hawn, Goldie, 149, 156
Hay, Virginia, 269
Hayden, Sterling, 269
Hayek, Salma, 152
Hébert, Anne, 71
Hebrew names, 127, 128. *See also*
  Names by origin
  altering, 53
Heese, Mark, 28
Hennessy, Jill, 149, 155
Henstridge, Natasha, 152
heritage, names reflecting, 39–40. *See
  also* Names by origin
Hewlett, David, 142
Hewson, Ben, 142
Hill, Faith, 157
Hilton, Paris, 139, 269
Hines, Cheryl, 157
Holden, Jody, 27
Hooper, Charmaine, 31
Howard, Blanche, 72
Howe, Gordie, 27
Hudson, Kate, 52, 149, 155
Huggan, Isabel, 73
humorous name, 8, 10, 180–181
Hungary, 87
Hunt, Helen, 158

I

Icelandic names, 63–64, 168
Igali, Daniel, 27
India, 88
India.Arie, 269
initials formed by names, 12
Inuit names, 53–54
invented names. *See* Created names
Ireland, Kathy, 269
Irish names, 105–107, 168
Irving, John, 64, 68, 78, 80, 81, 84
Israel, 87
Italian names, 108–111, 169

J

Jackson, A.Y., 36, 159
Jackson, Joshua, 144
Jackson, Marni, 75
Jackson, Michael, 2, 153
James, Jesse, 27
Japanese names, 112–114, 166, 213, 239, 274
    popular names, 169
Japanese traditions, 134
Jarrahy, Reza, 154, 155
Jewish traditions, 134
Jewison, Norman, 145
Johnson, Ben, 27
Johnson, Michael, 29
Johnson, Molly, 136
Johnson, Pauline, 75
Jolie, Angelina, 147, 159
Jordan, Michael, 29
Joseph, Larry, 158
Joyner-Kersee, Jackie, 31

K

Kain, Karen, 32
Karmazin, Lisa, 154
Keitel, Harvey, 154
Khanjian, Arsinee, 147
Kidder, Margot, 150
Kidman, Nicole, 152
King, Billie Jean, 30
King, William Lyon Mackenzie, 133
Kinsella, W.P., 71

Klum, Heidi, 158
Kogawa, Joy, 73
Korean traditions, 15
Koteas, Elias, 144
Kraus, Alanna, 30
Kutcher, Ashton, 142
Kuzyk, Mimi, 152

L

Lagasse, Emil, 158
Lambert, Nathalie, 33
Langdon, Royston, 155
last names, 179
    used as first names, 246–249
Laurence, Margaret, 74, 82
Laurier, Wilfrid, 133
Lavigne, Avril, 138, 147
Law, Jude, 144, 155
Leacock, Stephen, 70, 81
LeBlanc, Matt, 158
Ledger, Heath, 143
Lee, Christopher Khayman, 269
Lee, Jason, 134
Lefley-Hean, Mary-Ann, 280–281
Leinemann, Conrad, 27
LeMay Doan, Catriona, 30
Lemieux, Mario, 28
length of names, 8, 45, 65, 211, 231, 249
Lilly, Evangeline, 149
Limpert, Marianne, 32
lists, importance of, 11
literary names. *See* Authors' names
Locklear, Heather, 156
Lowry, Malcolm, 68

M

MacDonald, Ann-Marie, 71, 82, 83, 84
Macdonald, John Alexander, 133
Mackenzie, Alexander, 133
MacLeod, Alistair, 66, 76
Madonna, 138
Maguire, Gareth, 157
Maguire, Martie, 157
Maguire, Tobey, 146
maiden name, as first name, 280–281
Maillet, Antonine, 71
Maines, Natalie, 153

Mancuso, Donna, 31
Manitoba
   birth certificate application, 288
   favourite names, 84
   place names, 264, 265, 267, 271,
      272, 274
Manley, Elizabeth, 31
Marley, Bob, 140
Martel, Yann, 66, 71, 80
Martin, Chris, 156
Martin, Paul Edgar Phillipe, 133
Martin-Boyle, Alicia, 282
Mastropietro, Paolo, 155
McCormack, Eric, 142
McEnroe, John, 156
McGraw, Tim, 157
McLachlan, Sarah, 152, 158
McLean, Cheryl, 46
McLeod Rogers, Jacqueline, 73
McLuhan, Marshall, 68
McNabb, Donovan, 27
meaning of names, researching, 11
Meloni, Christopher, 154, 159
Melville, Herman, 64
Mercer, Rick, 146
Messier, Mark, 28
Messing, Debra, 155
Métis names, 54–59, 166
Michell, Chantelle, 31
middle names, 31, 39, 88, 124–125, 134,
   156, 163, 179, 181, 224
Milano, Alyssa, 138
Milne, A.A., 81
Minogue, Kylie, 150
mispronunciation, 101
Mistry, Rohinton, 70, 78, 79, 80, 82, 84
Mitchell, Margaret, 64
Mitchell, W.O., 71, 78, 79
Moder, Daniel, 155, 157
Montana, Joe, 27
Montgomery, Lucy Maud, 74, 80, 81, 83
Moore, Brian, 66
Moore, Demi, 140, 148, 158
Moore, Julianna, 150
Morissette, Alanis, 147
Morrow, Robert, 159
Moss, Carrie-Anne, 148
movie characters, 136–137
Mowat, Farley, 68, 78

Mullen, Larry Jr., 156
Mulroney, Martin Brian, 133
multiple births, 60–62
Munro, Alice, 71, 82, 83
Murphy, Eddie, 156, 159
Musgrave, Susan, 76
Myers, Mike, 138, 145

N

names, changing, 278–279
names by origin
   Abenaki, 47, 48, 50
   African-American, 29
   Algonquin, 47, 48, 49
   American, 26, 44, 192, 199, 203,
      205, 206, 207
   Arabic, 28, 41, 43, 52, 61, 186,
      192, 197, 198, 203, 205, 225,
      230, 244
   Aramaic, 209
   Assyrian, 41, 217
   Australian Aboriginal, 205
   Basque, 52, 197
   Bengali, 221, 223, 225
   Blackfoot, 47, 48, 49
   Celtic, 51, 187, 188, 193, 196, 206,
      207, 232, 236, 241, 243
   Cree, 47, 48, 49, 50
   Czech, 239
   Danish, 52
   Dutch, 62, 219
   English, 27, 29, 32, 33, 41, 42,
      44, 45, 51, 52, 60, 61, 62, 63,
      131, 187, 188, 189, 191, 193,
      194, 195, 196, 197, 199, 200,
      201, 202, 203, 204, 205, 206,
      208, 209, 210, 227, 232, 233,
      234, 235, 236, 237, 239, 240,
      241, 242, 243, 244, 245, 246
   French, 27, 28, 33, 34, 35, 41, 42,
      43, 44, 45, 50, 51, 52, 53, 59,
      60, 61, 62, 63, 132, 186, 188,
      190, 193, 194, 195, 196, 198,
      199, 200, 201, 202, 206, 207,
      208, 210, 234, 236, 237, 238,
      240, 241, 242, 243, 244, 245,
      246

Gaelic, 28, 32, 186, 187, 195, 200,
202, 236, 237
German, 27, 28, 29, 32, 35, 41,
43, 44, 50, 51, 52, 53, 59, 60,
61, 162, 187, 191, 197, 198,
199, 200, 201, 202, 204, 206,
207, 232, 234, 235, 236, 237,
238, 239, 241, 242, 243, 246
Greek, 32, 33, 34, 41, 42, 43, 44,
45, 50, 51, 52, 53, 59, 60, 61,
62, 63, 132, 186, 188, 189, 190,
191, 192, 194, 195, 196, 197,
198, 200, 201, 202, 204, 205,
207, 208, 209, 210, 217, 219,
222, 223, 225, 227, 228, 229,
230, 232, 234, 235, 236, 237,
238, 239, 240, 241, 242, 243,
244, 245, 246
Gwich'in, 47, 48, 49, 50
Hawaiian, 192
Hebrew, 27, 28, 29, 33, 34, 35, 41,
42, 43, 44, 51, 52, 53, 60, 61,
62, 63, 128, 129, 130, 134, 135,
163, 165, 168, 186, 187, 189,
190, 191, 192, 193, 195, 196,
197, 198, 200, 201, 202, 203,
204, 205, 206, 207, 208, 209,
210, 217, 218, 219, 220, 221,
222, 223, 225, 227, 228, 229,
230, 235, 240, 241, 243, 244
Hindu, 187, 207, 209, 217, 218,
219, 222, 225
Hungarian, 42
Irish, 27, 32, 43, 53, 187, 188, 189,
190, 193, 195, 199, 202, 204,
205, 206, 207, 208, 209, 210,
234, 235, 243
Italian, 28, 33, 34, 45, 62, 203,
206, 207, 210, 227, 239, 240,
241, 246
Latin, 28, 29, 34, 35, 41, 42, 43,
44, 50, 51, 52, 53, 59, 60, 61,
62, 165, 186, 187, 188, 189,
190, 192, 193, 194, 195, 196,
198, 199, 200, 201, 202, 204,
205, 206, 207, 208, 209, 210,
221, 222, 225, 232, 233, 234,

235, 238, 239, 240, 241, 242,
243, 244, 245, 246
Latvian, 225
Mi'kmaq, 50
Mohawk, 47, 48, 49
Muslim, 164, 187, 217, 219, 220,
221, 223, 225, 227, 228
Native American, 189, 201
Ojibway, 47, 48, 49, 50
Old English, 42, 60, 187, 233, 235
Persian, 44, 53, 62, 189, 191, 203,
227, 230, 244
Polish, 239
Portuguese, 29
Punjabi, 203
Russian, 52, 191, 225, 239, 246
Sanskrit, 230, 244
Scandinavian, 43, 188, 190, 198,
202, 235, 236, 240
Scottish, 28, 32, 44, 52, 59, 60,
186, 187, 188, 190, 193, 203,
204, 205, 206, 233, 235
Sikh, 203, 217, 218, 219, 227, 228
Slavic, 32, 35, 42
Southern Tutchone, 47, 49
Spanish, 33, 52, 63, 186, 193,
203, 206, 209, 242
Swedish, 188, 239
Welsh, 42, 189, 190, 195, 196,
203, 208, 210, 233, 236, 242
names to avoid, 182
Navratilova, Martina, 33
Neeson, Liam, 138
Nelligan, Émile, 68
New Brunswick
Acadian names in, 40
birth certificate application,
286–287
place names, 265, 266, 273
Newfoundland
birth certificate application, 287
place names, 264, 264, 265, 267,
268, 270, 272, 273
nicknames, 7, 12, 32, 36, 39, 88, 178,
184, 185, 224, 248
disadvantages of, 10
Northern Canada, popular names,
215

Northwest Territories
  birth certificate application,
    289–290
  place names, 264, 264, 266, 268,
    271, 272, 273
Norway, popular names, 170
Nova Scotia
  Acadian names in, 40
  birth certificate application, 287
  place names, 264, 265, 266, 267,
    268, 270, 271, 272, 273
  popular names in, 37, 275
Nunavut, 167
  birth certificate application, 290
  place names, 264, 271

O

O'Brien, Soledad, 154
old-fashioned names, 11, 231–245
Ondaatje, Michael, 65, 69, 76, 78,
    81, 83
O'Neal, Shaquille, 29, 180
O'Neal, Tatum, 156
Ontario
  birth certificate application, 288
  place names, 265, 266, 267, 268,
    269, 270, 271
  popular names, 215
opposites, 57
original names, 26

P

Pagan, Angelo, 159
Paltrow, Gwyneth, 148, 156
Parker, Mary-Louise, 150, 156
Parker, Sarah Jessica, 154
Pasdar, Adrian, 154
Paulin, Viveca, 155
Pearson, Lester Bowles, 133, 181
Pelletier, David, 32
Perreault, Micheline, 49
Perry, Luke, 145
Peterson, Oscar, 145
pets, 231
Pfeiffer, Michelle, 150
Phelps, Michael, 29
Phillippe, Ryan, 156

Phillips, Chynna, 156, 157, 158
Phoenix, Summer, 155
Pinkett-Smith, Jada, 149
Pitt, Brad, 142
place names, 179, 269–276
Polish names, 87, 114–117, 170
Polley, Sarah, 152
Pope John Paul II, 52
popular names, 9, 37, 127–139, 183–184,
    186–215
  around the world, 161
  in Australia, 162
  in Austria, 163
  in Canada, 159, 164, 212, 213, 214,
    215, 255
  in Denmark, 164–165
  in England, 165
  in Finland, 166
  in France, 167
  in Germany, 167
  in Iceland, 168
  in Ireland, 168
  in Italy, 169
  in Japan, 169
  in Norway, 170
  in Poland, 170
  in Scotland, 172
  in Spain, 173
  in Sweden, 173
  in Switzerland, 173-174
  in United States, 174
Porter, Kalan, 45
Portman, Natalie, 152
Prairies, popular names, 214
Préfontaine, Darren, 58, 59
Priestly, Jason, 145
prime ministers, 133
Prince Edward Island
  Acadian names in, 40
  birth certificate application, 287
  place names, 264, 266, 271, 273
  pronunciation, 129, 163, 211
Purdy, Al, 66

Q

Quaid, Dennis, 142
Québec
  Acadian names in, 40

birth certificate application, 288
place names, 264, 264, 266, 267, 268, 270, 272, 273
popular names, 16, 181, 212, 213
Quinn, Aidan, 138, 153, 156

R

Raymond, Brad, 154
Reece, Gabrielle, 31
Reeves, Keanu, 35, 144
Reisman, Rose, 75, 77
religious names, 216–229. *See also* Biblical names
Remini, Leah, 159
Reynolds, Burt, 142
rhyming names, 56
Ricci, Nino, 69, 81
Richard, Maurice "Rocket," 55
Richards, David Adams, 67, 80, 81, 82
Richards, Denise, 159
Richler, Mordecai, 69, 78
Robbins, Tim, 156
Roberts, Julia, 138, 149, 155, 157
Robinson, Chris, 155
Rock, Chris, 159
Rodman, Dennis, 180
Rogers, Linda, 74
Ross, Charlotte, 155
Roy, Gabrielle, 72, 82
Roy, Patrick, 29
royal names, 160
Rudolph, Wilma, 34
Russell, Kurt, 52, 156
Russian names, 87, 117–120
Ruth, Babe, 26
Ryan, Meg, 142, 150
Ryder, Winona, 269

S

Salé, Jamie, 32
Salinger, J.D., 64
Sambora, Richie, 156
Sarandon, Susan, 156
Saskatchewan
 birth certificate application, 288
 place names, 264, 265, 268, 272, 273

Scheel, Thaddeus, 157, 158
Schiffer, Claudia, 148, 153, 157
Schumacher, Michael, 29
Scotland, popular names, 172
Scott, Beckie, 30
Seal, 166
Service, Robert W., 70
sex, determining before birth, 15
Sheen, Charlie, 159
Shewfelt, Kyle, 28
Shields, Carol, 72, 78, 79, 80, 82, 84
shortening names, 7
siblings, 11
Simpson, Jessica, 138
Small, Sami Jo, 33
Smart, Elizabeth, 72
Smith, Will, 146, 149
Sood, Ashwin, 158
Sorbo, Kevin, 153, 156
Sorvino, Mira, 158
Sosa, Sammy, 29
Sossamon, Shannyn, 153
Spanish names, 120–124, 173
spelling, 9, 45, 77, 88, 129, 132, 140, 171–172, 178, 211, 261
Spielberg, Steven, 156
sports names, 26-30, 36, 79, 153, 231, 253–255
stereotypes, 9
Stern, Bonnie, 72, 77
Stewart, Jon, 155
Sting (Gordon Matthew Sumner), 35, 138, 146
St-Laurent, Louis Stephen, 133
strange names, 256
Stringfield, Sherry, 158
surnames, 277, 280–282, 282–286
Sutherland, Donald, 138, 142
Sutherland, Keifer, 126, 144, 157
Swank, Hilary, 149
Sweden, popular names, 173
Switzerland, popular names, 173-174
synonyms, 57

T

Tandy, Jessica, 143
Tennant, Veronica, 34
testing names, 14, 16–17

Theron, Charlize, 148
Thesen, Sharon, 76
Thompson, John Sparrow David, 133
Thurman, Uma, 152, 157
Tilly, Jennifer, 149
Timberlake, Justin, 138
traditional names, 11, 87–88, 125. *See also* Names by origin
Tremblay, Michel, 69
trendy names, 9, 250, 251-252
Trudeau, Pierre Elliott, 133
Trump, Donald, 158
Trump, Ivana, 158
Tupper, Charles, 133
Turner, John Napier, 133
Twain, Shania, 152
Tyler, Liv, 155

U

unique names, 8, 224
unisex names, 7, 65, 79, 185, 255–261, 278
United States, 88, 174
unusual names, 7, 176–177, 178, 179, 185, 224
Upton, Andrew, 154, 155
Urquhart, Jane, 73, 76, 77, 78, 80, 81, 82, 83

V

Vanderhaeghe, Guy, 68
Van Herk, Aritha, 72, 81, 83
Vardalos, Nia, 152
Vassanji, M.G., 69, 81
Vaughn, Matthew, 153, 157
Villeneuve, Jacques, 27
Vincent, Christian, 156, 159
Vogels, Josey, 73, 77
vowels, 9–10

W

Warren, Estella, 149
Watson, Alberta, 269
Watts, Naomi, 150
Websites, 215
Western Canada, popular names, 214
Wheeler, Winona, 46
Wickenheiser, Hayley, 31
Wier, Mike, 29
Williams, Robin, 146
Williams, Serena, 33
Williams, Venus, 34
Willis, Bruce, 140, 158
Witherspoon, Reese, 156
Wojtyla, Karol Jozef, 52
Womer, Melissa, 158
Woods, Eldrick (Tiger), 29, 274
Wright, Mary Kathryn, 33

Y

Yamaguchi, Kristi, 32
Yashinsky, Dan, 67
Young, Neil, 145
Young, Paul, 157
Yukon
  birth certificate application, 290
  place names, 265, 265, 266, 268, 269, 271, 273, 274
  popular names, 165, 255

Z

Zelman, Daniel, 155
Zeta Jones, Catherine, 157